Insurrectionist Wisdoms

ENVIRONMENT AND RELIGION IN FEMINIST-WOMANIST, QUEER, AND INDIGENOUS PERSPECTIVES

Series Editor
Gabrie'l Atchison

Environment and Religion in Feminist-Womanist, Queer, and Indigenous Perspectives is a series that explores the subject of ecofeminism from feminist-womanist, queer, and indigenous perspectives. The governing assumption of the series is that ecofeminism is not only a mode of scholarly discourse and analysis but also a hub for social formation and action. What distinguishes this series in particular is that it focuses on ecofeminism as a disciplinary matrix through which the voices of women, particularly women of color, and indigenous peoples can speak from their religious and spiritual traditions and practices to address the environmental challenges and concerns of the age. Volumes in this series will attend to the environmental and ecological issues that impact women, people of color, and indigenous populations, as these communities are, in almost all respects, the most immediately threatened by contemporary climate and ecological changes and catastrophes. Works in the series will focus on the history; scholarly resources and perspectives; constructive practices; religious, spiritual, and natural traditions from which these voices speak; and how these can provide alternative narratives, illuminate hidden agendas, and generate resistance to environmental and religious racism and exploitation.

Titles in the series

Insurrectionist Wisdoms: Toward a North American Indigenized Pastoral Theology, by Marlene M. Ferreras

Ecology, Spirituality, and Cosmology in Edwidge Danticat: Crossroads as Ritual, by Joyce White

Re-Indigenizing Ecological Consciousness and the Interconnectedness of Indigenous Identities, edited by Michelle Montgomery

Ecotheology and Love: The Converging Poetics of Sohrab Sepehri and James Baldwin, by Bahar Davary

Ecowomanism at the Panamá Canal: Black Women, Labor, and Environmental Ethics, by Sofía Betancourt

Mapping Gendered Ecologies: Engaging with and beyond Ecowomanism and Ecofeminism, edited by K. Melchor Quick Hall and Gwyn Kirk

In the Name of the Goddess: A Biophilic Ethic, by Donna Gianc

Insurrectionist Wisdoms

Toward a North American Indigenized Pastoral Theology

Marlene M. Ferreras

LEXINGTON BOOKS
Lanham • Boulder • New York • London

Published by Lexington Books
An imprint of The Rowman & Littlefield Publishing Group, Inc.
4501 Forbes Boulevard, Suite 200, Lanham, Maryland 20706
www.rowman.com

86–90 Paul Street, London EC2A 4NE

Copyright © 2023 by The Rowman & Littlefield Publishing Group, Inc.

All rights reserved. No part of this book may be reproduced in any form or by any electronic or mechanical means, including information storage and retrieval systems, without written permission from the publisher, except by a reviewer who may quote passages in a review.

British Library Cataloguing in Publication Information Available

Library of Congress Cataloging-in-Publication Data

Names: Ferreras, Marlene M., 1980- author.
Title: Insurrectionist wisdoms : toward a North American indigenized pastoral theology / Marlene M. Ferreras.
Description: Lanham : Lexington Books, 2022. | Series: Environment and religion in feminist-womanist, queer, and indigenous perspectives | Includes bibliographical references and index.
Identifiers: LCCN 2022037104 (print) | LCCN 2022037105 (ebook) | ISBN 9781793645463 (cloth) | ISBN 9781793645487 (paperback) | ISBN 9781793645470 (epub)
Subjects: LCSH: Mayas—Religion. | Work—Religious aspects—Christianity. | Corporations, Foreign—Mexico. | International business enterprises.
Classification: LCC F1435.3.R3 F46 2022 (print) | LCC F1435.3.R3 (ebook) | DDC 305.89742072—dc23/eng/20220913
LC record available at https://lccn.loc.gov/2022037104
LC ebook record available at https://lccn.loc.gov/2022037105

∞™ The paper used in this publication meets the minimum requirements of American National Standard for Information Sciences—Permanence of Paper for Printed Library Materials, ANSI/NISO Z39.48-1992.

Contents

List of Figures	vii
Agradecimientos (Acknowledgments)	ix
Preface	xi
Introduction	1
1 ¿*Y qué crece en tu pueblo?* (What Grows in Your Town?)	9
2 From *Milpa* to *Maquila*, Mamá to Machine	29
3 *Primeramente Madre*: The Life-Bearing Gospel	61
4 *La Ciencia de la Lucha: ¡Sí se puede!* (The Science of Struggle: Yes We Can!)	99
5 *Ma'alob* (Goodbye and Hello)	135
Bibliography	151
Index	159
About the Author	171

Figures

Figure 1.1	My tiny research assistant	10
Figure 1.2	La palapa, the open-sided dwelling where we spent the majority of our day preparing meals and talking	13
Figure 2.1	A sewing machine in a home in the pueblo mágico	31
Figure 2.2	Henequen in the pueblo mágico	36
Figure 2.3	A campesino picking chiles in a milpa located in the pueblo mágico	43
Figure 2.4	Maquilas pay women lethal wages	54
Figure 3.1	Women with their children walking to the rancho	63
Figure 3.2	Maíz in a milpa located in the pueblo mágico	66
Figure 3.3	Tattoo of Maíz Goddess	76
Figure 3.4	Artist rendering of Maíz God/Goddess	77
Figure 3.5	La Virgen de la Asuncion in the pueblo mágico	89
Figure 4.1	After an afternoon thunderstorm in the pueblo mágico	112
Figure 5.1	Lxs hijxs de maíz as an image of pastoral care. Artwork by William Bredvik.	136
Figure 5.2	Orange groves in Redlands, California	146

Agradecimientos (Acknowledgments)

First and foremost, I wish to express my profound gratitude to the girls and women in the pueblo mágico. ¡Nos queremos vivas! Escribo esta historia, con la esperanza que haya redactado algo de la realidad que viven ustedes cada día. Son mi inspiración y mis maestras. ¡Sí se puede!

I am so grateful to both my mother and grandmother, Mayra and Mima. Mom, I learned to struggle not because it was a skill I desired but because we had no alternative. In the midst of loss, tragedy, betrayal, abuse, and scarcity we found life. Thank you for bringing me along to learn la ciencia de la lucha. How a single-parent Cuban refugee mother in the United States ever survived is beyond my ability to comprehend. Eres una mujer loca y rebelde, y así mismo te quiero con todo mi corazón. Mima, me enseñaste las tablas de multiplicar en un idioma que no reconocían en la escuela. Que cabrona eras, pero como me consentías. Siento mucho que no hayas vivido a ver que por fin terminé y escribí un libro. Tu rebeldía y forma de animarme con tus consejos aun vive en mi alma.

Many thanks to colleagues who engaged me in conversation and encouraged me to keep writing despite challenging circumstances: Josh Morris, Katherine Rand, Yara González-Justiano, Grace Vargas, and Erika Dunbar.

I am extremely thankful for relationships with mentors and teachers who read several drafts, engaged me in conversation, and provided valuable feedback. Their friendship and consistent support over the years has meant so very much to me: Papusa Molina, Kathleen J. Greider, Duane R. Bidwell, Fritz Guy, John Brunt, Maury Jackson, and Ulrike Guthrie. I am also extremely grateful for the graciousness and patience of editorial staff at Lexington Books: Michael Gibson, Mark López, Kasey Beduhn, Courtney Morales, and Emma Ebert. In addition, I am deeply grateful to a blind peer reviewer who provided excellent feedback and areas where the book could be improved.

Many thanks to the Forum for Theological Exploration and the Hispanic Theological Initiative. Your financial support made possible the relational research approaches this book exhibits.

Most of all I am grateful to my daughter, Xin Xin: Your bravery and curiosity never cease to amaze me. The familial bonds we share are the theological constructions I am most proud of. This book is dedicated to you and to fierce little girls everywhere.

Preface

The qualitative researcher, by virtue of her task, enters into the meaning-making world of individuals, communities, and individuals-in-communities to gain insight and understanding of particular situations. Postmodern theorists refute modernity's claim that the researcher can maintain a detached and objective position when conducting qualitative research. As an "outsider," the researcher comes with her own set of experiences and hence her peculiar framework for interpreting what she sees, hears, senses, and believes. However, the knowledge that emerges between the researcher and the subject is not one-sided. Subjects also participate in the investigation by bringing their own set of assumptions and frameworks for understanding the situation.

This dynamic interplay is described by twentieth-century philosopher Hans-Georg Gadamer (1900–2002). His hermeneutical theory contests the influential claims of modernity (1500–1800) that emphasize the objective role of the researcher and his[1] ability to discover truth by reason. Gadamer argues that interpretation, by its very nature, is a dialogical process in which two or more different "horizons" meet—the horizon of meaning in the text being interpreted and the horizon of meaning brought by the interpreter. In *Truth and Method*, Gadamer explains that humans are by nature interpretive beings who bring particular "prejudices" from their past to understand the present. He describes the "hermeneutical circle" as a person's horizon that moves back and forth and eventually creates a "fusion," at which point the person comes to an understanding and a broadening of her or his horizon as she or he makes meaning of the event.[2] Gadamer's metaphor of "fusing horizons" illustrates how meaning and interpretation take place.[3] The fusion of horizons is an exercise in intersubjectivity, a term used in social science to refer to the social interaction between persons and communities when they make meaning out of experiences and share their particular experiences in the process of constructing that meaning. I use this theory of fusing horizons as a framework for research design by overtly stating the biases I bring to the work and then inviting participants to bring theirs by reviewing and revising interviews and theoretical themes I write. The back-and-forth process of checking for accuracy is the fusing of horizons that causes me to reflect on the meaning that arises from the dialogue constructed between experience, theology, and cognate disciplines. While some qualitative researchers do not directly state their ontological, epistemological, axiological, and methodological beliefs,[4] I stand in the practical theological tradition that seeks to democratize theology, and so I do.[5] My reasons for doing so are based on my identity as a practical theologian dedicated to the work of bridging the wisdom of the pueblo and the academy. This bridge building activity, in my view, requires transparency and language that is conversant with audiences. Furthermore, Gadamer's theory underscores the emergent nature of knowledge. Because I believe knowledge is situated in particular contexts, I will begin by presenting the herstory[6] and "horizon" that bring me to this research topic and problem.

THE RESEARCHER'S HERSTORY AND "HORIZON"

I am an American-born child of Cuban refugees who immediately on arrival were granted political asylum and US citizenship. My grandfather died by suicide three months after arriving from Cuba in 1971. The cause of his death and the events surrounding the tragic loss is a topic my family does not discuss. In secret, some of the women tell me he died because he never found a job, and he feared his daughters would end up working in factories instead of getting an education. After his death, his fears came true. Three of his daughters did end up working on the assembly line of a multinational corporation.

Overcome with grief, my grandmother rarely left her bedroom and complained of constant migraine headaches until she died in January 2017 at the age of ninety-six. She never worked a day outside her home. I am not sure she was capable or felt she was able to face the world outside her home. One of the few benefits of being a Cuban refugee and consequently being granted political asylum is getting access to public assistance. She received money from Social Security every month, but it was not enough to sustain her and her four daughters. Economic need was only one of a long list of needs.

At the age of fourteen and while she was still enrolled at the local public high school, my mother, the youngest daughter in this family, began working in a bakery. Her three older sisters all went to work for the British multinational company Tecform Engineering Limited. At the time, they assembled airplane parts and earned $1.25 an hour, which was 25 percent less than the

California minimum wage of $1.65 set on February 1, 1968.[7] As new arrivals in the US, they say it was the only job available to Spanish-speaking Latinas. They worked in hopes of their future unborn children going to school and becoming professionals who would never have to work in a factory a day in their lives.[8]

Their physical scars attest to the commodification of their bodies. To see my aunt's left hand is to hear her story all over again. She had falsely reported her age to be eighteen and so began working in 1971 when she was actually only sixteen. While cutting steel for the airplane parts, she damaged her hand. Her hand never healed. She also never filed a worker's compensation case because she did not know and was not told she could. The factory job was difficult but my aunt says it almost seemed worse to be home without a reliable source of income. Regardless of belonging to the social group referred to as "the working poor," she says any payment —even a measly $1.25 an hour—is better than none. She learned to silence physical pain. After the factory fired her due to her decreased efficiency, and essentially "disposed" of her body much like industrial waste, she returned to a trade she knew: sewing. Prior to entering the factory, my aunt had been invited to join an independently contracted group of migrants who sewed dresses for a Mexican woman who in turn sold them in a store in Los Angeles. A Mexican family converted their garage into a factory and rented industrial sewing machines to migrants like my aunt who would then produce the clothes. The migrant family taught my aunt to sew and she left this job for TecForm because the pay was better in the large company. However, after injuring her hand, she returned to sewing, despite the lower wages and even longer work hours.[9]

My worldview is shaped by the evidence of these women's bodies that suffered physical, social, emotional, and economic harm as a result of working on a factory assembly line. As I witnessed this suffering, the faith community of the southern California Christian Seventh-day Adventist church to which I belonged promoted values and beliefs that gave me a lens by which to view the activity of labor. Most relevant to this discussion is the patriarchal eschatological vision of God as acting outside time, in control of an eschaton that only God could bring about, and a human's dependent need for God. The Spanish-speaking Christian Seventh-day Adventist church we attended concluded with impassioned appeals for baptism and conversion into the faith because this meant when Christ returned one would be given access to a new life. As a child, I recall prayers that pleaded with God to return to earth and take those of us who were baptized to heaven where justice would reign. In this theological framework, I exercised the only agency one seems to have—I was baptized and joined the community to "wait" for God. In this "waiting" period the emphasis was on orthodoxy: keep the Sabbath and the commandments of God in Exodus 20. The commands were a list of what not to do, and I spent much time, effort, and emotional energy carefully living within the limits of the tradition's rules. This embedded theology resulted in what I later identified as the internalized oppressor that preserved capitalism's desired telos ("end") in the here-and-now, while my/our suffering would be attended to in an afterlife. I/we patiently waited for reprieve in our daily lives and did not question this eschatology.

Yet my mother did question the church's eschatological view and did not accept the life-limiting view of God presented by our church community. Curiously, when I was a child she allowed me to live out my faith convictions while communicating to me how "ridiculous" and "impractical" the rules were. She violated the Sabbath in so many ways. Her wisdom and ability to subvert this dominant Christian narrative were rooted in the practical wisdom of her everyday life as a single-parent refugee mother. For example, I recall her purchasing a gallon of milk on the Sabbath; meanwhile I refused to enter the grocery store with her—shopping was a Sabbath violation—and sat in the car waiting. Believing that my mother's hope for liberation from this world was tied to her "right" action, I worried. Yet my mother's need to provide milk for her daughters was an authoritative source guiding her action (phronesis).

Wrestling with the indoctrination of Seventh-day Adventist religious education in my youth and the insurrectionist actions of my mother, during my undergraduate college years I began to investigate my faith critically. By reading theologians such as Walter Brueggemann, I came to understand the conflicting economic systems presented in Exodus. One system presents a capitalistic view of the land. Land is a possession to be bought and sold. The goal in this system is to acquire more. A second system has a covenantal view of land. Land is an inheritance, a birthright, that is only a portion of a larger promise that is for all God's people. In this second system, land is then to be shared so neighbors and heirs all benefit from its produce.[10] The struggle for me was identifying, or perhaps developing a growing awareness of, how my family's life experience was anchored in possession of land that, ironically, we never seemed to acquire. We assisted others in increasing their wealth at our expense.

All this brings me to the topic of women's identity, preferred futures, and Christian praxis with a lifetime of experience that reaches back into my family's migration story. I am skeptical of labor law, free trade agreements, and public policy because in my experience the documents' interests did not serve my family's immediate needs. In tandem with this cynicism is the underlying Christian theological framework that renders our suffering invisible. While I certainly respect the intellectual genealogy[11] of Christian theology, I also recognize the white, western, European, androcentric context of its development. For this reason, I instead privilege liberation theologies that seek to emancipate human beings from "applied theology" by acknowledging that knowledge is *performative*.[12] That is to say, one can learn what a faith community's values and beliefs are by studying the embodied actions of the people. As a practical theologian, I therefore bring to this qualitative research the beliefs that: a) practice and theory cannot be separated; and b) marginalized communities enter into a process of conscientization[13] as part of their liberation from historically violent and oppressive structures that were never intended to function for their benefit.

While what I bring to this research project is rooted in my own lucha and I believe this helps me recognize la lucha in the pueblo mágico, I want to be careful not to colonize the experience of working-class Maya mexicanas whose lucha, while similar to mine, has its own shape. I locate my religious identity along the margins of Seventh-day Adventism, a tradition that has influenced my values and ethics in ways I am sometimes unaware. The early influence of Christian orthodoxy prejudices how I approach daily living; for example, I keep dietary laws that I violated for the first time when I was living in the pueblo.[14] While my action to approach research was deliberative, I did spend time reflecting on actions and tending to feelings of guilt. In many ways this research resulted in a deconstruction of my Christian orthodoxy and was somewhat disorienting. The research changed me as I immersed myself in this quest.

I must also note that I identify myself as a "Cuban born in exile" because I do not experience myself as fully embraced by North American culture. I feel like an unwelcome outsider but when I travel to South America or Cuba, I realize I am not from that place either. In these locations I confront my American-ness and how my everyday life in the United States is tied to the realities of Latinoamérica, namely the economic privileges that Gustavo Gutiérrez names, which depend on the exploitative practices of the US in Latinoamérica (dependency theory).[15] I, however, do not really know what citizenship and life outside the US is like. I am a perpetual outsider, which is both an advantage and a disadvantage.

This book is intended for three publics. First, I aim to attract and inform practical and pastoral theologians teaching pastoral care and counseling in a seminary to students enrolled in MDiv and MA programs. Second, the book is useful for postgraduate students designing research in practical theology. The methodology of the book serves as an illustration of practical theological research and furthermore presents a transnational feminist commitment to understand and uncover the relationship between nations and the flow of labor and commodities, the latter including women's bodies. Finally, the relevance for pastoral care sections seeks to attract spiritual caregivers by offering them practices of care with working-class women of color and other marginalized communities struggling with similar circumstances as well.

NOTES

1. The masculine pronoun is used by Gadamer to refer to humanity and this reveals his own patriarchal view, not mine.
2. Hans-Georg Gadamer, *Truth and Method*, rev. ed., trans. Joel Weinsheimer and Donald G. Marshall (New York: Continuum, 2004), 304–305.
3. Gadamer, *Truth and Method*, 304–305.
4. John W. Creswell, *Qualitative Inquiry and Research Design: Choosing among Five Approaches*, 3rd ed. (Thousand Oaks, CA: SAGE, 2013), 19–22.
5. Elaine Graham, Heather Walton, and Frances Ward, *Theological Reflection: Methods* (London: SCM Press, 2005), chap. 6, Kindle.
6. I use the term "herstory" as opposed to history because this is a narrative guided by the stories of women, not men. The women are the protagonists in this saga and ought not to be regarded as victims or invincible heroines, as "*his*tory" might depict them. They are neither. They are subjects, consistently devising plans to survive given the realities of multiple converging systems of power and control.
7. "History of California Minimum Wage," State of California Department of Industrial Relations, accessed October 30, 2017, https://www.dir.ca.gov/iwc/minimumwagehistory.htm.
8. Hulda Duran, interview by author, Riverside, CA, October 19, 2017.
9. Maritza Aoyagi, interview by author, Riverside, CA, October 19, 2017.
10. Walter Brueggemann, *Sabbath as Resistance: Saying No to the Culture of Now* (Louisville, KY: Westminster John Knox Press, 2014), 38.
11. Dána-Ain Davis and Christa Craven, *Feminist Ethnography: Thinking through Methodologies, Challenges, and Possibilities* (Lanham, MD: Rowman & Littlefield, 2016), 10.
12. Graham, Walton, and Ward, *Theological Reflection*, chap. 6.
13. Paulo Freire, *Pedagogy of the Oppressed*, 30th anniversary ed., trans. Donaldo P. Macedo (New York: Continuum, 2000), 47–48.
14. Seventh-day Adventists practice dietary laws based on Leviticus 11 and Deuteronomy 14, which make a distinction between clean and unclean meats. While living in the pueblo, I ate whatever food was offered to me without asking questions. On more than one occasion I knowingly ate pork, a meat considered "unclean."
15. Gustavo Gutiérrez, *A Theology of Liberation*, 15th anniversary ed. (Maryknoll, NY: Orbis Books, 1988), 51–54.

Introduction

Neocolonialism in the twenty-first century takes the form of multinational corporations that exploit and abuse the land, multimillion-dollar corporations that build their factories and then employ women of color to labor in unjust, death-producing assembly-line conditions. Through practical theological and anthro/gynopological methods, this book offers an analysis of the situation of working-class Maya mexicanas living in Yucatán, México, and working on the assembly line of a multinational corporation. Drawing on a decolonial approach to pastoral theology and feminism, the book proposes Lxs Hijxs de Maíz as an image for pastoral care and counseling.

Pastoral theologians have previously explored similar questions about care in the context of the neoliberal age and colonialism as an aspect of suffering. Less literature in practical theology, specifically in the subdiscipline of pastoral theology, addresses the care of Hispanics living in North America. While this literature is useful and even helpful for understanding care of communities with historical trauma linked to colonialism, the contextual realities of such US Hispanic communities are quite different from those of communities in Latinoamérica. The questions of assimilation, Catholic devotional life, and immigration in the US are central to pastoral theologians' reflection on caring for Hispanics in the US, but for many Latinoamérica communities these contributions are far removed from the realities of their everyday lives.

CLOSELY RELATED LITERATURE

Similarly, Latina feminist theologians like Ada María Isasi-Díaz, who like me uses ethnography as a method for doing theology, focuses on Hispanics in the US.[1] While her reflections, like those of pastoral theologians more specifically, are useful for helping the field understand the significance of family, la lucha, la vida cotidiana, solidarity, and un poquito de justicia, these are all concepts that are developed within a privileged Christian framework. Even the work of Maria Pilar Aquino, while much more focused on interculturality and the wisdom of communities of women in Latinoamérica, begins with an assumption of Christian, and specifically Roman Catholic, theology.[2]

When I arrived in pueblo mágico, the pseudonym women gave their hometown, I came informed by the aforementioned literature, but quickly realized that this framework was insufficient for the context and that I needed a different one. A postcolonial and decolonial framework assisted me in resisting the temptation to impose my US-born Christian identity and theology onto the situation in pueblo mágico. The context of pueblo mágico is such that the women from whom I sought to learn continue to practice rituals linked to their Mesoamerican spiritual tradition. However, they claim a Catholic identity in name and are critical of the Christian tradition whose ecclesiology they experience in the one cathedral in pueblo mágico.

Though I believe I am contributing to the discussion of care in the neoliberal age and also care of Hispanics and Latinx communities that work in similar conditions in US sweatshops, I position my work within postcolonial and decolonial pastoral theology. I am not proposing a theory. Rather, what I am doing is suggesting an experiential approach to pastoral care and counseling. Care informed by working-class Maya mexicanas suggests to pastoral theologians that they consider indigenous epistemologies that practice corazonando (understanding life through their heart) as a means to support women's ethical positions that challenge the values of neoliberal capitalism and by extension its imperial spread.

METHODOLOGY

This qualitative research project acknowledges that centuries of colonialism, racism, and globalization have produced new forms of inequalities. Beyond the traditional feminist focus on gender relations, I approach this study with a transnational feminist commitment to understand and uncover the relationship between nations and the flow of labor and commodities, the latter including women's bodies.[3] This book begins to decentralize such dominant power by democratizing the production of knowledge through proposing a transnational feminist ethnographic methodology. The methodology I use combines an anthropological approach (critical ethnography) and a practical theological approach (mutual critical correlation) to learn about women's experiences and eschatological practices.

Women in pueblo mágico do not relate to an approaching eschaton or a chronological destination. They understand and experience the eschaton as a communal/topological phenomenon that's emerging in the present through their primary identity as life bearers or, as they say, "primeramente madre." As a pastoral theologian I'm using the term "eschatology" to discuss the dimensions of a person's spirituality. I am speaking of eschatology as a longing, desire, possibility. I am emphasizing an understanding of eschatology that has been subjugated throughout Christian history. I am recovering an understanding of eschatology as the negotiation of the configuration of present circumstances in order to open up possibilities of conservation, survival, and human flourishing. In that sense, it can be connected to an Aristotelian teleology rather than the hegemonic Hegelian teleology of neoliberal globalization.

SCOPE AND LIMITATIONS

I realize that there are many complex factors that can be explored in this book, so I begin to narrow those by identifying several topics I will not be discussing. Multinational corporations create environmental harms that exacerbate pollution and thus global warming and public health concerns. I am aware of this reality and yet only address the pollution of women's bodies and their ways of life in order to focus on the care of persons. I am prioritizing care of the individual not because it is of greater value but because I must start my work somewhere. As will become clear in subsequent chapters, these women share a spiritual relationship with the earth that is rooted in their Mesoamerican spiritual tradition; in this sense, by studying the women I am also studying the earth. Similarly, though I draw on Mesoamerican spirituality and religious multiplicity, I am using these very important resources to better understand the everyday experiences of the women in pueblo mágico, I do not go in-depth with either of these themes. I use these themes to help me enrich the description and also interpret experiences.

Neither will I discuss sexual assault, for though it is pervasive and the women shared with me many intimate stories of suffering, the suffering of sexual violence was a pain so deep that they informed me for the purpose of helping me stay safe and also to tell me that inside the maquila the realities of sexual assault were present. The reader might wonder why I choose not to narrate such an important context that relates to violence. I heard these stories of sexual assault after our formal interview conversations had concluded. After shutting off the recorder and thanking the women for engaging in such honest conversation, on more than one occasion women then proceeded to tell me of an incident of sexual assault. I did not perceive that they wanted these conversations recorded, and for that reason I simply urge the careful reader to understand that the backdrop to all that is contained in the following pages is a context of sexual violence. Women's souls die in more ways than one, and they also survive and thrive to tell truths. I collected stories of struggle, some so jarring I lay awake in my hammock at night crying and also wondering if I myself was safe from harm. This research invited me to practice faith in a community of women who desired life. I came to believe that though I was not safe from harm, I was secure in a matriarchal community that would teach me both how to live under the constant threat of violence and how to birth life in death-producing contexts. I must also note that I did come to them with some prior knowledge of how to live in such a context. My mother was my first teacher.

I am also not writing in a vacuum. I began this research in November 2016 on the eve of the presidential election of a businessman and multimillionaire as the forty-fifth president of the US. The ensuing xenophobia, racism, sexism, and Christian nationalism of his presidency have limited and also focused my research. I suspect that discussion on migration to the US was carefully considered by the community in pueblo mágico. Most of the community in pueblo mágico was born in pueblo mágico and discussed generations of their family living in that same pueblo. It is not a community that experiences or even sees a lot of migration. However, the men in pueblo mágico do talk about migrating to the US to work and sending money home to their families. Their mothers, wives, and sisters live in a constant agony of fear that the men in their lives will make the dangerous journey north. Some men who go are never heard from again. Presumably they die on the journey or arrive in the US and begin new lives. No one knows for sure—and that is an agony in itself. There are some homes in pueblo mágico that have tiled floors and walls made of cinder block. The children in pueblo mágico tell me that these homes belong to women whose husbands send money home from the US. My host family tells me that on two separate occasions a coyote has come promising to take their father to the US to work. The coyotes ask for a down payment to secure their father's trip and then leave without fulfilling their promise to the family but with the money. In some cases, these payments pull families deeper and deeper in debt, as is true of my host family. Even so, one of the sons in the host family speaks of going north. So why do the men travel north? The men travel in spite and because of it being a dangerous journey and, as the son in this family tells me, because men need and want to do something to help their mothers, wives, and children have a better quality of life. With desiccated crops due to the import of corn, campesinxs also look for opportunities to make more money so their families can have a better quality of life.

Unfortunately, I did not interview these or any men. While I did observe and learn much about the lives of men in pueblo mágico and by extension their work in the multinational company, my research focused on the experience of women. Men work in similar conditions and future research could explore their experiences. While this research is informed by men's experience inasmuch as they are part of the community being observed, more research is needed to understand their unique challenges and perspectives.

I do not develop two of the five themes that arose from the study. I chose three themes based on the importance evident in the frequency of their emergence in the interviews. The first theme, dehumanization, provides the content of chapter two and describes the problem this book seeks to address, in so doing supplying important contextual information. The second and third themes of mothering and la ciencia de la lucha are chosen because of the centrality of these practices in the lives of the women. I leave the fourth and fifth themes, desire and education, for future exploration and subsequent research and writing as I gathered insufficient evidence to engage them in a meaningful way here. What follows is a modest but I hope nonetheless important contribution to the development of pastoral care through the privileging of non-Western thought and practice.

ORIGINALITY AND CONTRIBUTIONS

In a chapter titled "Globalization, Internationalization, and Indigenization of Pastoral Care and Counseling," Emmanuel Lartey anticipates the indigenizing of pastoral theology. This book is a contribution in that direction.[4] I aim to present non-Western practices for Western pastoral care and counseling to consider as caregivers offer care particularly to working-class women of color. This is a small beginning to a much larger project; I envision a growing body of literature in Latina practical theology informed by epistemologies of the south. While practical and pastoral theology have attended to issues of race, class, gender, and globalization, the voices and experience of Latinas in pastoral care and counseling are largely absent from the discipline's literature. Most recently, Rubén Arjona contributes to the growing body of literature through his doctoral dissertation by presenting a more adequate form of pastoral care for exploring desire with young Mexican men.[5] I am particularly hoping to contribute to the field of literature begun by feminist and womanist pastoral theologians like Pamela D. Couture, Chanequa Walker-Barnes, Phillis Sheppard, and Sharon Thornton,[6] who draw attention to the intersection of identity and social contexts. Suffering that is created by humans can also be decreased by humans' efforts to assume responsibility and devise ways to reduce the violence and oppression under which people live.

OUTLINE OF CHAPTERS

Following this introductory chapter, chapter 1, "¿Y qué crece en tu pueblo? (What Grows in Your Town?)" introduces the reader to pueblo mágico and to the problem of neoliberal capitalism, sexism, and racism. Then chapter 2, "From *Milpa* to *Maquila*, Mamá to Machine," traces the movement of working-class Maya mexicanas from life sustained by crops in the milpa that nourished their families and community to becoming assembly-line workers in a multinational corporation increases that corporation's bottom line while deprioritizing the well-being of its employees. The chapter begins by connecting the story of neoliberal capitalism to the colonialism of fifteenth-century Spaniards in the Yucatán. I focus on the common features of the encomienda system, the hacienda system, and the present-day maquila industry in the Yucatán. Keeping a focus on the case of pueblo mágico, I demonstrate how a multinational corporation appropriated an indigenous ritual and desecrated the spiritual connection of the Maya and their relationship with the land. I present five broad strategies maquilas use to subjugate working-class Maya mexicanas. Maquilas (1) assign to individuals the traits of machines; (2) effectively incarcerate women; (3) implement a culture of surveillance to produce pressure and "cansar" (to tire); (4) pay women lethal wages; and (5) advance the religion of the colonizer.

Chapter 3, "*Primeramente Madre*: The Life-Bearing Gospel," presents the life-giving gospel of the women who live in pueblo mágico. I acknowledge the multivalent uses of the term "gospel" and recover the term's usage in pre-Christian military contexts to demonstrate how working-class Maya mexicanas bear life and lay claim to their territory by opposing the gospel of the maquila. Using the theological loci of theological anthropology and eschatology, I analyze the experience of women, of Mesoamerican spirituality, and the eschatological practices of women. Women's identity as lxs hijxs de maíz assists them in focusing on their understanding of themselves as connected to life in an ecosystem where the anchor to their existential questions is linked to their role as primeramente madre (mothers first). As mothers, they care for life that is vulnerable in their pueblo, which includes their children but extends to the land and to tending to life in matriarchal communities where they are strengthened by practicing solidarity with one another and teaching their children la ciencia de la lucha (the science of the struggle). This chapter concludes with relevance for pastoral care and counseling that attend to the bearing of life by participating in advocacy, political activism, and nurturing women's wisdom as caregivers of life in their communities.

Chapter 4, "*La Ciencia de la Lucha: ¡Sí se puede!* (The Science of the Struggle: Yes, We Can!" explores the anatomy of hope. I explain that hope lives in women's literal bodies—in their anatomy. Taking a decolonial approach, I use the concept of sabidurías insurgentes (insurrectionist wisdoms) and the ability of lxs hijxs de maíz to corazonar la vida (understand life through the heart) found in the Maya sacred text Popol Vuh as it is explained by Ecuadorian anthropologist Patricio Guerrero Arias. I advocate for approaches to care that embrace the creation of a pluriverse, or what the Zapatistas explain as "un mundo donde quepan muchos mundos" (a world where many worlds fit). The chapter imagines a dialogue between Latina feminist Christian theologians (Marcella Althaus-Reid and Ivone Gebara), indigenous texts, and working-class Maya mexicanas' experiences. Reflecting on the Christian theological concepts of salvation (death, life, and resurrection), I describe women's eschatological strategies of hablando, ignorando, insistiendo, and renunciando. This chapter concludes with the study's relevance for and frameworks of pastoral care and counseling while also contributing to practices of pastoral care and counseling that honor the wisdom of the heart.

Chapter 5, "*Ma'alob* (Goodbye and Hello)," summarizes the relevance of this research for the discipline of pastoral theology and identifies possibilities for future research that build on the content of this book. This final chapter is also a reflective move that returns to an analysis of how this research lived in my body from early childhood experiences in my family of origin to the research adventures that took place from November 2016 to December 2018. Because pastoral care and counseling is also about the personhood and formation of the practitioner as she or he provides care, I reflect on how the search to live into the questions this book pursues shaped me and increased the personal resources I bring to the caregiving relationship and to teaching in this field.

NOTES

1. Ada María Isasi-Díaz, *Mujerista Theology* (Maryknoll, NY: Orbis Books, 1996); Ada María Isasi-Díaz, *En la Lucha/In the Struggle: Elaborating a Mujerista Theology* (Minneapolis: Fortress Press, 2004).

2. María Pilar Aquino, *A Cry for Life: Feminist Theology from Latin America*, trans. Dinah Livingstone (Maryknoll, NY: Orbis Books, 1993); María Pilar Aquino and Maria José Rosado-Nunes, eds., *Feminist Intercultural Theology: Latina Explorations for a Just World* (Maryknoll, NY: Orbis Books, 2007).

3. Dána-Ain Davis and Christa Craven, *Feminist Ethnography: Thinking through Methodologies, Challenges, and Possibilities* (Lanham, MD: Rowman & Littlefield, 2016), 26–27.

4. Emmanuel Y. Lartey, "Globalization, Internationalization, and Indigenization of Pastoral Care and Counseling," in *Pastoral Care and Counseling: Redefining the Paradigms*, edited by Nancy J. Ramsay (Nashville: Abingdon Press, 2004), 87–108.

5. Rubén Arjona, "The Minister as Curator of Desire: A Model of Pastoral Accompaniment with Young Mexican Men" (PhD diss., Princeton Theological Seminary, 2018).

6. See, Pamela D. Couture, *Blessed Are the Poor? Women's Poverty, Family Policy, and Practical Theology* (Nashville, TN: Abingdon Press, 1991); Chanequa Walker-Barnes, *I Bring the Voices of My People, Prophetic Christianity* (Grand Rapids, MI: Eerdmans, 2019); Phillis Isabella Sheppard, *Self, Culture, and Others in Womanist Practical Theology, Black Religion/Womanist Thought/Social Justice* (New York: Palgrave Macmillan, 2011); and Sharon G. Thornton, *Broken Yet Beloved: A Pastoral Theology of the Cross* (St. Louis, MO: Chalice Press, 2002).

Chapter One

¿Y qué crece en tu pueblo? (What Grows in Your Town?)

"¿Maestra? ¡Maestra!"[i] a wide-eyed, dark-haired three-year-old girl called to me from behind the wooden door to the nah[ii] that I had shut to keep the afternoon thunderstorm rain from coming in. "¡Maestra, déjame entrar!"[iii] she insisted, her tone growing increasingly annoyed by my having excluded her from participating in the research. I had locked her out of the room where I was interviewing a woman who worked on the assembly line of a multinational corporation. She forcefully tugged on the door and demanded, "¡Maestra, déjame entrar!"

    I went to the door, let her in, and told her that Sofia and I were talking about work and life in pueblo mágico. She looked into my eyes confirming she understood and then confidently entered the nah. She sat down, nestled between Sofia and me, and motioned for us to continue. She knew I was collecting stories from the women in town who worked in the maquila where her mother and father worked. I did not invite her to participate; she appointed herself to be my assistant. I did not believe I needed an assistant and certainly not a toddler with a fierce temper. She had a different opinion and ignored my ignorance. She followed me everywhere, asking questions and carrying on conversations as I went about observing, interviewing, and participating in daily life in pueblo mágico. Her mother asked me to teach her English. She was only three so I taught her to say "Hello" and how to write the first letter in her name. She was a good student. In the evenings before dinner she sat at the table and asked me to help her write her letter again. She covered several pages in my research journal with the first initial of her name.

---

i. Teacher? Teacher!
ii. Mayan word for a traditional home or thatched-roof hut built of sascab.
iii. Teacher, let me in!

As I look back on her constant companionship, I am grateful she made sure I did not venture out to see her pueblo without an appropriate guide. What would I have done without her? I am indebted to her persistence and assertiveness. Thankfully she slipped her tiny fingers around my jean shorts belt hook, and stayed latched on for three months. She walked with me, showed me around her pueblo, and taught me to approach research as play. She introduced me to friends, and her very presence taught me not to take myself too seriously. She was the best research assistant a new researcher like myself could ever hope for.

Figure 1.1. My tiny research assistant. Photo taken by the author.

My three-year old research assistant's home, which for the purposes of this book I identify only as pueblo mágico, is a small village with 456 inhabitants located eight miles from a larger town in Yucatán, México. There is only one paved road running through the center of the pueblo, and it is in desperate need of repair. For the last two years, the people have implored the city to fix this road because campesinxs need a well-paved road by which to transport their chiles to the markets in the nearby town in the beds of their pickup trucks. I understood the struggle of the pueblo when I could not find a taxi cab willing to take me the five miles from the nearby town to pueblo mágico. Cabdrivers told me they did not want to damage their tires and besides, they explained, there was nothing to see in pueblo mágico. I imagine this was part of the reason why the familias in pueblo mágico often asked me, "¿Cómo es que nos encontraste? ¡Si nosotros no estamos ni el mapa!"[i] To me, that seemed a curious question since a Google search did in fact yield the location of their pueblo. But maybe that was beside the point. Maybe what their question revealed to me was their experience of being invisible and the perceived dispensability of their lives.

Once I arrived in pueblo mágico, it was difficult to leave. There is no form of public transportation. Few families own a vehicle, and those that do use it sparingly. Owning a mode of transportation is not all that necessary except if one works in the multinational corporation in town or if campesinxs need to go to the nearby town to sell their produce. When people in pueblo mágico want to go to town, they hitchhike and stand by the one road in the pueblo waiting for a car traveling through the pueblo toward one of the two larger towns located to the north and south to give them a ride.

La plaza (town square) in pueblo mágico has three main buildings. Situated directly in the center of town and a few feet from the one paved road is la catedral (the cathedral), an old Spanish-style building that seats roughly one hundred people. On either side of la catedral is a small market with a refrigerator to keep soda pop, water, and Yoplait yogurt cold, and la escuela primaria y pre-escolar (elementary and preschool). Past the small market, at the very end of a dirt road lined with casas de paja (straw-thatched houses) is la casa de Doña Lucía and Don Santiago, the grandparents of my tiny research assistant. This is the home that welcomed me, a stranger. They shared their food, their familia, and their lives with me.

MEETING LA FAMILIA

My tiny research assistant's mother and father live in the pueblo mágico and work in the nearby multinational corporation, called a maquila in México.

---

i. How is it that you found us? We do not even appear on the map!

Her grandmother, Doña Lucía, takes care of her while her parents work. Doña Lucía is similar in age to me; she is only in her late thirties yet has four sons and six grandchildren. When I met la familia for the first time, I realized how odd I must appear to them because I have neither children nor grandchildren. I also did not know how to make tortillas, and when asked, "¿Y que crece en tu pueblo?" (What grows in your town?) I did not know. I tried explaining how I survived without cooking skills and attempted to describe my life as a single, never-married professional woman living in the United States.

I explained that I am the American-born eldest daughter of Cuban refugees raised in southern California. I live in Redlands, a town with a population of 71,554 in San Bernardino County,[1] and the only things I could recall growing in my pueblo are . . . buildings. Five miles down the road from my concrete-walled house, I see construction workers making "progress" on the construction of a new outlet mall that is located at the intersection of two major freeways (210 and 10) headed into the larger city of Los Angeles. That's why when my tiny research assistant's grandmother asked me, "What grows in your town?" I did not know what to say. Doña Lucía asked me this question as she showed me the herbs she plants around the outside edges of her home.

As she kneels in the dark brown soil and smells the fragrance of the herbs she is introducing to me, she's also telling me I must go see the milpas where corn, jícama, plátanos, chiles, and sandía grow. I know nothing about planting and harvesting. I do not see that kind of growth around my home in Redlands, not because it does not exist but because I am so disconnected from the soil. I lack the relationship with the earth she seems to cultivate, so all I see is how industrial businesses and a nearby newly constructed gated community with model homes grow. Doña Lucía and I strain to listen and understand the world in which the other lives, but despite my strange outsider status la familia welcomes me into their home and seats me at their dinner table. This was the first of many conversations in this place.

After teaching me about the herbs that surround her home, Doña Lucía takes a seat behind her candela[i] and starts to tortear (make tortillas out of corn). She kneads the dough and pounds her fist into the large ball of yellow masa (dough) as she asks about the purpose of my visit to her pueblo. I explain, "Estoy escribiendo una historia para un libro. Mis maestros lo van a leer y quizá mucha otra gente también lo lea. La meta es contar esta historia para los que no conocen [este pueblo] y como es vivir aquí."[ii] Prior to opening her home to me and allowing me to live with them for three months, her sister

---

i. A furnace where she burns wood to heat the surface where she makes tortillas and boils pots, mostly for stew and soup.

ii. I'm writing a story for a book. My teachers will read it and maybe many other people will read it too. The goal is to tell this story for those who don't know [this pueblo] and what it is like to live here.

Figure 1.2. La palapa, the open-sided dwelling where we spent the majority of our day preparing meals and talking. Photo taken by the author.

Doña Valentina told her of my interest in interviewing women who work in the maquila and wanting to know more about everyday life in pueblo mágico. I also described to Doña Lucía the doctoral dissertation process as a series of exams and assignments judged by a group of three experts. At that point her daughter-in-law, my tiny research assistant's mother, came in to help tortear. Doña Lucía asks me to explain to her daughter-in-law what I have just told her. The two laugh and tease me about this odd assignment I describe. They ask why anyone would want to hear the stories of pueblo mágico. I understood this to be yet another way they felt forgotten and insignificant to the rest of the world. Yet they reassure me, "Maestra, no se preocupe. La vamos ayudar con su tarea."[i]

Doña Lucía and the women first help me by reframing what research is—*tarea*, a homework assignment. There is something comforting in thinking of academic work (research) as homework. There really is an aspect of this project that is about presenting the wisdom of "home" here in pueblo mágico to the academic discipline of religion and theology.

---

i. Teacher, don't worry. We are going to help you with your homework.

My primary audience is practical and pastoral theologians who are concerned with neoliberalism's effects on women of color and how to offer care that is informed by strategies created by the women themselves. While this is my primary audience, I am also writing for postgraduate students designing research in practical theology. The methodology of this book serves as an illustration of practical theological research and furthermore presents a transnational feminist commitment to understand and uncover the relationship between nations and the flow of labor, the latter including women's bodies.

Writing to these two audiences is challenging, first because in the writing I attempt to take a multidimensional experience and place it on to a two-dimensional page without flattening the rich complexity of life in pueblo mágico; second, because as I write I hear the assertive matter-of-fact voice of my tiny research assistant in the back of my mind entreating me "¡Maestra, déjame entrar!"[i] Her ever-present voice reminds me that while I am writing about my experience, I am also writing about my experience in *her* pueblo. Her words provoke me to wrestle with the question posed to the Western academy by Indian scholar, literary theorist, and feminist Gayatri Chakravorty Spivak, "Can the subaltern speak?"[2] I do not pretend to suggest that what follows in these pages fully accomplishes this goal. What I am claiming is the ability to stand in the gap between the Western academy and pueblo mágico. I do this by allowing the questions and the very speech of the community in pueblo mágico to be present on these pages. I am weaving a conversation between unlikely conversation partners, unlikely due to the realities of racism, misogyny, and classism. I did not always understand what was being communicated to me in pueblo mágico, but I did the best I could to ask questions and pay attention to what I was seeing, hearing, feeling, touching, and smelling. Where the reader and I find ourselves puzzled, I believe, is an opportunity to recognize our privilege, our distance from these voices, and the importance of our sitting with not-knowing while straining to understand.

My tiny research assistant consistently invited me to practice not-knowing. She asked me questions like, "¿Qué estás haciendo? ¿Por qué haces eso? ¿Qué dices? ¿Dónde vas?"[ii] These questions repeatedly caused me to pause and reevaluate my daily activities and purpose. My answers rarely satisfied her queries and frankly her persistence led me to believe that perhaps there was some wisdom in living into the questions. At some point (I am not entirely sure when it was) I grew to be less concerned with the answers and more present with the practice of cultivating curiosity with regard to all I did not understand. I think her questions invited me into this experience and practice, and it is into this experience that I am inviting the reader.

---

i. Teacher, let me come in/enter.
ii. What are you doing? Why are you doing that? What are you saying? Where are you going?

A third challenge was my research plan versus the actual experiences of research, which forced me to revise my plan, as I will show in due course. I want to be as honest as I can in my writing and retelling of these stories. I came to pueblo mágico with an idea of what I expected to learn, a defined timeline to "collect data," and research methods I trusted to guide this research project. However, what I soon came to realize is that research is first and foremost a relational process, and that this research project was indeed *homework*, an act of labor accomplished by a familia co-authoring a story that begs to be told. The "home" of this "work" is in the in-between relational space that sits between myself and the women of pueblo mágico. It is "la herida abierta" (the open wound) that provides the starting point for the theorizing of Chicana cultural, feminist, and queer theorist Gloria Anzaldúa (1942–2004).

LA HERIDA ABIERTA

Anzaldúa's text, *Borderlands/La Frontera*, presents a theory of what she terms "the new mestiza." She explores the topics of identity, land, conquest, and culture to explain how consciousness emerges along "borders." Beginning with a history of US imperialist expansion, Anzaldúa emphasizes the border as a site of trauma where "the Third World grates against the first and bleeds."[3] The friction she depicts is both literal and figurative. To understand this, I first explain the US-México border as a geographical space defined by historical events.

Geographical Borders

Anzaldúa begins her theorizing by analyzing the impact of the US-Mexican War. She notes how the geographical border separating "the Mexican people" from the US "was born on February 2, 1848 with the signing of the Treaty of Guadalupe-Hidalgo."[4] That day, México lost a third of its territory on account of US president James K. Polk's imperialist agenda to expand west, referred to in US history as Manifest Destiny. The newspaper editor of the *New York Democratic Review*, John L. O'Sullivan, in an article published in 1839, describes the "divine destiny" of the United States.[5] He writes,

> For this blessed mission to the nations of the world, which are shut out from the life-giving light of truth, has America been chosen; and her high example shall smite unto death the tyranny of kings, hierarchs, and oligarchs, and carry the glad tidings of peace and good will where myriads now endure an existence

scarcely more enviable than that of beasts of the field. Who, then, can doubt that our country is destined to be the great nation of futurity?[6]

O'Sullivan's article reveals the Christian nationalism and white supremacy supporting the expansionist motives of mid-nineteenth-century America. This notion that the US, in its conquest of territory, was fulfilling some divine mandate resulted in literal bloodshed. Many families in my own community share stories of how "the border crossed us," and though they never moved, the land where their relatives have lived for decades went from being part of México to becoming US territory. Many lives were lost in the process. Anzaldúa, a native Texan, understood this lived reality where history itself established a geographical border that not only separated her from her people but also desecrated the land of her ancient Indian ancestors, the Azteca.

In addition to separating individuals from their tribe and people, the border and trade policies have further contributed to the "grating" that causes such suffering along the border. At various times in its history, the US has enforced immigration laws and trade agreements that allow Mexican workers to enter the US as farm laborers. One such time was between 1942 and 1964. During this period, a number of laws allowed mexicanos (mostly men) to cross into the US for work. It is significant that this program began as US men were being drafted into service for World War II, creating a vacuum in the US labor force, which both US women and immigrants filled. Alongside internment camps, a number of strikes related to unfair pay and working and living conditions occurred during this twenty-two-year period. A full discussion of these realities is beyond the scope of this project. However, it is important to note that exploitative wages and inhumane working conditions for mexicanxs employed by US companies began as far back as 1942. This book focuses on the change from mexicanxs in the Bracero program working in the US to the emergence of maquilas—US-owned companies establishing factories in México that could take advantage of cheap labor and lax labor laws—which took place when the Bracero program ended in 1965.

The Emergence of Maquilas

The maquila was birthed in Ciudad Juárez, México, in 1965, as a result of the end of the Bracero program, the beginning of the Border Industrialized Program (BIP), and a growing globalized economy heavily influenced by the 1944 Bretton Woods meetings, which resulted in the establishment of the International Monetary Fund (IMF) and the World Bank. A "twin city" to El Paso, Texas, Ciudad Juárez is an attractive area for multinational corporations to establish maquilas and benefit from the tax incentives of the 1994 North American Free Trade Agreement (NAFTA) between Canada, the US, and México.

Ostensibly, NAFTA[7] promised to address the issue of mass unemployment in México by providing jobs, not incidentally at the same time increasing profits for US companies that could ship goods in and out of México free of tax and employ workers for wages below the US minimum-wage standards. There was a boom in the maquila industry and the auto, technology, and textile industries that moved into México, and a consequent drain on the agricultural sector, most notably in the production of the staple food of México: maíz (corn). Thus, NAFTA resulted in highly subsidized corn produced in the United States being imported to México. México's more than two million small farmers could not compete with the cost of corn, which had fallen so much that the cost merely of planting corn exceeded the price at which it could be sold in México.[8] The US had anticipated this impact of NAFTA on campesinxs (peasants, small farmers)[9] and expected that out-of-work campesinxs would supply the maquila with labor on its assembly line.[10] Clearly, then as now, the terms of free trade and the open market disproportionately favored the US while harming México.[11]

In addition to policy agreements that invite and indeed encourage businesses to establish factories along the US-México border, migration and US immigration law play an important role in the steady employment opportunities there. The end of the Bracero program discouraged migration northward, for the US no longer granted guest worker visas to migrants. Consequently, guest workers returned to México and added to the number of unemployed Mexican citizens. The BIP was an effort to respond to this growing economic crisis by creating jobs. At the same time, refugees were migrating north to flee political and civil wars in El Salvador, Guatemala, and Honduras, and they too added to the number of persons seeking employment in maquilas. The city of Ciudad Juárez soon became overpopulated by both eager workers and maquilas. Rafael Luévano reports that Ciudad Juárez became a shantytown with four times the population of El Paso.[12] The abundance of willing workers, public policy agreements such as NAFTA, and the age of globalization created conditions in which multinational corporations could make incredibly high profits by employing workers at extremely low wages, a pattern sometimes referred to as "the race to the bottom."[13]

What begins to occur in such a sociopolitical economy is what the German philosopher Karl Marx identified in *The Communist Manifesto*: capitalism produces a form of struggle between class groups that Marx names "the bourgeois and proletarians," between the owners of the means of production[14] (the bourgeois) and the working class (the proletariat).[15] Marx argues that societies typically are made up of a majority of the population that lives suppressed by an elite group of people who benefit from exploiting the larger group's labor and gaining and accumulating profit for themselves. Marx goes on to explain that eventually the proletariat comes to an awareness of this exploitation and it revolts.

Practical and pastoral theology[16] is increasingly concerned about both (1) death-producing sociopolitical and socioeconomic structures (pastoral theology), and (2) the care of persons-in-community living within these structures (pastoral care and counseling). Literature in the field is moving toward care that understands not only personal and interpersonal suffering but the entire systemic social ecology of suffering as the domain of practical theology and pastoral care and counseling.[17] Anzaldúa's theory of the border as figurative is helpful in elucidating how la herida abierta (the open wound that is the border) is also a border site of suffering inside our bodies.

Borders as Identities and Consciousness

Anzaldúa theorizes that "borders" are also figurative spaces in culture contexts where distinctions are made between insiders and outsiders. Borders "distinguish *us* from *them*," and privilege defines and protects those who belong inside from those who are outside the acceptable bounds. This too is a source of suffering and consciousness raising. Anzaldúa explains how a third space is created where "los atravesados" (the traversed) live in la herida (the wound), which "before a scab forms [la herida] hemorrhages again, the lifeblood of two worlds merging to form a third country—a border culture."[18] The border culture is where los atravesados live. She lists the multiple communities who belong to los atravesados: "the prohibited and forbidden . . . the squint-eyed, the perverse, the queer, the troublesome, the mongrel, the mulato, the half-breed, the half dead; in short, those who cross over, pass over, or go through the confines of the 'normal.'"[19] In such bodies, the border is an analogy for internal conflict caused by norms and individuals' transgression of defined cultural expectations. This transgression is la herida abierta that is continually re-injured even as it gains the ability to right the wrongs by speaking its truth. Anzaldúa claims that while the border is the site of suffering, the border is also where acts of rebellion by los atravesados move humanity toward a more just end. She posits that mestiza identities emerge in the borderlands and create a third space, a borderland. Mestizas, according to Anzaldúa, generate wisdom for attending to the wounds of la herida abierta responsible for suffering.[20]

Working-class Maya mexicanas are part of the community of los atravesados. This book focuses on a community that lives closer to the southern border of México. The Yucatán is near the borders with Belize and Guatemala. However, its geographical proximity to the northern port cities such as Galveston, Texas, and the growing capital city of Mérida that includes an international airport prompted the Yucatán interim governor Víctor Manuel Cervera Pacheco to invite the maquila industry to consider the region as "México's other maquiladora frontier."[21] The solicitation of multinational corporations by México's governor is intended to produce business negotiations that benefit the region's economy by employing its working-class citizens. I will argue that the maquila industry is an extension of colonialism and that practical and pastoral theologies interested in understanding and attending to this particular suffering can draw on the wisdom of women who work on the assembly line of Yucatán's maquila, women such as the ones I interviewed in what follows.

The eleven working-class Maya mexicanas who collaborated on this study went from sewing *hipiles*[i] in their homes to becoming seamstresses on a multinational corporation's assembly line. The particular corporation studied is a large North American–owned supply chain that manufactures twenty-three brands of clothing. I focus on one particular source producing brand-name clothing in Yucatán, México, near the pueblo where the women live. The manufacturing company began employing workers in the local area in 1997. Over the past twenty-plus years, many maquilas have moved from the northern border of México to the southern border due to increased border violence in the north and the endless pursuit of cheaper labor. As the first free-trade region established by the signing of the North American Free Trade Agreement[22] in 1992, México became a sort of test case for free-market capitalism and neoliberal ideology.

In discussions on free trade, proponents of the system argue that "individual freedoms are guaranteed by freedom of the market and of trade."[23] Conversely, those who are critical of neoliberal capitalism argue that supporters of the system have disguised the economic system's desire to reestablish an elite class by highlighting the political values of human dignity and individual freedom to support and advance its agenda of making an ever-increasing profit, in this case on the backs/bodies and at the expense of the spirit and communal culture of the indigenous working-class people of Yucatán, México, and specifically its women.[24] Fifty years ago, the Peruvian theologian and Dominican priest Gustavo Gutiérrez identified the consequences of neoliberal capitalism on the lives of people living in Latin America as the central concern of liberation. He writes, "The dynamics of the capitalist economy led to the establishment of a center and a periphery, simultaneously generating progress and growing wealth for the few and social imbalances, political tensions, and poverty for the many."[25] As a pastoral theologian, I seek to understand the suffering of "the many" and my complicity in that

---

i. This is the traditional garment worn by Maya women. The garment has a rectangular form and is embroidered with a floral border along the neckline of the dress.

suffering, not only so that I can provide better care but also in an attempt to recover my own humanity.[26] There was something in my own body and soul that led me to this project.

DEAD BODIES: A PRACTICAL AND PASTORAL THEOLOGICAL PLEA

Beginning in 1993, several hundred dead, mutilated bodies of female maquila workers have been discovered along the bus routes to and from the maquilas in Ciudad Juárez, México. Various reports describe from a couple of hundred up to 740 bodies found between 1993 and 2009.[27] This variation is a result of some investigators claiming that many crimes against women go unprosecuted and thus unaccounted for.

It was this alarming news story on National Public Radio that caught my attention one morning as I was driving to class the first semester of my PhD program at Claremont School of Theology. The five-minute segment sent chills up my spine, and as a pastoral theologian concerned with how violence against women is reinforced by Christian doctrine, I determined then that I would investigate the everyday lives of working-class mexicanas on the assembly line of a multinational corporation. In line with a practical theological commitment to study practices, I decided I would move into a pueblo in México where women work in a multinational corporation.

My initial desire was to go to Ciudad Juárez. However, the violence along the border posed a potential risk that led me to consider maquilas in the Yucatán. The Yucatán peninsula presented a different aspect of studying a "border town." While the Yucatán does not share a geographical border with the US or even its southern neighbors, Belize and Guatemala, the maquila business is a "borderland" between México and the US. Governor Víctor Manuel Cervera Pacheco invited the maquila industry to consider expanding into the Yucatán peninsula not least because of its topological advantages: an international airport in the capital city of Mérida; the port city of Progreso and its proximity to major ports of entry along the Texas border; and a stable (meaning less migratory) population of workers. In essence, what began as a maquila business along the northern border expanded into the interior of the country and became another example of the colonial bite of US imperialism.

The community in the Yucatán is of Maya descent. The multinational corporation that employs women from pueblo mágico is a US textile company. It is important that we keep in mind that weaving in Mesoamerica and Maya culture has a heritage that is passed down through the lineage of women. In short, a US textile company invaded a region in which the art of weaving stretches far into the cultural roots of Maya women. The maquila has appropriated this cultural heritage and simultaneously exploits women and extracts resources from them. As a pastoral theologian, I wondered what I could learn about suffering in this neoliberal context and what these women might help me learn about how to provide spiritual care for them and others who suffer under similar conditions.

THE MYTH OF THE THIRD WORLD WOMAN

As a practical and pastoral theologian, over the years I had grown increasingly concerned and troubled by practices that extract worth from women of color and by the complex dimensions of suffering to which they are subjected. Melissa W. Wright's language of "myth" assisted me in locating this issue as a theological concern. During my undergraduate education, I read excerpts of the work of Romanian historian of religion and philosopher Mircea Eliade, in which he explores religion as a phenomenon. Professor of Geography and Women's Studies at Pennsylvania State University Melissa W. Wright examines "the myth of the third world woman" as a woman who is both dispensable and valuable within the global capitalist market.[28] As I read Wright's work, I began to recall what Eliade had said in his book *Myth and Reality*. Eliade clarifies that though the term "myth" is often used to denote a fable or falsehood, in the histories of religions "myth" is more properly understood as a story about a people's sense of the sacred and the sacred's relationship with reality. He writes,

> Myth tells how, through the deeds of Supernatural Beings, a reality came into existence, be it the whole of reality, the Cosmos, or only a fragment of reality—an island, a species of plant, a particular kind of human behavior, an institution. Myth, then, is always an account of a "creation"; it relates how something was produced, began to be.[29]

Though Wright is not writing as a theologian, she is engaging in a conversation about creation, that is to say, how women's dispensability in the two-thirds world came to be.

Wright presents the metanarrative (myth) that young women, through the process of working in multinational factories, gradually lose the very qualities—the psychospiritual, physical, and mental capabilities—that made them attractive to their employers in the first place. Through qualitative interviews, Wright records the rhetoric of multinational company managers in China and México who describe women as temporarily valuable for production due to their "dexterity," "docility," "patience," "attentiveness," and "cheapness."³⁰ A woman is hired to work on the assembly line based on these qualities that are attractive to the employer because assembly-line work demands that she reach her quota of items produced within a given workday. For example, she may need dexterity, attentiveness, and patience to be able to sew the inseam of one pair of jeans every twenty seconds in order to assure that by the end of her eleven-hour workday she has completed twenty-five bundles of seventy pairs of jeans each—a total of 1,750 pairs of jeans (interview with a maquila assembly-line supervisor, November 3, 2016).³¹ Besides the more obvious physical injuries, such as carpal tunnel syndrome, tendonitis, shoulder and back pain, and eyestrain, such stress-filled repetitive work can also cause psycho-spiritual injury.³² The dehumanization to which women are subjected by their maquila supervisors obscures women's humanity and the connections they share with the land and their people. Both kinds of injury, physical and psycho-spiritual, together tend to lead first to the eventual depreciation of her value and then to her dismissal and replacement. She becomes "industrial waste." But on this almost inevitable path to becoming "industrial waste" and eventually being replaced by another willing worker, she produces products of value to satiate corporate and consumer greed.³³

Wright's myth of the third world woman illustrates the dangerous trope on which systems of power and oppression depend. These systems create a complex "living web"³⁴ of constructed meaning, in which human beings navigate their power and subjugation simultaneously. Pastoral theologians are increasingly making more use of intersectionality theory as a metatheory that can aid pastoral caregivers in caring for the complex and interconnected needs of persons.³⁵ In the case of the women living in pueblo mágico, they are women of color living in the two-thirds world and in particular living in a country whose main trade partner is the US. While the current exploitative realities are troubling, this extractivist relationship with the US is part of a long history that illustrates how the imperial bite of the US in México is nothing new. Anzaldúa reminds us that the relationship between the US and México is replete with acts of violence that geographically, psycho-socially, and spiritually injure both individuals and collective communities. She describes the US-México border as "una herida abierta"³⁶ (an open wound) and goes on to explain both the literal border and the border as an analogy by describing individuals-in-communities' experience, identity, and history. Anzaldúa's theory continues to influence scholars in the humanities and social sciences not least because she explains how the place of harm is also the place where there is potential for the work of healing to begin.

There is much conversation on healing in the field of pastoral theology. When I use the word "healing" I am alluding to *sabidurías insurgentes*, which will be expanded on in chapter 4. There is a difference between resiliency, or survival, and healing by way of insurrection. The women whose stories you will encounter in this book practice a deep spirituality that is life-giving. They recognize the importance of building relationships with other women in the maquila and through small everyday emancipatory practices of faith they temporary dismantle the powers of racism, sexism, and capitalism. Admittedly, these emancipatory practices of faith do not eradicate the systemic oppression under which they live; however, even if only for a moment, they exemplify what Italian philosopher Giorgio Agamben describes as inoperative potentiality.

Agamben, influenced by Foucault's understanding of power, draws on Aristotle's concept of potentiality. For Aristotle, potentiality is not only about having the capacity to be but also to *not* be. Agamben develops his political philosophy of inoperativity in conversation with Aristotle's potentiality to discuss freedom and how subjects can enhance their freedom by rendering the apparatus, in this case neoliberal capitalism, inoperative.[37] In the absence of a labor union, the women whose stories you will read in the following chapters connect with other women on the assembly line and emphasize the importance of building good relationships. The "goodness" is based on both women protecting each other's interests and earning pay for work they are not completing. So that, for example, when an article of clothing arrives at a department store in southern California with imperfect stitching it is placed in a discount bin at the back of the store where a single mother struggling to clothe her children can purchase clothing at a discounted price and the profit expected from the product is lost. Capitalism is not entirely dismantled, but the system is subverted by women's practices. It is these practices, along with others, that draw on women's wisdoms (her ability to think-feel through life's complex systems) that free her (if even for a moment) from functioning as a cog in the capitalist machinery. This is an insurrection of nonviolent inoperativity that renders aspects of neoliberal capitalism as inoperative.

The following chapter explains how pueblo mágico went from working on their maize fields (milpas) to assembly-line work in the multinational corporation. The goal is to describe the conditions of working-class indigenous women in Yucatán, México, the better to understand how these women perceive themselves and imagine their preferred futures. Through their experiences, I assess the claim that free trade agreements advance human freedom by considering the case of indigenous female assembly-line workers living in a pueblo in light of one such agreement—the North American Free Trade Agreement (NAFTA). As will become clear in chapter 4, by *wisdom* I mean the thinking-feeling a woman does when she is perceiving a way to move through complexities in life. I believe there is a distinction between surviving and being fully alive. On the one hand, resiliency is the ability to adapt to complex suffering in order to resist destruction, and in this way, it is a form of survival. On the other, subversive wisdom goes beyond resisting death to discern where and how she can thrive and experience the fullness of life as she envisions life to be.

NOTES

1. United States Census Bureau, "QuickFacts," U.S. Department of Commerce, accessed December 16, 2018, https://www.census.gov/quickfacts/fact/table/redlands citycalifornia,US/PST045217.

2. Gayatri Chakravorty Spivak, "Can the Subaltern Speak?" in *Marxism and the Interpretation of Culture*, edited by Cary Nelson and Lawrence Grossberg (Urbana: University of Illinois Press, 1988), 271–313.

3. Gloria Anzaldúa, *Borderlands/La Frontera: The New Mestiza*, 4th ed. (San Francisco: Aunt Lute Books, 2012), 25.

4. Anzaldúa, *Borderlands*, 29.

5. Marlene M. Ferreras, "Women's Agency in the Context of Neoliberal Capitalism," in *What's with Free Will? Religion and Ethics after Neuroscience*, edited by Philip Clayton and James W. Walters, 110–111. Used by permission of Wipf and Stock Publishers, www.wipfandstock.com.

6. John L. O'Sullivan, "The Great Nation of Futurity," *United States Democratic Review* 6 (November 1839): 426–430, cited in John C. Pinheiro, *Missionaries of Republicanism: A Religious History of the Mexican-American War* (New York: Oxford University Press, 2014), 56.

7. NAFTA Secretariat, "North American Free Trade Agreement," https://www.nafta-sec-alena.org/Home/Texts-of-the-Agreement/North-American-Free-Trade-Agreement. See also U.S. Customs and Border Protection, "North America Free Trade Agreement," Department of Homeland Security, https://www.cbp.gov/trade/nafta.

8. Anjali Browning, "Corn, Tomatoes, and a Dead Dog: Mexican Agricultural Restructuring after NAFTA and Rural Responses to Declining Maíze Production in Oaxaca, Mexico," *Mexican Studies / Estudios Mexicanos* 29, no. 1 (Winter 2013): 89–91.

9. Analiese Richard, "Withered Milpas: Governmental Disaster and the Mexican Countryside," *Journal of Latin American and Caribbean Anthropology* 13, no. 2 (November 2008): 387–413. Richard specifically notes the consequences of neoliberal capitalist discourse embedded in NAFTA, discourse that emphasizes the "rights and responsibilities of the individual," and how this leads campesinxs to accept policies such as NAFTA as "natural and inevitable." More damaging and important, in my view, is the way this discourse misleads the individual to believe they are to oppose and resist these policies in isolation rather than in collectives.

10. Ferreras, "Women's Agency in the Context of Neoliberal Capitalism," 111–112.

11. Sergio Zermeño, "Desolation: Mexican Campesinos and Agriculture in the 21st Century," *NACLA Report on the Americas* 41, no. 5 (October 2008): 28–41.

12. Rafael Luévano, "A Living Call: The Theological Challenge of the Juárez-Chihuahua Femicides," *Journal of Feminist Studies in Religion* 24, no. 2 (Fall 2005): 67–76.

13. This phrase is used in several books and articles to explain the rapacious economic systems that seek workers who are vulnerable for a variety of reasons. See, for example, Robert J. S. Ross, *Slaves to Fashion: Poverty and Abuse in the New Sweatshops* (Ann Arbor: University of Michigan Press, 2004), 113–20. The term was coined by Supreme Court Justice Louis Brandeis in his dissent in *Liggett Co. v. Lee* in 1933. The race to the bottom is a socio-economic term that describes incentives such as deregulation and taxation laws that benefit corporations and the economic goals of the state without regard to or valuing of small corporations or individual laborers. Nicolas Meisel, *Governance Culture and Development: A Different Perspective on Corporate Governance* (n.p.: Development Centre of the Organisation for Economic Co-operation and Development, 2004), 41, http://books.google.com/books/about/Development_Centre_Studies_Governance_Cu.html?id=N57VAgAAQBAJ.

14. The means of production refers to the ownership of factories, workers/labor, machines/tools, and materials used to produce.

15. Karl Marx and Friedrich Engels, *Communist Manifesto*, trans. Harold Joseph Laski (Chicago: Charles H. Kerr, 1946).

16. Among a variety of definitions for *practical theology*, Bonnie Miller-McLemore suggests that *practical theology* is an activity of believers, a curricular area, a method in theology and religious studies, and an academic discipline. I use the term to refer to a method in theology and religious studies that is concerned with knowledge for the purpose of "enriching the life of faith in the world." See Bonnie Miller-McLemore, "Practical Theology," in *Encyclopedia of Religion in America*, edited by Charles H. Lippy and Peter W. Williams, Vol. 3 (Washington, DC: CQ Press, 2010), 1739–1742. The distinction between *practical theology* and *pastoral theology* varies in use throughout the discipline. I use *pastoral theology* to refer to the subdiscipline of pastoral care and counseling.

17. A significant shift in the literature of the field of pastoral theology and care is the move to consider macro systems and individuals', families', and communities' suffering as a result of these systems, inequities and harms. See Pamela D. Couture, *Blessed Are the Poor?* (Nashville: Abingdon Press, 1991); Larry Graham, *Care of Persons, Care of Worlds* (Nashville: Abingdon Press, 1992); Philip B. Helsel, *Pastoral Power Beyond Psychology's Marginalization* (New York: Palgrave, 2015); Ryan LaMothe, *Pastoral Reflections on Global Citizenship* (Lanham, MD: Lexington Books, 2018); Bruce Rogers-Vaughn, *Caring for Souls in the Neoliberal Age* (New York: Palgrave, 2016); and Archie Smith, *The Relational Self: Ethics and Therapy from a Black Church Perspective* (Nashville: Abingdon Press, 1982).

18. Anzaldúa, *Borderlands*, 25.

19. Anzaldúa, *Borderlands*, 25.

20. Ferreras, "Women's Agency in the Context of Neoliberal Capitalism," 112–113.

21. Eric N. Baklanoff and Edward Moseley, eds., *Yucatán in an Era of Globalization* (Tuscaloosa: University of Alabama Press, 2008), 92.

22. Senate Committee on Finance, U.S. Congress, *North American Free Trade Agreement: Hearings before the Committee on Finance, United States Senate; One Hundred Second Congress, Second Session; on Labor Issues, Business and Labor Views, and Agriculture and Energy Issues Concerning NAFTA; September 8, 10, 22, and 30, 1992* (Washington, DC: U.S. Government Printing Office, 1993), 1–458.

23. David Harvey, *A Brief History of Neoliberalism* (New York: Oxford University Press, 2005), 7.

24. Harvey, *A Brief History of Neoliberalism*, 19.

25. Gustavo Gutiérrez, *A Theology of Liberation*, 15th anniversary ed. (Maryknoll, NYk: Orbis Books, 1988), 51.

26. Ferreras, "Women's Agency in the Context of Neoliberal Capitalism," 113.

27. Claire Laurent, Michael Platzer, and Maria Idomir, eds., *Femicide: A Global Issue That Demands Action*, 2nd ed. (Vienna: Academic Council on the United Nations System, Vienna Liaison Office, 2013), 118, http://www.genevadeclaration.org/fileadmin/docs/Co-publications/Femicide_A%20Gobal%20Issue%20that%20demands%20Action.pdf. Though there is variance in the total number of murdered women, Rafael Luévano argues there is an increase based on the independent studies of both Diana Washington Valdez and Rosa Linda Fregoso. See Luévano, "A Living Call," 67. Valdez estimates 470 girls and women were the victims of violent crime in Mexico between 1993 and 2005. Diana Washington Valdez, *Harvest of Women: Safari of Women* (Burbank, CA: Peace at the Border, 2006), 359–373. Compare that number with Fregoso, who estimates that 37 women were murdered between 1985 and 1993. Rosa Linda Fregoso, *Mexican Encounters* (Berkeley: University of California Press, 2003), 2.

28. Melissa W. Wright, *Disposable Women and Other Myths of Global Capitalism* (New York: Routledge, 2006), 27–30.

29. Mircea Eliade, *Myth and Reality*, trans. Williard R. Trask (New York: Harper & Row, 1963), 5.

30. Wright, *Disposable Women*, 25.

31. This interview with a supervisor in Yucatán, México, was confidential, and the name of the interviewee is withheld by mutual agreement. I recognize the inconsistency of the supervisor stating there is an eleven-hour workday and later in my account the women reporting that they work regular twelve-hour workdays plus obligatory overtime, which means at times they work a 24-hour day. My goal is not to harmonize information but to present multiple perspectives even when they contradict each other. These contradictions themselves are interesting and add complexity to the realities being described.

32. Wright, *Disposable Women*, 23.

33. Wright, *Disposable Women*, 2. Ferreras, "Women's Agency in the Context of Neoliberal Capitalism," 109–110.

34. Bonnie Miller-McLemore, "The Human Web: Reflections on the State of Pastoral Theology," *Christian Century* 110, no. 11 (1993): 366–369.

35. Nancy J. Ramsay, "Resisting Asymmetries of Power: Intersectionality as a Resource for Practices of Care," *Journal of Pastoral Theology* 27, no. 2 (November 21, 2017): 83–97, https://doi.org/10.1080?10649867.2017.1399784.

36. Anzaldúa, *Borderlands*, 25.

37. Sergei Prozorov, *Agamben and Politics: A Critical Introduction* (Edinburgh: Edinburgh University Press, 2014), 30–38.

Chapter Two

From *Milpa* to *Maquila*, Mamá to Machine

My first encounter and conversation with Araceli is in her home while her preschool-age son—the youngest of three—plays on the floor near our feet. My eyes are immediately drawn to her bandaged wrist; when I ask, she tells me it is an injury from working at the maquila for the last two years. Her station along the assembly line is in the area of cerrar bolsas (closing pockets). She explains to me the repetitive task she does twelve hours a day, four days a week. "Haste cuenta que con esta mano lo jalamos. Lo jalo, lo doblo, lo subo en la máquina, lo cierro y le hago así [motions how she tosses over her opposite shoulder] y cae en un cajoncito que está al lado de la máquina."[i] Araceli performs this same operation between 4,200 and 4,800 times a day and earns $16.66 US[1] a day. I look again at her wounded wrist and ask about the injury. She tells me, "Cuando lo quise tirar así en la canasta, para tirarlo así, este dedo se me quedo abajo de la máquina . . . y se dobló mi mano así . . . Es que tenía, bueno, como pesa el bulto, hay que hacerlo con fuerza porque para tirarlo."[ii] Araceli was treated for a fractured wrist at the maquila by a physician employed by the maquila who gave her a note excusing her from work. Although it is a work injury, she receives no financial compensation on the days she is home recovering and can only return to work if this physician signs a form that says she can work. She tells me she has some money saved but she's worried because she has not earned anything for the last fifteen days. She hopes that when she returns to her station, her wrist will tolerate

---

    i. "Imagine that with this hand I pull the material. I pull it, I fold it, I lay it over the sewing machine, I close it and I do this . . . and it falls into a bin that is next to the sewing machine." I wish I could better envision this description. Even my experience doing piecework in a Carter's factory isn't enough to help me see it.

    ii. "When I wanted to throw it in the bin, to throw it like that, this finger got caught under the machine . . . and I bent my hand like that . . . It was that I had, well, since the material is heavy, you have to do it with force/strength because you have to throw it."

the thousands of times of day she will pull, fold, sew, toss, pull, fold, sew, toss, pull, fold, sew . . .

Araceli's case illustrates the rule: maquila work wears on women's bodies and souls. Itzel doesn't sleep. Ximena is so allergic to the pelusa (lint) at work that she sneezes constantly and her eyes swell. Celeste and Teresa complain of headaches. Natalia's hands and feet are tired. María says she feels anxious and stressed and has a hernia, a painful neck, and frequent fevers related to kidney stones. Teresa says she feels so depressed and unmotivated to do anything or go anywhere that when she is not at work she stays cooped up in her home. Veronica faints, suffers from constant pain in her shoulder, and says that feelings of depression wash over her periodically. Paloma tells me that she and the women work for as long as their bodies can aguantar (hold on/endure). She explains,

> Terminas lesionada, así que te duele tu espalda, que te duele esto, y yo pues desde que aguantas, pues duele mucho tus manos. Si. Yo te diría . . . a veces, tengo un problema aquí, que cuando voy a trabajar, siento mucho dolor de cabeza. Y es, como te digo, ¿cuánto tiempo aguanto? Porque no sé cuánto tiempo más voy a seguir soportando que me llega a doler acá. Porque cuando estoy descansando, no me duele. Cuando estoy trabajando es cuando siento el dolor . . . A eso me refiero, a cuánto tiempo más aguante el cuerpo.[i]

This chapter tells the story of how women moved from the milpa (maíz field) to the maquila. It is a story about how Maya mexicanas went from being mamas to machines. I will demonstrate how the maquila subjugates working-class Maya mexicanas through a process of dehumanization that renders them objects and threatens to distort their relationships with the land, themselves, and their communities. It is a story that has a long history.

It is, in many ways, the story of capitalism in southern Mexico, which some believe is capable of influencing "human instincts such as gluttony, greed and the desire for wealth and power for the benefit of all."[2] If this is true, then the effects of capitalism in general and recent free trade agreements ought to positively impact the lives of diverse individuals and societies and provide them with equal freedoms. The measure of this promise can be judged by the lives of eleven working-class Maya mexicanas employed by a transnational corporation.

---

i. "You end up injured, your back hurts, this hurts you, and you hold on/endure, your hands hurt a lot. Yes. I'm telling you . . . sometimes, I have a problem here, and when I go to work, I get a strong headache. And, like I'm telling you, how long can I hang on for/endure? Because I don't know how much longer I can continue to endure these headaches. Because when I am resting, it doesn't hurt. It's when I'm working that I feel the pain . . . That's what I mean when I say how much longer can my body hang on/endure."

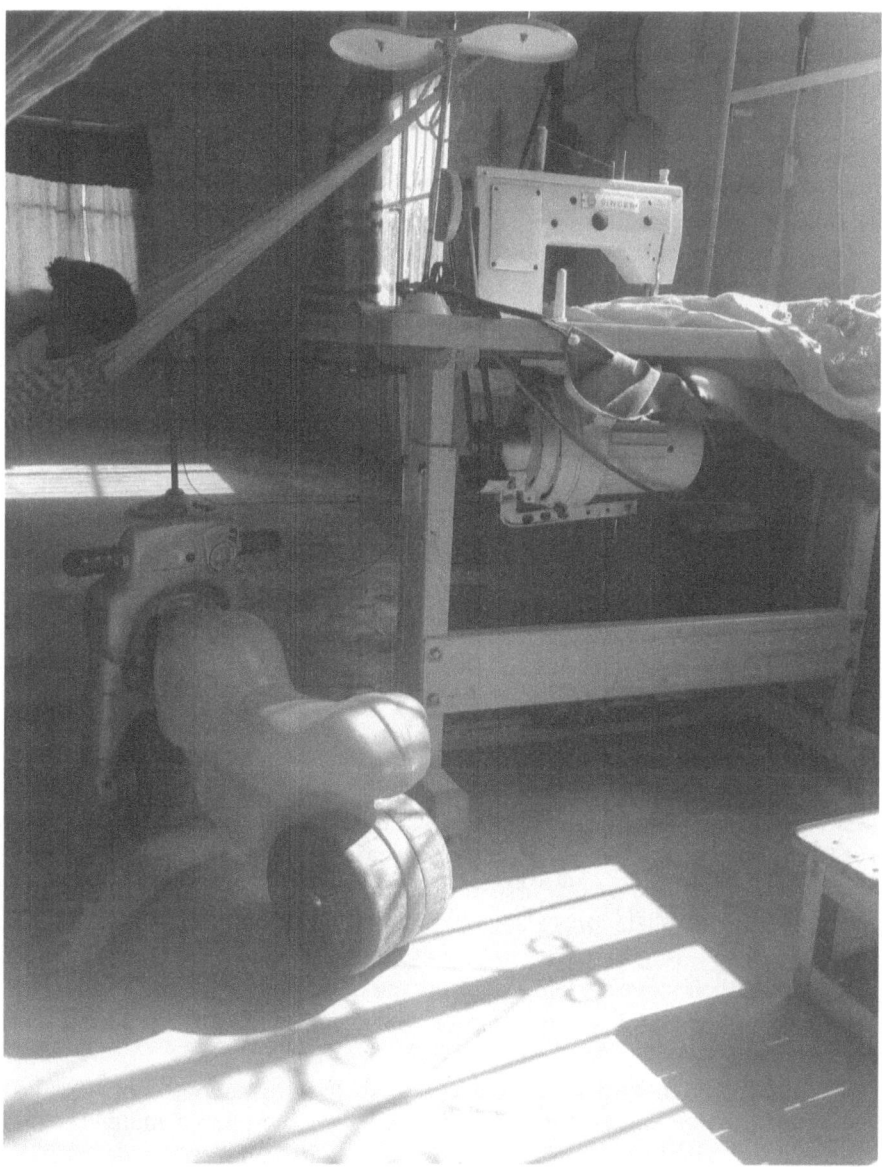

Figure 2.1. A sewing machine in a home in the pueblo mágico. Photo taken by the author.

FROM ENCOMIENDA TO HACIENDA

Spaniards arrived in what for them was the New World (the Americas) and established what C. H. Haring identifies as an exploitation colony.[3] The exploitative colonies occupying the Yucatán extracted the native indigenous resource, Kí.[4] These colonies relied on the interrelationship of three distinct powers to impose their punitive actions: the crown, divine authority, and social stratification. In Spain, as in other nations around the world, the king supposedly ruled by divine authority, as did other men with political authority. The king's subjects practiced passive obedience to the crown and to political and ecclesial authority.[5] A brief overview of how this took root is important for us to identify the persistent patterns of colonization that are entrenched in the process of extracting wealth and resources from the land and the people.

Juan de Grijalva arrived on the Yucatán coast in 1517 in search of gold and slave labor.[6] The encomienda system, an exploitation colony, imposed on Muslims in Spain during the Reconquista[7] and replicated in the occupation of the Caribbean islands beginning in 1492, was a deeply entrenched method of exploiting the local resources of land and people. The conquistadores who arrived in the New World were already well coached in viewing agricultural and mining labor as "a demeaning occupation,"[8] beneath them, so it is unsurprising that they forced those they conquered to labor for their profit and regarded them—particularly as the locals were non-Catholics—as subhuman.

Encomenderos stripped the pueblo indígena from owning weapons, forced them to wear clothing of "reasonable men,"[9] and obligated them to bring their children twice a week to be instructed in Christian education. The conquistadores forced the pueblo indígena to learn to read and write in Spanish, to make the sign of the cross, participate in confession, recite the Pater Noster, the Credo, the Salve Regina, and, in many cases, to be baptized and to attend weekly religious services.[10] With no regard for the integrity of the pueblo indígena, the conquistadores also submitted the people to long hours of labor in the fields and in gold mines to provide food and riches for the Spaniards. They veiled their slave system by paying the pueblo wages according to what they deemed to be a fair wage.[11] In short, the encomienda was a feudal system in every way.

Among the many atrocities the encomienda system brought, the arrival of the Spanish occupiers also affected the health of the pueblo indígena. Diseases such as smallpox, measles, malaria, and yellow fever had devastating effects on the pueblo indígena. Infections spread and birth rates declined as infant mortality rates increased.[12] It was obvious that the encomienda system was killing the pueblo indígena. The system was almost abolished by the advocacy of the missionary, diplomat, historian, and encomendero[i] Bartolomé de Las Casas, who arduously campaigned for freedom of Indians in the encomienda after he himself witnessed the grave injustices of the encomienda system as a result of his own participation in the system.[13] De Las Casas was an encomendero in Cuba between 1502 and 1512. Through the preaching of Dominican friars and a growing awareness of his violent actions, he sought absolution and was rejected because he was an encomendero. In *Brevíssima Relación*, de Las Casas describes the brutality of the encomienda on the pueblo indígena that finally awakened his conscience and drew him to confession. Surprised that his continued role as encomendero was the basis for not receiving absolution for his sins, de Las Casas decided to devote the remainder of his life to correcting his action by advocating for the freedom of the pueblo indígena.[14] He was somewhat successful in that by May 1520 the encomienda system was eliminated, but conquistadores in New Spain protested that they could not survive without the labor of the Indians. As a compromise, the order was altered in November 1526 to state that laborers work voluntarily, be paid, and could remain in an encomienda as free persons if "it was thought necessary for their conversion."[15]

The encomienda system took root in the Yucatán by the authority of the royal cédula that defined Spanish-Indian relationship and ascribed a rather incomprehensible meaning to the freedom of the pueblo indígena:

> Whereas, the King my Lord and I agree, in the instruction which we commanded given to Don Fray Nicolás de Ovando . . . that the Indian inhabitants of the island of Española are free and not servile . . . and whereas we are now informed that because of the excessive liberty enjoyed by the said Indians they avoid contact and community with the Spaniards to such an extent that they will not work even for wages, but wander about idle and cannot be had by the Christians to convert to our Holy Catholic Faith; and in order that the Christians may not lack people to work their holdings for their maintenance and extract the gold that there is on the island . . . and whereas we desire that the said Indians be converted to our Holy Catholic Faith and taught in its doctrines; and whereas this can better be done by having the Indians live in community with the Christians of the island and go among them and associate with them, by which means they will help each other to cultivate, settle, and reap the fruits of the island, and extract the gold which may be there, and bring profit to my kingdom and subjects,
>
> [Therefore], I have commanded this my letter to be issued on the matter in which I command you, our said governor, that beginning with the day on which you receive my letter you will compel and force the said Indians to associate with the Christians of the island and to work on their buildings, and to gather and mine the gold and other metals, and to till the fields and produce food for

---

i. One who owns an encomienda.

the Christian inhabitants and dwellers of the said island; and you are to have each one paid on the day he works the wages and maintenance which you think he should have . . . and you are to order each cacique to take charge of a certain number of the said Indians, so that you may make them work wherever necessary, and so that on feast days and such other days as you think proper they may be gathered together to hear and be taught in the things of the Faith . . . This the Indians shall perform as free people, which they are, and not as slaves. And see to it that they are well treated, those who become Christians better than the others, and do not consent or allow that any person do them any harm or oppress them.[16]

In short, the encomienda system enslaved and murdered the pueblo indígena while the colonialists, by supposed divine authority, justified their actions. More important, in my view, is that the colonialists offered a definition of "freedom" that obscured the pueblo indígenas' moral agency to act out of their own conscience and knowledge of the divine. In this way colonialism is not only responsible for the genocide of the pueblo indígena but also what economist and legal scholar Boaventura de Sousa Santos calls "epistemicide." Citing de Sousa Santos's definition, sociologist and decolonialist Ramón Grosfoguel explains epistemicide as "the extermination of knowledge and ways of knowing."[17] Epistemicide is an indictment on the practices of colonialism that judge knowledge produced from particular world regions, cosmologies, and people as inferior to those of white Western men.[18] The royal cédula sanctions a double violence on the pueblo indígena, both physical and epistemic. The assault on the pueblo indígena is an attempt to eradicate not only the physical body but the ancestral wisdom and knowledge tradition of the Maya.

FROM HACIENDA TO MAQUILA

A second system, the haciendas, emerged in the Yucatán during the nineteenth century. The haciendas in México—large estates built by the Spanish on stolen land—were privately owned by a hacendado or patrón (predominantly of European descent) but operated by an administrator. Land laborers were forcibly drawn from local peasants or campesinos. These private estates were established for the production of various kinds of native produce. In the Yucatán, the henequen or agave plant proved to be a rich resource for the Spanish Empire. With a sudden increase in demand for henequen from Europe and the United States, the Spanish saw an opportunity and used the hacendados and their system of forced labor through a debt peonage system to subjugate and enslave Mayas. Allan D. Meyers and David L. Carlson use Friedrich Katz's definition of debt peonage to understand the context of labor in haciendas in Yucatán. Katz writes that debt peonage "is a form of forced labor which develops when a number of social and economic prerequisites for bondage in agriculture (such as a powerful group of large landowners, a shortage of labor, etc.) exists but the state officially refuses to implement bondage while tacitly tolerating and acknowledging it under another name."[19] Campesinxs were technically free to leave, but only after their debt to landowners was paid—and wages were such that campesinxs needed to borrow from the hacienda in order to survive. Peones (campesinx laborers) would even increase their debt by requesting an advance on their wages and/or food rations.

The Yucatán peninsula has a very thin layer of topsoil covering limestone rock. Its vegetation is largely a low-lying tropical forest. Kí or agave grows in this dry and stony terrain where other crops fail that rely on more rainfall or on the irrigation systems that depend on cenotes, the peninsula's water-filled sinkholes and cisterns. The indigenous plant of the Yucatán, known as Kí in Maya, was already cultivated on the peninsula before the arrival of Columbus in the late fifteenth century. The Mayas manually scraped the yard-long Kí leaves to make the raw fiber they then used for hammocks, mosquito nets, bags, and rope. The community lived off the local land and shared resources in this way until the conquistadores arrived and established Spanish colonies, which exploited the land and the people.

Several factors in the nineteenth century led to a boom in the production of henequen in the Yucatán; however, I focus on the second industrial revolution (1870–1914) because it marks the beginnings of a trade relationship between the US and the Yucatán. The industrial revolution was spurred by labor-saving inventions such as the mechanical reaper known as the McCormick Harvesting Machine, co-invented by enslaved African American Jo Anderson, which harvested grain and used wire to tie bales of crops together for ease of transport and storage. Metal bits of wire contaminated the feed of farm animals, which was harmful to the animals. To rectify this problem, the company adapted the machinery to use henequen, also called binder or baling twine, which was safe for livestock to consume but still held the bales together admirably.[20] As the demand for McCormick reapers increased in North America and Europe, so too did the demand for henequen. Yucatán's haciendas consequently turned away from the long-established production of staples like livestock and maíz[21] (which was already starting to decline) to produce the region's latest "green gold"[22]—henequen.

Exportation of henequen made Yucatán one of the richest states in México during the early 1900s, creating an economic upper class. Twenty to thirty families owned the exporting houses, while 400 families owned 200 million pesos each, along with debt from loans they took out from Banqueros de

Figure 2.2. Henequen located in the pueblo mágico. Photo taken by the author.

Nueva York.[23] Why does this matter? The hacienda system established an upper class that named itself "casta divina" (divine caste) and abandoned the tradition of raising livestock and maíz to produce henequen for the consumption not of its surrounding community but for a global market. This urgency to keep up with the demand when it was at its height also encouraged the invention of machines that could produce goods efficiently.[24]

The haciendas' henequeneras resembled their encomienda predecessors in that "La mano de obra, peones mayas encasillados, trabajaba en condiciones de semiesclavitud que se perpetúaban junto con deudas impagables."[25] Haciendas invaded pueblos by first constructing edifices that resembled European mansions, equipped with a chapel that reflected the Catholic Christian religious agenda of the encomienda system. The pueblo indígena, here the Maya, were stripped of their everyday lives in the pueblo—cultivating maíz and honey, weaving—to work for the hacendados, who forced them to labor long hours chopping the native plant and learning to use machinery that altered their ancestral skills of shredding Kí and creating hammocks, mosquito nets, bags, and rope. The introduction of machines and industrialization pulled campesinxs from their traditional relationship to the land to a context where the land was an object from which to extract resources for the growing greed of henequeros seeking riches. The identity of campesinxs went from being a human in an ecosystem to being an indebted slave in the production of henequen.

The greed of henequeros should also be understood in its larger context, that of a Mexican political system that facilitated the taking of land and enslaving of the pueblo. The American journalist John Kenneth Turner exposed the abuse of the pueblo indígena and the corruption of the hacienda system in his book *Barbarous Mexico*.[26] Here, Turner attributes the unjust system to then-president of México Porfirio Díaz. He does not dismiss its Spanish colonial roots but argues that under Díaz "slavery and peonage were reestablished in Mexico" after the indigenous people were given some freedom in the Declaration of Independence of 1810.[27] Turner accuses Díaz of "land robbery" for the sake of accumulating wealth for himself and his immediate family and friends, and identifies this as "the direct step in the path of the Mexican people back to their bondage as slaves and peons."[28] Turner describes the government of Mexico as having only one branch—the executive, meaning the president of the country, the governor of each of the twenty-seven states who answers to the president, and the jefe politico (political boss) of the district, who answers to both the governor and the president. While the judicial and legislative branches exist in name, they are governed by the executive and have little power themselves.[29] The implication of such a structure is that there is no mitigating power that can advocate or even safeguard the people from the tyranny of the president and his inner circle. Consequently, Díaz's method of requiring land registration in order to claim rights to land facilitated the stripping of ancestral land from the pueblo. When Díaz enforced the 1856 Reform Laws, he did not send out persons to inform the pueblo that this new "modern"[30] requirement was being enforced; instead he organized land companies headed by his father-in-law and comprised of members of his government to scout the land and "select the most desirable lands in the country, register them, and evict the owners."[31] This resulted in the loss of land for thousands of campesinxs and the beginning of an elite ruling class in México. A significant cultural shift provoked by the Reform Laws was the transition from communal inherited land to private individual ownership.[32] In particular, the Maya living in the region of Yucatán suffered devastating effects from the Díaz government granting the 43,000 square kilometers of Quintana Roo to eight Mexican politicians. The land in this area is rich in not only henequen but also valuable dyewoods, and is expected to produce tobacco at a rate that could compete with the neighboring country, Cuba.[33] The Maya responded peaceably. When land rich in sugar cane was destroyed during the Caste War, the Maya fled to the monte (forest jungle) in the southeast of the Yucatán, where they lived in autonomous communities, thus allowing the henequeros to take over the lands in the northern region around Mérida and establish haciendas.[34]

Land robbed from the pueblo indígena allowed the hacendados to profit from the fertility of the soil, the labor of the people, and the protection of a government that supported the pillage of people and property. With the gradual decline in demand for henequen, the state government began to promote and recruit maquilas to provide jobs and continue the ideology of profiting from extraction of resources of land and labor for the advantage of an elite ruling class.

As noted in chapter 1, the maquiladora industry began in the north along the Texas–Ciudad Juárez border. Yucatán marketed its territory by promoting three advantages to US companies. First, in comparison with Tijuana, Ciudad Juárez, or Mexicali, shipping to New York or destinations on the east coast is less expensive from Yucatán. Second, the transportation infrastructure of the region is relatively good, with easy access to ports of entry that can facilitate transportation of goods. Third, the population in the region gives maquilas access to cheap nonmigrant labor that is stable, which in turn saves costs associated with training new workers. The state government incentivized the US maquila companies by offering them urban territory at low or no cost. As a result, in 1997, maquilas invaded thirteen impoverished municipalities: Tekit, Tekantó, Motul, Cholul, Tahmek, Izamal, Seyé, Tekax, Tecoh, Mocochá, Suma, Chicxulub Pueblo, and Temax.[35] A unique characteristic of the maquilas in Yucatán in comparison to those along México's northern border is that they rely on manual labor more than on technological/electrical machine skilled labor.[36] It is important to keep in mind that "la maquiladora es la única fuente de empleo industrial en la localidad," which leads to workers being described as "mucho más leales a la empresa."[37]

Maquilas use five broad strategies to subjugate Maya working-class women, dehumanizing them through a process that renders them objects and threatens to distort their relationships with the land, themselves, and their communities. Activists from Ciudad Juárez confirm that these strategies seem universal across México, with regional variations. There may be similarities with men's experience in maquilas, but since I did not interview men, I limit my discussion to women's experience. Maquilas: 1) assign to individuals the traits of machines, 2) incarcerate women, 3) implement a culture of surveillance to produce pressure and "cansar" (to tire), 4) pay women lethal wages, and 5) advance the religion of the colonizer.

Sowing Pernicious Seeds: The Invasion of Indigenous Land by US Transnational Corporations

The women refer to the maquila as "la planta." I understand this analogy from my own experience living in the geographic location of southern California. There is a non-native, invasive plant known as iceplant that has recently spread along the coast of California from Humboldt County to Baja California. It "forms a large, thick mat that chokes out all other native plants and alters the soil composition of the environment . . . it competes with many endangered, threatened, and rare plants"[38] that die as a result of its presence. It is an invasive species. "La planta" is like iceplant. The intrusion of maquilas, while bringing jobs and commerce to the region, also endangers indigenous life. The maquila begins by planting the seed of capitalism in the region's sacred land, and capitalism devastates the collectivism of tribal life. Capitalism is both an economic system and an ideology.[39] Academic definitions of capitalism abound but I prefer to define the system and ideology with the words of those who live under capitalism's tyranny. Radio Zapatista, an autonomous colectivo (collective), describes capitalism as a social system where

> hay unos pocos que tienen grandes riquezas, pero no es que se sacaron un premio, o que se encontraron un tesoro, o que heredaron de un pariente, sino que esas riquezas las obtienen de explotar el trabajo de muchos . . . exprimen a los trabajadores y les sacan todo lo que pueden de ganancias . . . el capitalismo hace su riqueza con despojo, o sea con robo, porque les quita a otros lo que

ambiciona, por ejemplo tierra y riquezas naturales. Al capitalismo lo que más le interesa son las mercancías, porque cuando se compran y se venden dan ganancias. Y entonces el capitalismo todo lo convierte en mercancías, hace mercancías a las personas, a la naturaleza, a la cultura, a la historia, a la conciencia. Según el capitalismo, todo se tiene que poder comprar y vender. O sea, en el mercado vemos mercancías, pero no vemos la explotación con las que se hicieron.[i]

In this description of capitalism, I hear Zapatistas naming imperialism's rapacious economic system of death, also known as neoliberal capitalism.[40]

The link between racism, sexism, and capitalism is designed to exploit not only women living in the two-thirds world but also women of color living within the United States. Political theorist Cedric Robinson introduced the concept of racial capitalism in his influential book *Black Marxism*, which is essential to understanding global capitalism and its entrapments in the colonial project. Robinson encountered the term "racial capitalism" from South African intellectuals he was in conversation with during his sabbatical in England. Building on the understanding of racial capitalism as a description of a specific system (apartheid), Robinson broadened its meaning to trace the history of racism inherent in modern capitalism. Capitalism, he argues, is not a departure from feudalism; capitalism evolved from within the feudal system and gained momentum in a society that was already entrenched in racism. In other words, racism predates capitalism and European proletarians experienced colonization and slavery as racial subjects.[41]

In the 1980s, there was a reconstruction of capitalism, or what is called neoliberal capitalism.[42] This new articulation of capitalism emphasizes policies of liberalization, privatization, and deregulation, retaining Adam Smith's claim that "the hidden hand of the market" is capable of influencing "human instincts such as gluttony, greed and the desire for wealth and power for the benefit of all."[43] If this is true, then the effects of free trade ought to impact the lives of diverse individuals and societies positively and provide them with equal freedoms. I assess the benefits of neoliberal capitalism by focusing on one free trade agreement, the NAFTA,[44] and judge the freedom of the market based on the lives of eleven working-class Maya mexicanas employed by a transnational corporation.

---

i. "La Guerra Capitalista," Radio Zapatista, September 18, 2017, https://radiozapatista.org/?p=22934&lang=en. Translation: "There are a few who have great wealth, but it is not that they got a prize, or that they found a treasure, or that they inherited from a relative, but that those riches are obtained by exploiting the work of many . . . they squeeze the workers and they take everything they can from profits . . . capitalism makes its wealth with dispossession, that is robbery, because it takes away from others what it seeks, for example, land and nature's riches. Capitalism is interested in goods, because they are bought and sold, they give profits. And then capitalism turns everything into goods, because when they are bought and sold, they give profits. And then capitalism turns everything into goods, makes/transforms people, nature, culture, history consciousness into goods. According to capitalism, everything has to be able to buy and sell. In other words, in the market we see merchandise, but we do not see the exploitation with which they were made."

POLLUTING AGRICULTURAL RITUALS: FROM MILPA TO MAQUILA

One afternoon, as Doña Nayeli and her sister's daughter-in-law were washing dishes, they invited me to take part in the daily ritual that protects their family from disease and keeps order in the palapa. Doña Nayeli placed the plates and cups in a large bucket filled with soapy water. She took her hand and rubbed the food-stained surface of the plates before handing them to me and instructing me to rinse them in a separate bucket filled with water. The other woman then took the plates and cups from me and dried them with a rag. The daughter-in-law's children played in the palapa along with other children whose parents were working at the maquila. These children joined us for a meal. When we ate, any child or adult who was near our home was invited to join. There was always enough. When Doña Lucía prepared food she never worried. She told me, "Le agregamos agua. Si hay bastante. Vengan a comer."[i] There was always room at the table to feed one more child whose parent was working.

As we washed dishes, the women told me about a ritual the maquila colonizes. Every year these campesinxs practice the Wáajil kool, an agricultural ritual that preserves the Maya belief in equilibrium and interrelationship between humans, nature, and the gods. The ceremony is a communal ritual that asks the ancestors for their blessing of the land. It is an act of gratitude for the harvest and also a petition for the continued prosperity of the crops. Doña Nayeli told me that if the Wáajil kool is not done, then the land "le da hambre"[ii] and culebras (snakes) and other animals drive out people from the land and no crops are produced.

Once a year the campesinxs make an offering to the god of rain, Chaac, during the Wáajil kool ritual. Campesinxs come to the milpa with their shovels, cooking pots, and jicaritas (the shell of the fruit jícaro that is used as a cup), and their families participate in the ceremony. The owner of the milpa offers the first portion of the harvest of the field to Chaac and the remaining harvest is used to make a communal meal for the campesinxs to share with the entire pueblo. The meal is prepared by dividing the tasks among the men and women in the pueblo. The women cook chicken and kol (a corn paste) to make pib, a meal that is also prepared for Hanal Pixán (Day of the Dead) and placed on altars for the dead ancestors to eat. The men gather large leaves from the trees in the monte (forest) and bring them to the women to fill with kol and chicken. The pib that is made to offer to Chaac is filled with thirteen pepitas (pumpkin seeds), which represent the maximum offering a campesino

---

i. "We'll add water. Yes, there's enough/a lot. You all come eat."
ii. Gets hungry.

is able to make. After the leaves are filled, the men tie the leaves and the pib is ready to cook.

In order to cook the pib, the men dig a hole in the earth. They line the edges and fill the bottom with stones. Then they lay firewood and start a fire. Once the stones are warmed, the burnt wood is removed and the pib are laid on top of the stones. Additional wood is used to cover the pib and then dirt is piled on top to create an underground oven in which the pib bakes. After a few hours, the men dig up/unearth the pib and serve everyone in the pueblo pib with Báalche, a red drink made from the bark of a tree and mixed with honey. The pueblo shares, eats, and sees that creation is very good.

In 1997, capitalist owners located the maquila in a nearby town where campesinxs and their families had long safeguarded and perpetuated a strong cosmic connection to the land where they grew their crops of jicama, plátanos, maíz, and chiles. This was a strategic choice based on where the transnational corporation could extract profit from the land without regard to environmental harm. Additionally, the maquila planted itself in a place where the pueblo indígena has lived for centuries.

Its presence disturbs the people's historic and cultural practice of trading goods. The pueblo's economy is based on the exchange of goods for the sake of the community. Prior to the colonial invasions of Spanish and US transnational corporations, the pueblo exchanged resources, and the women in particular preserved the ancestral skill of weaving as part of that economy. But the pueblo's way of life (its communal economy) cannot compete with globalization and the expansionist practices of neoliberal capitalism. When la planta set its roots in the land, it polluted the rich cultural, economic, social, and spiritual lives of the pueblo. In my view, this pollution begins with capitalism's desecration of the sacred, especially the indigenous, communal spirituality and the rites that express and maintain it.

The maquila is aware of the campesinxs' sacred connection to the land where it plants its industrial edifice and preys on cheap labor. The US-based company spreads its imperial power by changing the local economy of the place. Whereas previously the campesinxs traded their crop with one another, life changed when the maquila came into the town. The campesinxs cannot compete with the global market economy. As the price of fertilizer and costs of maintenance of land rise, campesinxs are ripped from their land and essentially thrown into the maquila assembly line to produce goods for the consumption of North American customers. They now sow a harvest they reap to satisfy the global market economy's greed, not for their own limited needs. I suspect that the maquila's owners must have some fear of the sacred

Figure 2.3. A campesino picking chiles in a milpa located in the pueblo mágico. Photo taken by the author.

connection campesinxs have with the land, and so, just in case their relationship to the soil is real and just in case failing to practice the Wáajil kool means the crop/produce will be devoured by snakes, the maquila co-opts the Wáajil kool. When I wondered out loud about this, I was told "lo hacen porque son campesinos los que trabajan."[i] What I understood the woman to be saying is that campesinxs are appeased by the maquilas' practice of the Wáajil kool because whoever occupies the land should observe the ritual. The maquila modifies the Wáajil kool by introducing the element of what Zapatistas call "el monstruo" (the monster): capitalism and patriarchy.

Once a year, los gerentes (managers), los jefes (bosses), and la de calidad (quality control supervisor) plan a Wáajil kool. They meet and decide who will be responsible to contact and hire a x'men to make the offering to Chaac. The women I spoke with know this is done but they do not know what is said or how the meal is prepared because they are not invited to participate in the ceremony. There is no shared time to prepare a meal. There is no communal eating. There is no cup from which all in the community drink. No one shares, eats, and sees. Instead they are relegated to a passive role where they are merely told that the maquila intercedes on their behalf, and those who have ears to hear begin to discern capitalism as a poisonous plant.

Maquilas Assign Individuals Traits of Machines

Once the maquila plants itself in the terrain, it begins to grow roots through its primordial value for efficiency and production. Campesinxs are gradually divested of human characteristics and reduced to docile, obedient, competitive, and cheap industrialized operators. In essence, the assembly-line workers become the latest technological invention of the globalized economy.

Mariana explains what made her apply for work at the maquila, "Uno, ¿por qué lo hace? Por necesidad. Porque como no estudié y entonces pues necesito sacar a mi familia adelante y ese trabajo está cerca, lo solicité."[ii] When a potential worker applies for work, she fills out paperwork and waits to hear from the maquila. When a person's application piques the interest of the maquila, she is called in to take "la prueba," or the test.

What would pique such an employer's interest? The research of Melissa W. Wright uncovers the rhetoric of multinational company managers and the qualities they identify in potential employees. Wright cites previous authors who confirm the language she hears employers use to describe the qualities

---

i. They practice the Waajil kool because they locate factories here and its campesinxs that work here.

ii. "Why do I/we do this? Out of necessity. Because I didn't study and I needed to help my family survive and this job is nearby. So I applied."

they seek in an employee as "dexterity," "docility," "patience," "attentiveness," and "cheapness."⁴⁵ She notes that in 2006, women workers "represented one of the world's best bargains," earning a mere eleven cents per hour.⁴⁶ The transnational company accepts applications from women in the local community and then gives them a test.

Natalia tells me about la prueba. "Te dan una tablita donde vas a ir metiendo los palitos y van a ir midiendo que tiempo que vas a estar presentando el examen . . . te ponen a competir entre tú y uno más. Y así lo van a ir metiendo en los huequitos . . . El que terminó mas rápido, quiere decir que es el más rápido para producir."ⁱ She tells me that on the day she was called in to take la prueba, she was put in competition with a male. She tells me she won the competition because she is a woman; she knows how to accomplish several tasks simultaneously and quickly because she is a well-trained mother. "Yo en que estoy en casa trabajando mis labores domésticos, pues yo trato de hacerlo lo más rápido que yo pueda para que yo pueda terminar antes de que mi nene despertar . . . lave trastes, ya barrí, ya cociné, ya trapeé, en mi casa, y termine eso de lavar."ⁱⁱ Natalia speaks without taking a breath as she tells me everything she does. Her eyes widen as she emphasizes how fast (rápido) she does all these tasks. I hear Natalia's explanation and I interpret this to mean she has a supernatural power to do many things at once. I understand her conception of herself as a woman with godlike qualities of omnipotence, omniscience, and omnipresence. A mother is all-powerful, all-knowing, and everywhere. She is a life bearer. One who can create conditions for life. The maquila employs her simply for these qualities and then extracts from her the production it needs.

Paloma describes the nature of the assembly-line production: "El trabajo repetitivo, nos ocasiona problemas."ⁱⁱⁱ Veronica warns me, "Mucha gente está empezando a tener problemas de desgaste en los huesos, por el tipo de trabajo que hacemos."ⁱᵛ The women's physical bodies wear down in this act of labor. Physically her ability to produce is diminished. She either quits or is fired for her lack of production. She becomes "industrial waste" discarded after her ability to meet the daily quota becomes impossible due to physical injuries *sustained on the job*. The women are discarded and replaced as if they are cogs in a machine that need to be regularly replaced for the mechanism to operate optimally. Additionally, as the transnational corporation grows, it

---

    i. "They give you a small board where you will go putting the sticks and they will measure how long you will be doing the exam . . . they put you in competition between you and one more person. And so, the two of you will be putting them in the little holes . . . The one that finishes first, means that they are able to produce faster."
    ii. "When I am at home doing my domestic work, I try to do it as fast as I can so I can finish before my baby wakes up . . . I finish washing dishes, sweeping, cooking, mopping, and washing clothes."
    iii. "The repetitive work causes us problems."
    iv. "Many people are starting to have bone wear problems, because of the type of work we do."

employs more people, each doing smaller, more discrete, and more repetitive tasks along sections of the assembly line. When the company first opened, one worker did two or three operations, whereas now each operation is done thousands of times a day by a single worker.[i]

A woman working on the assembly line is part of the machine. She is no longer a mother, wife, or sister. Familial ties that once bound the community together are now torn apart. Itzel explains, "Ya entrando ya, aquí no hay marido, esposo, no hay nada. Todos somos compañeros."[ii] The women still work alongside each other, but now, as in the entrance test or prueba, they are in competition with one another to sate the greed of a consumerist culture that wants to buy more for less and to satisfy the company, which needs to maximize its profits to keep its shareholders happy.

Maquilas Incarcerate Women

Once a woman is hired after passing la prueba, she becomes an employee and lives in the encierro (enclosed space). Teresa says, "Es mucho el encierro. Es como que te encerraron en la cárcel . . . Es como estar encarcelada . . . te cierran una reja donde están los vigilantes. Una vez que entres, ya te cierran la puerta."[iii]

The gated entrance of the maquila is an automatic iron-railed gate with a security tower. When I visited, I was escorted by one of the women who worked cleaning the managers' offices and running errands for management. We pulled up at the security tower in a pickup truck and were asked for identification by a uniformed security guard. He had a walkie-talkie and notified the maquila that I was requesting access. After getting clearance, he asked that I log in and reminded me not to take pictures inside.

The gate opened and we drove in and parked. I got out and walked to the entrance of the reception room. The bright cobalt blue colored room displays the company's logo. The floor is of bright white tile. A receptionist sits behind a glass window, much like in a bank. Behind her desk is an open lobby with a coffee machine and managers' offices along the sides. There is the outline of one door that leads to the production floor. In order to go into the production area, guests and workers wear protective clear plastic goggles and small orange ear plugs that feel like sponges. I am instructed to do all this before the ingeniero gives me a guided tour. Again, I am told not to take pictures.

---

i. On a drive into the pueblo, a taxi cab driver who had worked for the maquila told me about his experience as an assembly-line worker and why he had quit.

ii. "Once we enter, here there is no husband (marido), husband (esposo), there is nothing. We are all co-workers/partners."

iii. "The confinement is too much. It's like they locked you in jail . . . It's like being imprisoned . . . they close a fence where the guards are. Once you enter, and there they close the door."

As I walk in, all the color in the world fades away. The walls are painted gray. There are no windows, and the air that circulates is from the central air-conditioning unit that is working at full capacity. The floor is smooth and made of cement painted a glossy gray. There is a red stripe that designates where I can walk, and the inner area where the workers are is outlined separately. I recognize some of the women and we make brief eye contact but it is clear that they have to stay within that line. Araceli tells me that once you clock into work, you cannot leave. She says, "Una vez que estés allí, sin permiso no sales. Necesitas una hoja de permiso para salir, firmado por recursos humanos. Por ellos, la supervisora, sí."[i] It is not clear to me whether she is able to leave her station for a bathroom break or not. Activists in Ciudad Juárez tell me women are not given any breaks for twelve hours.[47] Celeste elaborates on this policy that theoretically permits breaks but is not kept in practice. She also notes that even during the break time designated for workers to eat, they dine in an enclosed area. "Nada más a las horas de comida salimos y de hecho es si quieres salir. Si tienes el tiempo de salir a una pequeña palapa donde ya entonces no está cerrado. Porque si ya sales nada mas de comedor, igual, no vas a ver nada."[ii]

The ingeniero giving me the tour walks me around the perimeter and into a dining hall that looks like a small cafeteria. It is hard for me to hear him speak above the noise of sewing machines and other sounds of pounding that echo through the gray room. He says this is where the women eat on their lunch break. These walls are blank white walls with cheap dinner tables organized in three long rows. There is a door that leads to a palapa[iii] with a long table. As he speaks, I have flashbacks of conversations in the pueblo around the dinner table. The campesinxs laugh at the cold sandwiches served at the maquila, "¡Eso no es comida!"[iv]

The enclosure of the maquila resembles the structure of institutional buildings that are designed to impose control over workers. These edifices, panopticons (*pan*-all, *opticon*-observed), are described by the eighteenth-century philosopher and social theorist Jeremy Bentham (1748–1832). The panopticon is an architectural structure that organizes power and transforms people into objects that self-surveil.[48] Entering into this sort of configuration is terrifying. Workers like Ximena have a similar sense that in the maquila

---

i. "Once you are there, without permission you do not leave. You need a permission slip to leave, signed by human resources. By them, the supervisor, yes."

ii. "Only during the hours we eat do we take a break and in fact it is if you want to take a break. If you have time to go out to a small palapa where you are not enclosed. Because if you only go to the cafeteria, just the same, you are not going to see anything."

iii. This is an open structure with a thatched roof made out of dried palm leaves that provides shade. This palapa is the only structure that resembles the building structures of the pueblo.

iv. "That's not food!"

they are entering a place from which they cannot escape and out of which they cannot see:

> Al momento de entrar como te da miedo. Te da miedo. Básicamente el encierro. Porque ya cuando entras, no ves nada. No, no ves nada por fuera . . . Estás muy lejos de, a distancias de la carretera, de la gente y de todo que pasa a veces por ahí. Pues, yo la primera vez que entré allá, como "ay, no voy a durar allá." Me sentía así. Pero ya con el tiempo lo fui agarrando más la onda, como se dice, y ya me acostumbré.[i]

This culture of confinement takes on an added dimension when supervisors are suspicious of workers and search their person to be sure nothing is stolen from the maquila. Workers are suspects, potential criminals, and treated as incarcerated convicts. Itzel explains, "Todo te están chequeando cuando sale uno . . . Nada puedes agarrar. Ni un botón que agarres, te pasan allá a la oficina para que te llamen la atención . . . porque según estas robando en la planta."[ii]

The women know the "gaze" of the oppressor, whether it is in their pueblo, the church, or on the assembly line. The men, the supervisors, "te andan vigilando."[iii] They pressure her to agree to behave in the given context in a way that profits the institution at her expense. The women tell me about "el turno nocturno" (night shift), which is voluntary in theory but in practice is required if you want to keep your job. Indeed, the practice is that one "volunteers" to work a full twenty-four hours at one stretch.

> Me dijo el que estaba, el ingeniero de producción, "Recuerda que firmaste a apoyar cuando la empresa la requiera. Y va haber nocturno mañana. Y no es obligatorio," te dice, "Pero recuerda que firmaste." En pocas palabras como que no te cabe de otra, tienes que ir.[iv]

---

i. "When you enter, like, you feel fear. It scares you, basically the confinement. Because when you enter, you cannot see anything. No, you can't see anything outside . . . You are very far from, at a distance from the road, from people and from everything that sometimes happens there. Well, the first time I went in there, like 'Oh, I'm not going to last there.' I felt that way. But over time I got the hang of it, as they say, and now I'm used to it."

ii. "When you leave work they check everything . . . You cannot take anything. Not even grab a button, they will send you to the office to talk to you about it . . . because according to them you are stealing in the maquila."

iii. "They are watching you."

iv. "The one who was there, the production engineer, told me, 'Remember that you signed to give your support when the company required it. And there is night shift tomorrow. And it's not obligatory,' he says, 'but remember you signed.' In a few words he was saying: you have no choice; you have to go."

Women tell me they typically signed the contractual paperwork without reading it either because it was too much or because some of them do not read Spanish.[i]

The structure of the panopticon, as Bentham describes it, also separates individuals into "cells" or "workrooms" in a circular building with a watchtower at the center. The "sovereign" or guard inside the watchtower is not visible to the prisoners, but has the ability to see each individual at any point in time. French philosopher and social theorist Michel Foucault (1926–1984) noted that in Bentham's panopticon persons are "alone, perfectly individualized and constantly visible."[49] Here, in the maquila, a similar architectural structure is present. Separate workstations are surveyed by supervisors who walk the perimeter, and a system is in place that quantifies the productivity of each worker each day. The Maya seamstresses are cut off from all forms of relationality. The strong ties that connect her to the land, her community, her children, her spouse, and even her comadres who ostensibly work alongside her are severed when she walks through the iron gate and takes her place on the assembly line. Here, she is alone.

That each woman is separated from all these relationships is strategic. Forced to assume a role as an individual with but one task on the assembly line, without a communal context of how she and her work are part of the larger operation of the maquila, she is deprived by the maquila of the ability to judge and consequently normalize her experience with respect to that of others. This is a form of social control that forces her to submit to the maquila without the threat that she might question whether the maquila bosses are violating some moral standard. Ultimately the standards that prevail in the maquila are those of the global market economy that desires to produce the goods that are in demand for the cheapest cost to the business and the greatest profit to these transnational corporations and their stakeholders. The women do not see the "invisible hand of the market" acting upon their lives; its sovereign reign is invisible to them. Yet the rules of the maquila—efficiency, production, and competition—are clearly the rules of the market. This structure creates the conditions for self-subjugation. The subject objectifies herself by self-surveilling. In other words, the internalized oppressor exerts its oppressive power first by imposing certain rules and practices, and eventually the individual internalizes these rules and practices and self-monitors compliance, meaning the corporation has to do very little to enforce its desires.

---

i. One woman commented on the IRB paperwork, the informed consent forms, that the paperwork looked like what the maquila gave them to sign.

Maquilas Design a Culture of Surveillance to Produce Pressure and "Cansar"

I began to understand how this internalized oppressor self-monitors when listening to Sofia talk about her experience. Sofia is eighteen years old, and she is still in the training/trial period in the maquila. She did not want to work in the maquila. When she finished primaria, she pleaded with her father to let her go to the nearby town to attend secundaria. The pueblo does not have education beyond primaria and very few people go to the neighboring town to pursue an education in hopes of going to college. Sofia's father denied her request. She recalls him telling her, "Como te voy a pagar tu carrera si después a mitad de año ya buscaste un novio por ahí te casas y el dinero que ya invertí por ti ¿quien lo va devolver?"[i] La lucha de Sofia is the one her mother had as well. Sofia says about her mother's experience, "Igual su papá no la dejaba . . . igual su papá, mi abuelo, no la apoyaba."[ii] Sofia understands that her father's reason for not sending her to school is "por ser mujer," and her mother counsels her that if she wants to get an education she needs to work in the maquila, earn money, and find a way to finance her own education. Sofia's mother had a similar dream of going to school, but life didn't work out because "el apoyo familiar es importante," and without that support it is very difficult to accomplish anything. Sofia is confronting a long-held belief that educating a woman is a waste of time, money, and effort. This belief is passed down through every generation; women's lives are predictable: they get married, have babies, take care of their homes, and attend to the needs of others.

Despite her father's refusal, Sofia's mother supported her daughter's dream and convinced her husband to allow her to travel to town and complete la secundaria and el bachiller. Though this is more education than the average child pursues in the pueblo, Sofia has her heart and mind set on pursuing a vocational calling. She knows her father will not and, in some sense, also cannot finance a college education. After all, he is a campesino affected by free trade and genetically modified seeds (GMO) entering Mexico through companies such as Monsanto. He cannot afford to grow corn anymore. The funds needed to purchase fertilizer and compete with GMO production are out of reach, and besides, he does not even own his own land. Sofia's father is a day laborer hired to pick chiles on land owned by another man. Day to day, he does not know when he will be offered work; during the harvest season, he simply hopes the dueño (owner) will visit his house and give him work.

---

i. "How am I going to pay for your career if midway through the year you find a boyfriend and you marry, and the money I already invested in you, who will repay me for that expense?"

ii. "Her father didn't let her either . . . her father, my grandfather didn't support her."

Sofia understands the uncertainty and financial strain under which her father struggles. She knows his life is also part of la lucha, and she expresses compassion and empathy for him. She believes he can be a better father, but she recognizes he is doing what he can in a difficult situation. Like many of the men in the village, Sofia's father gets drunk on the weekends, and when he comes home intoxicated he is violent. The first week I came into the pueblo, I was asked if I would be staying over during the weekends. I initially found this to be a rather peculiar question since the family I lived with and the neighbors showed great hospitality toward me. As the weekend drew nearer, a couple of the women in the pueblo told me stories of rape, sexual assault, and domestic violence. I perceived they were cautioning me to be prepared or perhaps reconsider my stay over the weekend. The men come home from the milpa on Friday and begin drinking. They continue on Saturday while watching baseball, and the women in the pueblo brace for what is sometimes a tragic fight for their safety.

Sofia summarizes her experience of entering the maquila as shocking, soul-crushing, and tiring. She says, "La primera semana estaba yo como en shock. No aceptaba lo que había pasado. Porque siento la presión. Como que prácticamente obligada a estar allí, a hacer todo lo que dicen."[i] At the end of a workday, Sofia echoes the sentiment of every woman I interviewed: "Llegando del trabajo lo único que quiero es dormir. Dormir. Porque no puedo. No me da. Mi cuerpo no me da para más."[ii]

The workday is a constant push for rapidez (speed). To do "lo máximo que puedas"[iii] despite the fact that sometimes "nos regañan, nos gritan."[iv] There is a growing frustration among the women that the maquinas (machines) on the assembly line need repair, and the mechanic ignores their requests. Their ability to produce is tied to the functioning of the maquina. The metaphysic at work here is that the woman and the maquina are one. The supervisor demands that Itzel make her daily quota and questions her ability to work because her production is down, and Itzel draws the supervisor's attention to her broken machine, "¿Quieres que te saque mi meta? Repárame mi maquina!"[v] The women struggle to separate themselves from the production. They note how they are undervalued and Paloma counsels the maquiladora: "Que piense más en nosotros. Y que no nos vea solamente como unos simple operarios que estamos para sacar la meta, una meta que realmente ellos se favorecen

---

i. "The first week I was in shock. I did not accept what had happened. Because I feel the pressure. Practically forced to be there, to do everything they say."
ii. "Coming home from work, the only thing I want to do is sleep. Sleep. Because, I can't. My body does not allow me to do any more."
iii. Paloma says, "To do the maximum you can."
iv. Itzel says, "They scold us, they yell at us."
v. "Do you want me to meet the quota? Repair my machine!"

más que nosotros."[i] Paloma alludes to the knowledge among the workers that they are merely cogs in a machine that functions for the benefit of others, not themselves. The women know they earn some money, but in reality, the profit and the advantages of their work is mostly for the unseen Other who accrues riches at their expense. Their bodies suffer from aching backs, broken wrists, sore shoulders, pain that radiates from their elbow to their hands, loss of sleep, miscarriages, allergies to the material, and chemicals that make them sneeze and their eyes swell. One worker is reportedly having lung surgery from the constant exposure. Others experience ringing in their ears from the constant noise, as well as loss of hearing, problema de nervios (anxiety), stress, hernias from lifting heavy material, and kidney stones. Paloma uses two words to describe the results of working in the maquila, "Terminas lesionada."[ii] There is no evading this impending telos. A woman works "todo el tiempo que aguante . . . porque no sé cuanto tiempo mas voy a seguir soportando que que me llega a doler acá."[iii]

There are rumors that the maquila might close but Araceli does not know if it is true or simply another tactic to get the women to feel the pressure to produce more: "No podemos decir también si es cierto o no, pero eso dicen, que si sigue así y no sale la producción que están pidiendo así, que a lo mejor se cierra."[iv] Is this a threat to keep the women under submission, or is it true? they wonder. What would it mean for the women to lose this income?

Maquilas Pay Women Lethal Wages

The daily income of a woman working at the maquila is simply not enough for survival. La vida es cara (life is expensive). The most common cry from the women is their children's need for leche (milk). Teresa tells me she works in the maquila

> [por] la necesidad. O sea, el gasto no me daba así, a la semana. Si lo que gana mi esposo no alcanza para nada . . . A veces nos falta. A veces nos falta porque digo de sobrar, nunca sobra. Sabes que el día nunca sobra.[v]

---

i. "Think more about us. And don't see us as only simple operators that are there to meet the goal, a goal that really favors them more than us."

ii. "You end up injured."

iii. "All the time that I can endure . . . because I do not know how much longer I will continue to endure the pain that hurts here."

iv. "We cannot say if it is true or not, but they say that if it continues like this and the production that is asked for doesn't come out, that maybe it will close."

v. "Need. That is, the weekly expenses were too high. What my husband earns is not enough. Sometimes we lack. Sometimes we are lacking. Sometimes because I'm talking about having enough to spare, there is never anything left over. You know that there is never extra for the day."

The women who are married have husbands who work on the assembly line of the maquila, as campesinos, as construction workers, or as security guards. I often saw men who worked in the maquila come home, eat a meal, and head out to the milpa to make more money. The men in the pueblo work hard just to meet their daily needs for food and shelter. Yet they alone cannot provide financially for the everyday needs of their family and this prompts women to go to work. Women enter the maquila in hopes of alleviating their families' financial strain and learn "no caro te pagan. Cuando vayas a mercado a comprar mercancía, esta caro. Esta caro la vida, le digo."[i]

As I walk through the drugstore located near the maquila, I see what the women in the pueblo are telling me. *Nestle Nido Leche Entera Fortificada*, an eighteen-liter can of powdered milk, costs 221 pesos, which is equivalent to $12.27.[50] Depending on how many children a woman is raising, the costs of her home (including utilities), and the needs of her aging parents and in-laws, it is quite understandable that the price of milk would stress her. Mariana explains the kinds of choices a mamá has to make: "Pero así que yo diga, 'Le voy a comprar su ropa a mis hijos' semanal o mensual, no. No hay. Con lo poco que agarro que yo este que yo gano con eso tengo que comprar leche."[ii] Maria explains to her children that this week there is no money for milk and so they cannot ask for leche. She says, "Pasamos muy difícil porque los niños están llorando, 'leche.' No piden si no tienen dinero. Están llorando, 'leche.' Pues como vas a comprar leche."[iii] Yet the women reason that they work in the maquila because they are the daughters of campesinxs and they have no education. Veronica says of the maquila, "Es un infierno."[iv]

Each woman works for the maquila and she is paid according to the number of pieces she completes, and wages are also calculated based on the area of the assembly line in which they work. For example, a woman sewing pleats makes less than the woman sewing pockets. This creates competition between workers.

---

i. Maria says, "They don't pay you very much. When you go to the market to buy merchandise, it's expensive. Life is expensive, I'm telling you."

ii. "But for me to say, for instance, 'I'm going to buy clothes for my children,' weekly or monthly, no. There isn't enough. With the little that I get, that I'm the one that, that I earn, with that, I have to buy milk."

iii. "We go through lots of difficulty because the children are crying, 'milk.' Do not ask, there is no money. They are crying, 'milk.' Well, how are you going to buy milk?"

iv. "This is hell."

Wages Reported by Women

Name	Number of children	Number of pieces produced per week	Pay per week (USD)	Wage per piece (USD)
Veronica	2 daughters	16,800–22,400	$44.44–$55.55	$0.006
Paloma	1 son	8,400 to 9,800	$55.55–$61.11	$0.006
Natalia	3 sons	9,120	$50.00	$0.005
Mariana	2 sons	21,120	$29.33	$0.003
Teresa	2 sons	10,800	$31.11–$55.55	$0.005
Araceli	3 sons	19,200–21,000	$66.66	$0.003
Maria	2 sons, 1 daughter	10,800	$50.00–$52.77	$0.005
Celeste	1 daughter	8,400	$13.88–$14.44	$0.002
Ximena	0	8,424	$66.66	$0.008
Sofia	0	6,960	$38.88	$0.005
Itzel	2 daughters	3,150–3,640	None reported	None reported

Figure 2.4. Maquilas pay women lethal wages. Created by the author.

Maquilas Advance the Religion of the Colonizer: Catholicism's Deadly Silence

Yes, this is hell. The conversion from mamá to maquina is an ontological assault on the theological claim that life is sacred. This practice is a negation of the claim that creation shares in the creative and generative labor of the divine. This is a complicated story. The Spanish colonizers imposed Christianity on the Maya through the encomienda system. When the encomienda system transformed into the privatized agribusiness of the hacienda, the Maya became the indebted peones who worked the land. The modern-day maquila repeats this tragic story. It invades foreign land, turns mamás into machines by making them little more than cogs in the production of goods, incarcerates, and subjects them to a context where they internalize the voice of the oppressor through self-surveillance. All the while, the laborer's life is being threatened, their autonomy eroded. What kind of gospel is this?

Veronica tells me that religion prescribes rules for women to live by; it disciplines her appetite, desire, and appearance: "Si creo en Dios, pero no, o sea no me ata como para hacer cosas de que no voy a salir, o no me voy arreglar, o no debo de comer esto . . . porque hay religiones que prohíben todo eso. La manera de vestirse."[i] This Christian orthodoxy she finds unhelpful. Maria emphasizes its uselessness when she says, "No me ayuda, eso no."[ii] When I become curious about her experience in the church, she changes the subject of conversation and doesn't elaborate on her brief comment about rejecting reli-

---

i. "Yes, I believe in God, but no, my belief doesn't tie me to do things like not going out, or not doing my hair and makeup, or that I should eat this . . . because there are religions that forbid all that . . . the way I dress."

ii. "Doesn't help me, that, no."

gion as a source of help/support. The church, according to Celeste, demands loyalty to one religion and this is problematic to her relationships with family and her community. Celeste was raised in the Catholic tradition and married a man who identifies as a Jehovah's Witness. Now she doesn't practice either faith. She wants to be both and her husband won't agree to hybrid religious identity and she finds the rhetoric coming from the Jehovah Witness temple to be extreme. She says,

> Supuestamente para ellos no existe la Virgen de Guadalupe. Solamente es Dios, es Dios y es Dios. Que . . . o sea, la Virgen de Guadalupe para ellos, según hasta me ha contado mi esposo, es una víbora disfrazada de mujer . . . ah ha . . . Tiene hasta un video donde muestran esas cosas así. ¡Exagerados![i]

As I hear her talking, I am reminded of the church's depiction of sin and evil entering into the world through the act of a woman.

Even more concerning are the descriptions Araceli and Paloma give. They underscore the church's disconnection from the reality of the everyday lives of the pueblo. Araceli says,

> Pues la verdad, no. No tiene nada que ver . . . Pues ellos hasta ahora no nos apoyan en nada.[ii]

Paloma similarly states,

> Pero no, no se habla del trabajo. No, no hablan del trabajo. No veo que no se mete en nada que ver con el trabajo . . . No se involucran en el trabajo. Nada. Nada que ver.[iii]

This disengaged church is colluding with the imperialism of corporate greed, if nothing else, by its negligence. The Christian gospel being proclaimed is one of either prosperity for the rich or devastation for the pueblo, depending upon from which angle one is reading and evaluating these claims. What is the gospel here in Yucatán, México? This land and its people are under the reign of greed. What is "the good news" rising up from this place? The resources of corn and henequen are being extracted from their native land. But those who have "eyes to see and ears to hear"[iv] know this news is nothing

---

i. "Supposedly for them there is no Virgen of Guadalupe. It's only God, God and God. That is it, in other words, the Virgen of Guadalupe for them, my husband told me this, is a viper disguised as a woman . . . ah ha . . . They even have a video where they show this. Such exaggerators!"

ii. "Well, the truth is, no. It has nothing to do . . . Well, to this day they don't support us at all."

iii. "No, work is not talked about. No, they don't talk about work. I don't see that they get involved with anything to do with work . . . They don't get involved with work. Nothing. Nothing to do with it. No relationship."

iv. I recognize this phrase as ableist and acknowledge the harm this phrase supports. And yet I quote this phrase due to its repetitive use in both the Hebrew Bible and Christian sacred texts to reference Christian praxis and bodily knowing.

close to "good" for the pueblo. The prophetic cry of the children for leche (milk) redirects our moral conscience to assess the "goodness of creation."

The cries of these women's babies are a plea for justice-making. These are sacred cries rising from children and to mamás who know within their bodies the sensation of a growing embryo and the labor pain of bearing life. They cannot ignore their children's cries. In similar fashion, Hebrew Bible scholar Walter Brueggemann talks of the power of a grieving mother's refusal of consolation. He traces the echoes of Rachel's grief from the loss of her sons in Genesis to Jeremiah's cry in the midst of violence: a burnt temple, city walls and royal court destroyed, plus the many people taken to Babylon where women and children faced the brutality of the Babylonian armies.[51] The writer of Second Isaiah pauses to allow the poet to give voice to the tragic telos that conveys the images of how "the sweep of imperial death takes all."[52] Again in Matthew, the gospel writer interrupts the narrative of the death of infant boys with a reference to Rachel weeping for her children. This weeping has no consolation. This cry refuses to be comforted with hope that is not based in the here and now. The struggle, for me, is to stay present to this weeping without reducing it to being the sound of "a mad prophet or a poor suffering soul."[53]

The following chapter will privilege the voices of the women, much as this chapter did. However, now that I have described the process of dehumanization that renders women objects and threatens to distort their relationships with the land, themselves, and their communities, I will turn next to hearing the voices of women's resistance. In the midst of this life-threatening context, women birth life through their practice of mothering and they build solidarity in abundance. It is just not the mothering or the solidarity I imagined when I began this research project.

NOTES

1. In Mexico's currency this is 300 pesos per day. The exchange rate used is 18 pesos MX = $1 US.

2. David Harvey, *A Brief History of Neoliberalism* (Oxford: Oxford University Press, 2005), 20.

3. C. H. Haring, *The Spanish Empire in America* (New York: Harcourt Brace Jovanovich, 1975), 27. Haring describes two types of colonies: exploitative and farm colonies. Exploitative colonies are ones that extract resources indigenous to the land and enslave its inhabitants to labor for the profit of the foreign occupiers.

4. Maya word for the plant henequen. Also "sóoskil" in Maya.

5. Haring, *The Spanish Empire in America*, 3–4.

6. Lesley Byrd Simpson, *The Encomienda in New Spain: The Beginning of Spanish Mexico* (Berkeley: University of California Press, 2008), 23.

7. The Christian war over control of the Iberian Peninsula that lasted for more than seven hundred years, 718–1492.
8. Haring, *The Spanish Empire in America*, 38.
9. Simpson, *The Encomienda in New Spain*, 11.
10. Simpson, *The Encomienda in New Spain.*
11. Simpson, *The Encomienda in New Spain.*
12. Haring, *The Spanish Empire in America*, 41, 43.
13. Haring, *The Spanish Empire in America*, 44–46.
14. Simpson, *The Encomienda in New Spain*, 36.
15. Haring, *The Spanish Empire in America*, 47.
16. Communication of Isabella of Spain to Ovando, December 20, 1503, in Simpson, *The Encomienda in New Spain*, 12–13.
17. Ramon Grosfoguel, "The Structure of Knowledge in Westernized Universities: Epistemic Racisim/Sexism and the Four Genocides/Epistemicides of the Long 16th Century," *Human Architecture: Journal of the Sociology of Self-Knowledge* 11, no. 1 (Fall 2013): 73–90.
18. Grosfoguel, "The Structure of Knowledge," 75.
19. Allan D. Meyers and David L. Carlson, "Peonage, Power Relations, and the Built Environment at Hacienda Tabi, Yucatan, Mexico," *International Journal of Historical Archaeology* 6, no. 4 (December 2002): 225–252.
20. Rodolfo Canto Sáenz, *Del Henequén a las Maquiladoras: La Política Industrial en Yucatán 1984–2001* (México, D.F.: Instituto Nacional de Administración Pública, 2001).
21. Canto Sáenz, *Del Henequén a las Maquiladoras*, 56.
22. Lee J. Alston, Shannan Mattiace, and Tomas Nonnenmacher, "Coercion, Culture, and Contracts: Labor and Debt on Henequen Haciendas in Yucatán, Mexico, 1870–1915," *Journal of Economic History* 69, no. 1 (March 2009): 109.
23. Canto Sáenz, *Del Henequén a las Maquiladoras*, 56–57.
24. Canto Sáenz, *Del Henequén a las Maquiladoras*, 56. Some of these machines are rueda Solís, rueda vencedora, and máquinas de vapor.
25. Canto Sáenz, *Del Henequén a las Maquiladoras*, 56. The workforce, Maya laborers bound to a landlord, worked under conditions of semislavery that were perpetuated by unpayable debts.
26. John Kenneth Turner, *Barbarous Mexico* (Austin: University of Texas Press, 1969).
27. Turner, *Barbarous Mexico*, 120, 137.
28. Turner, *Barbarous Mexico*, 126.
29. Turner, *Barbarous Mexico*, 141.
30. Alston, Mattiace, and Nonnenmacher, "Coercion, Culture, and Contracts," 107. One of Porfirio Díaz's campaign promises was to "modernize" México. By "modern" Díaz meant miles of railroad and land dedicated to exporting goods for profit.
31. Turner, *Barbarous Mexico.*
32. Alston, Mattiace, and Nonnenmacher, "Coercion, Culture, and Contracts," 108.
33. Turner, *Barbarous Mexico*, 126–127.

34. Alston, Mattiace, and Nonnenmacher, "Coercion, Culture, and Contracts," 108.

35. Canto Sáenz, *Del Henequén a las Maquiladoras*, 78.

36. Canto Sáenz, *Del Henequén a las Maquiladoras*, 79.

37. Canto Sáenz, *Del Henequén a las Maquiladoras*, 77. "The maquiladora is the only source of industrial employment in town . . . [making workers] much more loyal to the company."

38. "Invasive to Avoid: Iceplant," California Department of Fish and Wildlife, accessed April 1, 2018, https://www.wildlife.ca.gov/Conservation/Plants/Dont-Plant-Me/Iceplant.

39. Thomas Piketty, *Capital and Ideology*, trans. Arthur Goldhammer (Cambridge, MA: Harvard University Press, 2020). Piketty makes the argument that markets, profit, and capital are historical constructs created and maintained through narratives that inform choices justifying social economic inequities.

40. Capitalism and mercantilism share similarities in that they are both exploitative systems. One functions without the intervention of government and the other increases the wealth of a nation through government regulation (e.g., high tariffs on imports, restriction of emigration of workers and capital, and use of the military to safeguard local markets and supply sources). Both systems are present in the situation of working-class Maya mexicanas, although this book does not go into a nuanced discussion of the nature and relationship of capitalism and mercantilism.

41. Cedric J. Robinson, *Black Marxism: The Making of the Black Radical Tradition* (Chapel Hill: University of North Carolina Press, 2000).

42. Neoliberalism is a contested concept. Since the 1980s, the term *neoliberalism* is used in a variety of theoretical and disciplinary contexts where it takes on different meanings and descriptions. Critics point to the need for examining the development of the concept and tracing the meaning of the term in order to clarify the concept and eliminate problematic contradictions. See, Kean Birch, *A Research Agenda for Neoliberalism* (Northampton, MA: Edward Elgar, 2017); Wendy Brown, *Undoing the Demos: Neoliberalism's Stealth Revolution* (Brooklyn, NY: Zone Books, 2015); and Daniel Stedman Jones, *Masters of the Universe: Hayek, Friedman, and the Birth of Neoliberal Politics* (Princeton, NJ: Princeton University Press, 2012).

43. Harvey, *Brief History of Neoliberalism*, 20.

44. The revised agreement, known as the United States-Mexico-Canada Agreement, was completed in 2018 after the research in this book was gathered.

45. Wright, *Disposable Women*, 25.

46. Wright, *Disposable Women*.

47. Susana Prieto, "Obreras Maquileras de Ciudad Juárez" (lecture, Chiapas, México, March 9, 2018).

48. Michael White and David Epston, *Narrative Means to Therapeutic Ends* (New York: W. W. Norton, 1990), 67–69.

49. Michel Foucault, *Discipline and Punish: The Birth of the Prison*, 2nd ed., trans. Alan Sheridan (New York: Vintage Books, 1995), 200.

50. The conversion rate used was $1 US = 18 pesos MX.

51. Walter Brueggemann, "Will Our Faith Have Children?" *Word & World* 3, no. 3 (1983): 275.
52. Brueggemann, "Will Our Faith Have Children?" 275.
53. Gloria Anzaldúa, *Borderlands/La Frontera: The New Mestiza*, 4th ed. (San Francisco: Aunt Lute Books, 2012).

Chapter Three

Primeramente Madre:
The Life-Bearing Gospel

Maria is the mother of three children. She has been working on the assembly line of the local transnational corporation (TNC) for two years now. She tells me she is motivated by the *hope* that her children might perhaps be able to get the kind of education that her own parents could not give her because they were campesinxs. She continues,

> Como solo es campesino nada más, ¿cómo voy a buscar dinero para que vaya a estudiar? Acá no hay secundarias. Solo no más la prepa. No solo queremos estudiar, pero no podemos. No hay dinero. Si salgo o no a estudiar, necesito dinero hoy. Pasajes. Me dice mi papá, "No, no podemos," dice. "Estás viendo. Solo no más en la milpa."[i]

Maria says that she tells her children,

> Yo no quiero que te pase así. Que yo quiero es que salgan adelante . . . Se pongan a estudiar . . . saber leer. Como nosotros no sabemos leer, es lo malo. No podemos entrar. Pero hay trabajo más pagan más mejor pero no podemos digo porque no sabemos leer. Quedamos como burros. Leer no sé. Escribir casi no. Pero de mi cabeza, inteligente tengo. ¡Pues tengo![ii]

---

    i. "He's only a peasant, just a peasant, how is he going to find money for me to study? There are no secondary schools here. Just elementary school. We want to study, but we can't. There is no money. If I go study, I need money today. Transportation costs. My dad tells me, 'No, we can't,' he says. 'Are you seeing? There's only the maíz fields.'"

    ii. "I don't want you to experience that. What I want is for them to forge ahead . . . they start studying . . . know how to read. Because we don't know how to read, that's a bad thing. We can't enter. But there are higher-paying jobs but we can't get those jobs because we don't know how to read. We are like donkeys. We can't read. We can barely write. But I'm intelligent/smart. I am!"

Maria completed an elementary education but her family's inability to pay the costs associated with school supplies and transportation meant she could not continue her education beyond that. The children in the pueblo have to travel to a nearby town if they want to continue school beyond the elementary grades. For many this is a limitation because campesinxs whose crops cannot compete in the global economy do not earn enough profit to send their children to school. However, Maria insists that she is "intelligent" and she wants her children to "forge ahead" (salgan adelante).

As I sat with Maria straining to listen and understand her words and checking for understanding by repeating what I was hearing her say, within my own soul I heard an echo of my grandmother's and my mother's voices. My feisty grandmother also concluded her education in a small town in Cuba at the sixth grade. Every morning she said goodbye from the threshold of our doorway with the battle cry, "Adelante!" Even as I grew up and went to college, when I called Mima[i] she always ended our conversation with that one word, *Adelante!* I was her hope, the one who was moving forward (adelante) into the vision she herself could not step into. My going was a result of my foremothers' labor and their knowledge. I was their present and ever-growing hope. So when I heard Maria say "Adelante!" I wondered how her labor and knowledge might *be* hope. I wondered: Is her hope somehow connected to the life of her children? I came to understand what I interpret to be Maria's hope by carefully observing pueblo life and listening attentively to the narratives of eleven women. In my view, Maria bears life in a context that is simultaneously life-giving and life-threatening. She catches an eschatological fragrance as she labors at her station in the assembly line. I use the term "eschatological fragrance" to describe how women sense the future that is emerging in the present. Similar to when one is preparing a meal, the reality of the meal is first sensed through its promising fragrance that is evidence of the meal in preparation. As Maria works/labors she re-visions the world she is creating for her children; she senses the future in her present work. She is not a seamstress; she is a mother in the process of giving life to her children, a life that would otherwise be denied to them because she will not allow her children to "quedarse burros."[ii] She knows what every other mother knows, she is "inteligente," and she wants her children to be free from the death-producing assembly-line work the neoliberal global economy has chosen for her.

This chapter will present the life-giving gospel—good news—that the women in the pueblo live, which bears life by embodying hope. In systematic theology, eschatology (the study of last things, an end) is tied to discussions of "hope."[1] I found that what working-class Maya mexicanas hope for is:

---

i. My grandmother.
ii. "We remained donkeys." [idiomatic phrase meaning "dumb"].

Figure 3.1. Women with their children walking to the rancho. Photo taken by the author.

1) a life free of violence against them and their community; 2) a casa (house) and an economic means to construct the life their children need and they desire; and 3) freedom for their children to make choices. These hopes are not realized in a future that exists *outside* of time; they are hopes rooted in the necessities of the present and the everyday actions of their labor. In this way, working-class Maya mexicanas present an eschatological hope that is rooted in place, not in time. This particular experience of time and liberation from suffering invites us pastoral theologians to enlarge our understandings of health, illness, and resurrection. I want to focus on health and illness and only touch briefly on resurrection, a topic I will expand upon in chapter 4.

This chapter contributes to the communal contextual and intercultural paradigms for pastoral care and counseling in pastoral theology by privileging the cosmology and anthro/gynopology of Maya women. I begin by presenting the narrative of the Maya creation myth in the Popol Vuh, the Maya sacred text, to narrate the story of beginnings, which links humans to maíz and humans' ability to be "keepers of the days" (time). This sacred and soulful connection between the fruitful earth and humans who bear life is a primordial matter that shapes the identity of Maya mexicanas as life bearers. However, life and the flourishing of the earth is always taking place in what is a complex ecosystem. There are multiple life-forms within the universe that are in flux and affect each other. To explain this cosmovision, I will draw on the ethnographic work of Sylvia Marcos, a mexicana with a postdoctoral degree from Harvard University in psychology and sociology of religions, and her elucidation of Maya cosmology as it relates to understandings of "illness" and "healing." Having established this important cultural context, I will present the hope-practices of working-class Maya mexicanas observed in the veneration of La Virgen de la Asunción. I will underscore how the practices of mothering yield hope by using the loci of theological anthropology and eschatology to interpret the women's words, assess the effects of the maquila, and note the practices the women employ to counter the harm the maquila inflicts on them and their children, harms discussed in the previous chapter.

THE MAYA CREATION MYTH[2]

In the beginning, so goes the Maya creation story, there was no light, land, plants, people, or animals. The only things that existed were stillness, silence, and water. Dressed in green and blue feathers, three pairs of deities lay in the waters: Tz'aqol and the B'itol, Tepew and Quetzal Serpent, and Xpiyacóc and Xmucané. These six deities assisted Hurakán (Heart of Sky) to create the Earth, and they called their creation Heart of Earth. Next, the deities created the sky by planting a ceiba tree. The roots of the tree formed the nine levels of the Underworld (Xibalba), the trunk formed the surface of the land, and the branches stretched to shape the thirteen levels of the Upperworld. Then the deities populated the Earth with plants and animals—but these were plants and animals that did not speak and could not worship, and this prompted them to begin creating humans who could honor the deities.

The creation of humans was accomplished through a trial-and-error process. First, the deities created human beings from mud, but were not content with this because these humans had no souls and they could not be good "keepers of the days" (a reference to the calendar, a central component of Maya spirituality). The deities sent a flood, destroyed the mud people, and started over. In their second attempt, the deities created humans from wood, but because those wooden beings were unable to worship the gods either, the deities destroyed them. But some of the wood people survived and became monkeys in trees. The third attempt at creating humans was successful. How it occurred is recounted as a narrative within a narrative.

Lxs Hijxs de Maíz

The Hero Twins, Hunahpu and Xbalanqu, like their fathers, Hun Hunahpu and Vucub Hunahpu, were great ballplayers.[3] The Hero Twins' father was defeated in a ball game, then decapitated and sacrificed. The two went to the Underworld, Xibalba, where Hun Hunahpu from a cacao tree spat into the hand of their mother and the twins were conceived. The Hero Twins grew up to be great ballplayers like their father and challenged the Lords of the Underworld to a game in order to bring their father back to life. The Hero Twins were told that the Lords of the Underworld would accept their challenge if the Twins survived the dangers of the Underworld. This the Hero Twins did. In the resulting promised ball game, they defeated the Lords of the Underworld and brought their father back to life as the Maíz God.

With their father now alive, the Hero Twins left Xibalba and returned to the Earth and continued up into the sky. They became the Sun and the Moon. With creation now including a sun and moon, the six deities formed human beings from white and yellow corn. This final creation of humans satisfied the deities because these humans had souls and could therefore be good "keepers of the days" and capable of worship.

Maíz and México

The people of México refer to themselves as "los hijos de maíz" (the children of maíz or what is called corn in the US). Maíz carries deep cultural symbolism, as we can see from this creation story. Maíz connects the Maya people with their ancestors and with the land. Just as the maíz crops are planted in soil, growing roots down into the earth, soaking up nutrients provided by rainfall and sunlight, and growing tall into stalks that bear fruit, so too do humans. The Maya mexicanas from the pueblo mágico are rooted in the pueblo where they were born; their herstory is planted in this place where it soaks up the nourishment from many generations of Maya mexicanas, foremothers who lived and struggled on this same land. One out of the eleven women interviewed was not born in pueblo mágico but met her husband and moved to the pueblo. She talked about how she had to learn to live life in the pueblo where women make their tortillas by hand and grind their own spices to season their food. She compared her new experience in contrast to purchasing items such as tortillas and seasoning packets made by machines or hands other than her own. These unseen hands that operate machines and produce items to be sold in the market are a symptom of neoliberal capitalism. As discussed in chapter 2, the system of neoliberal capitalism moves consumers further and further away from the sources of life—people, earth, and relationality.

The struggle for life described by the women grows amid mingled forces of life and death, threatened and yet thriving. Such coexistence of forces of life and death is inherent in all of creation. The Maya creation myth presents as complementary twin life forces throughout the universe: life/death, sky/earth, day/night, and sun/moon, among many others. The balance of life and death, illness and health, is always in flux, and cycles of one to the other make up the rhythms embedded in our ecosystem's constant motion. This sacred connection and movement between forces of life and death is an inheritance that connects previous generations and life-forms to the present. The soul of the people is a collective memory that nurtures women's bodies and souls. Juana Batz Puac, a K'iche' Maya, explains the significance of this interconnectedness by stating, "Maize is sacred to us because it connects us with our ancestors. It feeds our spirit as well as our bodies."[4] Consequently maíz is planted in the milpa and consumed at every meal. As we shall see, in some way or another, maíz permeates the waking and sleeping of the people. Maíz facilitates both community and the experience of solidarity birthed at the table and distributed to tables around the world.

Figure 3.2. Maíz in a milpa located in the pueblo mágico. Photo taken by the author.

México is the world's largest producer of maíz. México's campesinxs cultivate more than one thousand different types of maíz. Maíz is consequently a large part of the culture of México, and the main ingredient in most Mexican dishes. Everyday women in the pueblo boil the harvested kernels of maíz overnight so that in the morning they can wash them and take them to the molino (the mill) to grind so they have masa (dough) for the family's daily consumption of tortillas, sopes, tamales, and pozole. Every day after the cena (dinner), women prepare for the next day's meals by pouring kernels of corn into a pot of water and setting it to soak and simmer overnight. It is a ritual that concludes one day's activities and begins the next. But it is also an activity that takes place in the context of suffering. Imports of genetically modified corn and the devastating effect of NAFTA on the milpas threaten the livelihood of the golden crop of México and lxs hijxs de maíz who identify so intimately with this life-giving force. There is a shared illness in the people's milpas and their bodies as a result of neoliberal capitalist greed and impatience. Maya cosmology expounds on this interconnection between health and illness, humans and the universe.

MAYA COSMOLOGY

Sociologist and psychologist of religion Sylvia Marcos develops and supports what she refers to as "an antihegemonic-feminist practice, theory and hermeneutics"[5] through her study of indigenous women in Mesoamerican religions. In *Taken from the Lips: Gender and Eros in Mesoamerican Religions*, Marcos presents a framework for understanding the internal logic of illness and healing from a Mesoamerican[6] cosmological perception. She constructs this framework from both ethnographic fieldwork with curanderas (healers) and the study of historical research of pre-Hispanic documents such as Sahagún's *Historia General de las Cosas de la Nueva España*.

Sahagún was a Spanish colonizer who composed a Nahuatl-Spanish questionnaire to be administered in three towns and villages (Tenochtitlan, Tepepulco, and Tlalteloco) with the help of fellow colonizers. Responses to Sahagún's questionnaire were compiled into a codex and given as a gift to an Italian noble whose home gave the document its name: the Florentine Codex. Today, this pre-Hispanic document is recognized as "the most reliable source on the ancient Mexicans, the way they worshipped their gods and goddess, their myths, rituals, and curing practices."[7] In consultation with curanderas and the *Historia General*, Marcos identifies and explains four core concepts in Mesoamerican epistemology that help us to understand illness and healing among these people: fluidity, duality, symbolic representation, and proximity and similarity. My goal is not to explain each of these in detail but to highlight some unique features that contrast with my own western Christian North American cosmology (which is also the context of most literature in pastoral care and counseling), the better to understand a few aspects of illness and healing in the Mesoamerican context.

Fluidity

The body is part of the cosmos and not a separate entity apart from the environment. A human being's skin (epidermis) is not the border between what is the human body and the external world populated with other humans, plants, animals, land, water, sky, and so on. The body is part of the universe and "is porous, permeable, and open to the great cosmic currents."[8] Because of that permeability, illness and healing cross boundaries between all living things in the universe.

Duality

A central characteristic of Mesoamerican cosmology is the "polarity of complementary opposites."[9] There is an infinite pairing present in the universe, for example: god/goddess, life/death, sun/moon, feminine/masculine. These dualities, along with an infinite number of other dualities, are disparate poles that complement each other. These dualities are different aspects of the material and immaterial world that exist on a spectrum. Along that spectrum exist many possibilities, composed of varying amounts of each aspect.[10]

Symbolic Representation

Within the Mesoamerican epistemology, illness is "a categorical and immaterial entity" that "takes material forms."[11] The duality of health and illness exists on opposite poles, as does the material and immaterial world. A healer, such as a curandera, can assist in restoring equilibrium in the universe when she participates in curative practices such as sucking illness out of a person who is sick. Marcos supports this claim through findings from her ethnographic fieldwork and evidence in the *Historia General*, which document curing practices that illustrate how curanderas extract illness (immaterial) from one source to another. Healers explain, for example, that illness "came out, like little frogs"[12] and in this way the immaterial illness is given materiality that can be transferred from one material object to another material object. More crucially, because it takes on materiality it can also be "destroyed, burned, or thrown out."[13] What is central for us to note is how health relies "on the balance of the material and immaterial flow between the body and its environment."[14] Marcos underscores the importance of understanding the symbolism in such connections/flows of the interior and exterior realities. In short, there is a connection between all things in the universe, and health depends on the balance of these relationships.

Proximity and Similarity

Mesoamerican healing practices assert that the universe is intimately connected and therefore qualities of one being can be transferred to another, as I explained above. These connections in the universe also share "a relationship of reflection."[15] This relationship is a mirroring of images that are concrete reflections of the other. Through an example, Marcos explains how this is connected to the understanding of illness. A pregnant woman walking outdoors during an eclipse risks her child being born with a cleft lip because the moon is known to consume the unborn child's lip during an eclipse. Just as the moon's actions may explain illness (deformity, in this case), healing properties are also present in material objects that reflect one another.[16] Marcos gives an example of healing through a heart-shaped flower, doradilla, in the Tuxtlas region of Chiapas, México. Curanderas use doradilla, also called flor de corazón (heart flower), to assist women in childbirth, placing the flower under the laboring woman's pillow. Just as doradilla opens up when placed in water, so too it is believed that its proximity to the woman will help her uterus open and her child's birth to occur more quickly.[17]

These four core concepts of fluidity, duality, symbolic representation, and similarity and proximity in Mesoamerican epistemology provide insight into how the Maya understand illness and healing. While the women in the pueblo mágico did not overtly reference such concepts in their descriptions of the working conditions in the maquila or in the health of their bodies, I did hear them tell stories that connected their actions and bodies to the life of the land. These interconnections situated illness and health as part of a cosmovision (macro system), in which not only is the withering of the milpa reflected in the dis-ease of the women's bodies (the micro system) but so too is the continued lucha to bring forth health and whatever gives life. Equilibrium is the goal and is apprehended by healing permeating (through its fluidity) the universe and impacting the balance of complementary qualities present in the material world (duality). The Maya creation myth and cosmology are thus a helpful backdrop when listening to women's accounts of how their bodies are deteriorating and their spirits are failing due to the working conditions in the maquila.

WOMEN'S BODIES AND ASSEMBLY-LINE WORK

Beatriz Castilla Ramos, a social anthropologist and professor at Universidad Autónoma de Yucatán, is a leading authority on women working in the maquila industry in Yucatán, México. In *Mujeres Mayas en la Robótica y Líderes de la Comunidad: Tejiendo la Modernidad*, she documents the ethnographic research in Ormex de México, one of the largest US maquilas, located in the southeastern region of Yucatán. Her research underscores how sexist and racist attitudes toward Maya women are subverted by multinational and transnational corporations that employ women to operate expensive machines and provide them with opportunities to assume leadership roles in managerial positions, both of which used to be jobs/roles reserved for men. I am reiterating rather than agreeing with her claims. Castilla Ramos discusses the "recreación" (new creation) and support of ancestral customs by the maquila industry. She highlights the community-building that occurs in the context of maquila culture. Events such as the company picnic, la fiesta navideña (Christmas), and rituals (such as those that accompany a woman's promotion to a new work station) result in a family-like work culture.[18] The women who participated in Castilla Ramos's research used the analogy of "tejiendo y el bordado"[i] as a "manualidad"[ii] that is "como una especie de juego o pasatiempo que se transmite de madres a hijas."[19] Castilla Ramos makes this connection about women's work assembling high-precision nickel-titanium files for a dental company.[20] Her reflection on this metaphor of an inherited feminine craft emphasizes the cultural and symbolic nature of tejiendo for women. Tejiendo is women's work; this ancient practice of making intricate designs by hand is a cultural practice that is passed down from one female to another in the family. It is a helpful observation. But Castilla Ramos seems to ignore how this cultural practice is apprehended and appropriated by the corporation, how it is transformed into an exploitative practice that obscures the freedom and agency she proposes this employment offers women. The maquila takes advantage of women's skills for capitalist purposes and disguises the cultural and artistic significance of those skills.

Perhaps because the women living in the pueblo mágico work in a maquila that manufactures textiles they did not need to allude to similarities with tejiendo as did the women Castilla Ramos interviewed. The women in the pueblo mágico are keenly aware that their employment is based on their abilities as women to sew and that the low wages they are paid exploit those abilities for others' gain rather than to honor them. Their particular practice of tejiendo in their homes is an act of resistance, a way of maintaining their

---

i. Weaving and embroidery.
ii. Craft.

cultural heritage as women who weave and create hipiles with intricate bordados.

Prior to the establishment of the maquila near the pueblo mágico, women sewed and embroidered shirts and dresses to sell to tourists in Mérida or to dress their daughters for special occasions such as la fiesta del pueblo. However, in a globalized economy, tejiendo cannot compete with the technologies of a maquila that produces thousands of articles of clothing a day. Mariana explains, "Pues tarda en hacerlo y aparte después lo vas a . . . a veces cada mes, cada mes, viene la señora a buscarlo. Bueno pues no ganarías un poquito . . . bueno ganarías pero lo mínimo."[i] Mariana acknowledges that her continued sewing at home will yield little financial assistance for her family. However, the women are not governed by the market's value of efficiency and profit. They keep tejiendo because of *who* they are—Maya mexicanas. This is how the women have engaged en la lucha for generations. Celeste reflects on her mother's tejido,

> Mi mamá hizo todo para que pudiéramos [tears well up in her eyes] seguir estudiando. Pero pues, tampoco pudo. Ella pues sabe tejer a mano. Y aunque ella así, veías, noche y día con su lucecita [tears run down her cheeks] . . . tejiendo, para darnos, igual, para poder estudiar. Pero pues, es como dice ella, por acá casi no se compra. Hay muchos que saben hacer lo mismo, y ya no se compra.[ii]

Celeste's mother taught her to tejer. Celeste continues to tejer in her home on her days off from the maquila. She does this work because "mi mamá, de hecho, hasta me enseño a tejer."[iii] As I listen to her, I do not understand her to be describing tejiendo as a hobby or a form of play; I see this as an act of liberation, a hope that her identity and cultural inheritance will not be and cannot be completely colonized by the maquila. Celeste tells me she practices the art of tejiendo and recalls her mother's lucha "para darnos" (to give us) life.

Though Castilla Ramos interprets the work of women on the assembly line as play, at the same time she notes how women become the "brazos robóticos" for the production of modern high-tech products. Her argument is that this new "robotic" identity allows women to gain increased and specialized skills that give them freedom from unpaid domestic work.[21] According to Castilla Ramos, women who are employed by the maquila raise their status in the

---

i. "It takes time to do it and then later you go to . . . sometimes every month, every month, the lady comes to look for it. Well, you earn very little . . . well, you earn the very minimum amount."

ii. "My mom did everything so that we could [tears well up in her eyes] continue studying. But then, she also couldn't. She knows how to sew by hand. And although she likes that, you saw her, night and day with her little light on [tears run down her cheeks] sewing, to give us, just the same, to be able to study. But then, it is as she says, here almost nothing sells. There are many who know how to do the same thing, and no one buys it."

iii. "My mom, actually, taught me how to sew."

family when they become wage earners and this allows them to construct and repair their casas (homes).[22] I did hear women in the pueblo mágico speak with great pride of the number of pieces they produced at the maquila, but this was always immediately followed by comments about their aching bodies and insufficient wages. What Castilla Ramos does not say is that women's work is appropriated by the TNC and benefits the profit margins of the US company more than the assembly-line worker. It may be that the women who participated in Castilla Ramos's interviews are of a higher socioeconomic class, because the proficiency of their Spanish in her transcribed interviews is something I did not experience among the women in the pueblo mágico. Likewise, though the women in the Ormex maquila wanted to obtain higher pay by seeking managerial positions, not one of the eleven women I interviewed expressed any desire to ascend into any occupational role beyond that of assembly-line worker. Women in the pueblo mágico are proud of their work, their production, but always conversation about it was quickly overshadowed by sustained comments on how the work "cansa" (tires) them and how insufficient their wages are. Castilla Ramos may be right in noting that women become somewhat like robotic arms, but they themselves are not robots though they are treated as such by the maquila. The women are mothers who emphasized how much they wanted and needed to work not only for income to sustain their families but also out of a deep sense of obligation to contribute to their families' lucha, their historical struggle for life.

HOPE-PRACTICES OF WORKING-CLASS MAYA MEXICANAS

The lives of working-class Maya mexicanas are situated in a context of struggle for the basic necessities of life. Women do not work so they can purchase the newest cell phone model or the latest brand-name clothing. They work for the sake of feeding and clothing their children, who complain their shoes are too tight. They work because their parents are ill, their maíz fields are dry, their spouse's income is low; because they desire to build their own home; and perhaps above all because they desire to create a situation in which their children can choose a vocation other than that of assembly-line worker. Women pursue these hopes, these ends, not so much through their maquila employment as through the activity of mothering. Mothering, as described by the women interviewed, is an act of resistance that proclaims a life-giving "gospel"[23] that rivals the religious institution's "gospel."

The "gospel" of imperialism and the "gospel" of the pueblo mágico announce the birth of two very different systems that have taken root in the land. The gospel of the maquila we heard announced in chapter 2. Here, in chapter 3, we turn to the gospel of working-class Maya mexicanas. I am recovering the use of the term "gospel" from its pre-Christian military context to underscore la lucha of the pueblo indígena to lay claim to their land, ways of knowing, and culture. Above, I noted that the Maya creation myth valued lxs hijxs de maíz because they were good keepers of the days—a reference to an ideology of time among Maya mexicanas that informs their identity and eschatology.

Time, Identity and Eschatology: The Question of *Who* Is Present

Constructive theologian Loida I. Martell articulates what various other Latinx theologians also assert—that for Latinx communities, presence, not time, is the primary value. For Latinxs, an event, gathering, and/or occasion occurs because of the people gathered, not because the hour has come. As Martell accurately notes, "Eschatology is not the *when*,"²⁴ eschatology is about *who*, *what*, and *where*. *Who* is present in a common place initiates the time of any given event, gathering and/or occasion. La fiesta starts because *we* arrive, not when we planned or were requested to arrive. *What* happens in the place in which we are gathered together is what makes time sacred. Contrary to German systematic theologian Jürgen Moltmann's explanation of how "God" comes to meet us in the present from a future time,²⁵ for Latinxs, nothing *comes* toward us; we come to meet our future, present, and past in the moment. We live in a deeply incarnational world where the sacred is relational and dynamic, moving among all of creation and meeting with us when we are together with one another. Allow me to expand on the *who* of Latina eschatology, leaving the topics of *what* and *where* for the following chapter (chapter 4).

Primeramente Madre: Caring for Vulnerability

Veronica summarizes what women in the pueblo mágico say about their primary identity when she says, "[soy] primeramente madre."ⁱ Mother is a familial title, a noun, that describes a woman who gives birth to a child. But this is not what I understand Veronica to be saying. When a woman in the pueblo mágico is "primeramente madre," she behaves in ways that bear life to her hope for her community, which oftentimes means violating norms that might deceive her into assuming the experience-near identity of being a seamstress on the TNC assembly line. For example, Itzel tells me her daughter asks, "Mamá, van hacer mi fiesta de día de las madres, ¿vas a poder

---

i. "I am primarily/first Mother."

venir?"[i] The child asks with some knowledge that her mother's long absences are attributable to her assembly-line work and at times her bosses' abuse of imposing overtime night shifts that mean her mother comes home very tired and sometimes injured. Itzel hears this question from her daughter, and she is immediately caught in a dilemma. For asking for time off can result in losing her job, and yet for her daughter a fiesta celebrating día de las madres without her mamá present is no celebration. Itzel tells me she responds by telling her daughter, "Sabes una cosa, hasta ahorita no se si voy a poder venir,"[ii] but then she turns to her husband and says,

> Yo a ver . . . falto a mi trabajo o pido permiso, pero voy a venir ese día. Mi hija me va cantar y yo tengo que estar con ella . . . voy a ver cómo lo voy hacer. Voy a ver cómo . . . o si no, no me lo dan, pues ya no me presento a mi trabajo hasta el día siguiente ¡y yo voy a ir![iii]

Being a mother means finding a way to make present relationships fruitful. The primary concern is what action needs to occur in order for familial bonds to deepen. In this case, Itzel is not preoccupied with what *might* happen in the future; she is present in her resolve to *be* a mother now. One of the ways in which Itzel and the other women know that relationships are productive is by the mothering of that which is vulnerable: the land, plants, women, and strangers. When a woman is mother, life springs up.

I observed women caring for the land by planting small gardens near their homes. They grow small quantities of watermelon, lemons, and herbs, which they use to feed their families, share with their neighbors, and heal their family's illnesses with tilos y remedios (herbal teas and remedies). Women sweep the dirt roads in the pueblo mágico and clean up around the plaza and the campo de béisbol (baseball field). They do this work in part because there are no city dump trucks that collect the garbage. Every family in the pueblo mágico has an area of the pueblo for which they are responsible, and I see them working together to care for their environment.

Likewise, I benefited from women's care, in this case care of strangers. They instructed me to leave the pueblo mágico on weekends when the men come home from their work in the milpa and often drink alcohol to the point that they get violent and sometimes sexually abuse women. Caring for the vulnerable is central to who Maya mexicanas understand themselves to be. This identity informs their behavior and their hermeneutic. Women's life-

---

i. "Mom, my Mother's Day party at school is coming up, are you going to be able to come?"
ii. "You know what, right now I don't know if I'm going to be able to go."
iii. "I'll see . . . I'll miss work or ask permission, but I'll come that day. My daughter is going to sing to me and I have to be with her . . . I'm going to see how I'm going to do it. I'm going to see how . . . or if not, if they don't give me time off, I won't show up for work until the next day and I'm going to go."

bearing qualities are a result of what I recognize to be a feminist hermeneutic of suspicion applied to the Popol Vuh narrative and the maíz god/goddess.

Maya Anthro/Gynopology's Emphasis on Place and Relationship

Maya oral tradition among women in the pueblo mágico and Zapatista women in Chiapas personified the maíz god/goddess as a woman in oral storytelling and artwork. I found women with tattoos of an image that was half cornstalk, half woman. Similar images are painted on buildings at the Caracol de Morelia. When I asked women to explain the artwork to me, they told me that it was assumed the maíz goddess is a woman because the god/goddess has life-bearing qualities. Women bear life by cooking, birthing children, planting, harvesting, and cleaning up the trash that accumulates in the pueblo.[26] The life force of creation in this cosmovision takes on a predominantly female appearance that shares an intimate relationship with the soil and by extension in this artwork, maíz, and she generates life.

Women care for their newborns by planting their umbilical cord in the earth. A practice explained to me by a couple of women illustrates how life is rooted in place and how women are primarily responsible for its preservation. Celeste tells me that when her baby girl was born, they took a piece of her umbilical cord and planted it near la candela (the fire). "A mi me tiene dicho mi mamá que cuando es niña que de por si tienes que poner un pedacito debajo de tu piedra de candela . . . así para que aprenda así a tortear."[i] Likewise, "Si quieres que estudie y todo eso, que lo traes ha enterrar a la escuela."[ii] Similarly, a boy's umbilical cord is planted in the milpa. This explanation seems to fit within the core concepts of fluidity and similarity and proximity. The girl/boy child and her/his future role in the community are linked to the places where there is a dynamic exchange between the material body and the immaterial life force of qualities desired for her/his flourishing and that of the community. This Maya anthro/gynopology is combined with Christian anthro/gynopology that introduces patriarchy and hierarchical relationships in the universe. However, the women in the pueblo cling to identities that contribute to the good of the family and advance the collective group's lucha toward accessing resources that will facilitate their participation in civic life. Notice that when babies are born there are also places where their ombliguito (used here to reference the umbilical cord; directly translated as "belly button") is not buried, namely the maquila. No mother *hopes* her child will work in the maquila. The women resist the identity of assembly-line seamstress.

---

i. "My mom has told me that when it's a girl, that you have to put a piece under the stone of your fire . . . so she can learn to make tortillas."

ii. "If you want her to study and all that, you bring it and bury it at the school."

Figure 3.3. Tattoo of Maíz Goddess. Photo taken by the author.

Figure 3.4. Artist rendering of Maíz God/Goddess. Photo taken by the author.

Sharing Resources

Women practice sharing resources with one another in the pueblo, and this is a second practice of mothering. During the day, women share the responsibility of caring for the pueblo's children. Mariana explains the care of her children: "Mi mamá me los cuida. Sí me siento mal, porque a veces los dejo. Los dejo así, pero por necesidad lo tengo que hacer. Lo tengo que hacer por ellos. Bueno para sacarlos adelante."[i] I was often confused with familial relationship titles because there were four variations of the word *mother* used by the children: mami, mamita, mamá, and mamio. Veronica explains that her two daughters call her "mamá o mamita," their grandmother "mami," and her sister and sister-in-law "mamio." The care of Mariana's children, and those of the women in the pueblo mágico, is communal. Mariana explains that this communal care is expansive, "Tanto emocionalmente, económicamente me ayudan."[ii] She says she asks for support in raising her daughters by telling her family, "Me gustaría que me ayudaras en la educación de mis hijas."[iii] Moreover, she says, "Si ellos ven que mis hijas están hacienda algo malo, que les llame la atención."[iv] Mariana invites women to participate in bearing life through caring for her daughters.

Women's everyday activities in the pueblo mágico take place within matriarchal support systems where conversation and wisdom are shared. There are two molinos[v] in the pueblo, on opposite ends of the main dirt road. Every evening after dinner, women take corn kernels and boil them overnight to soften the outer layer of the corn. In the morning they drain the water from the pot and scrub the corn kernels before placing them in a large plastic bowl, which they carry to the molino. The molino nearest the home where I stayed belongs to a family who was able to help their son adelante (forge ahead). His father worked in the comisaría (police station) in the nearby town, and he heard about a scholarship for educational funding to study in Cuba. The family submitted their son's name for this scholarship and the women in the pueblo mágico say he is now a doctor and married to a woman in Cuba who is a Mexican woman from Michoacán who also studied medicine in Cuba on the same scholarship. The son sends them money and the women of the pueblo mágico tell me that's why they have a molino and sewing machines that sew very fast. The home where the

---

i. "My mom takes care of them for me. Yes, I feel bad because sometimes I leave them. I leave them like that but out of necessity, I have to do it. I have to do it for them. Well, so I can get them to go ahead [idiomatic phrase approximately meaning to help them forge ahead]."

ii. "Both emotionally and financially, they help me."

iii. "I would like you to help me in the education of my daughters."

iv. "If they see that my daughters are doing something bad, bring it to their attention."

v. Grinders/mills.

molino is located has tile floors and wooden doors similar to those I have seen in Mérida.

At the molino women wait for their corn to be ground into masa for their daily tortillas. As we sit and wait our turn, we talk about life. Conversations range from questions about an elderly relative's health to storytelling about events that took place in the pueblo. I learned which young woman "se escapo" (eloped) and went to live with a boy in town. The norm is for a girl to marry a boy at the age of twelve and have her first child by the age of fifteen. Young women are courted by a boy and then without notice the boy takes her away to his home for a week or two before returning to her home and notifying her family that they are now a committed couple. Religious ceremonies or marriage rituals are rare. Most couples begin their lives together cuando se escapan (when they escape). When couples return to their mothers' homes with their partner, mothers make room for their new family members and oftentimes a new baby a few months later.

Women in the pueblo mágico work together to generate more income for their families by building work cooperatives. The maquila irrevocably damaged their local commerce by establishing itself in the local town and employing campesinxs to produce products for extremely low wages, then ship them to the US generate high profits for the maquila but not the assembly-line workers. Campesinxs who once dedicated their lives to local agribusiness cannot survive from the sale of their crops. Though this often generates a sense of fear—that if the maquila relocates the workers will lose their jobs—Paloma is not concerned. She knows what she will do: "vender comida allí con mi mama. Como mi tía tiene su puesto, pongo un pequeño negocio, algo así. Porque no me puedo quedar sin hacer nada."[i]

It is a wonder the women have such a vision since their recent attempt to compete with the maquila has failed. Doña Nayeli, a woman considered too old to be employed in the maquila at age thirty-five, drafted a proposal requesting funds to open a small textile business in the pueblo. She submitted her proposal to the Comisión Nacional para el Desarrollo de los Pueblos Indígenas (CDI) Delegación Yucatán and was given two hundred and fifty thousand pesos. With the funding, a group of women from the pueblo built a small workroom where they envisioned purchasing several sewing machines and material needed to start a small business. They named themselves Las Mujeres del Mayab. Doña Nayeli, or "la presidenta" as they call her in the pueblo, communicated with a "teacher" in Huhí, Yucatán, to teach the women how to make bolsas (bags/purses/backpacks). In the Yucatán, towns are

---

i. "Sell food there with my mom. Since my aunt has her small business shop, something like that. Because I can't stay without doing anything."

dedicated to particular trades and this town is known for its bolsas. The teacher taught the women how to make the product, price and sell it, but she also offered to help the women find a large contract that could generate profit. The teacher did in fact bring a man to speak to the women about contract work, but then the teacher stole the contract from the women in the pueblo mágico by deceptively persuading the contractor to work with her more experienced group of women from Huhí. This happened twice. After the second time, the women closed shop and distributed the sewing machines among themselves. This is the struggle: to keep working toward a future they desire and believe the struggle is life and to live means to struggle, while at the same time denouncing the evil that causes them to struggle—greed, dishonesty, and the threat to their communal life together. Women teach their children how to struggle by teaching their children to see and interpret the maquila through *their eyes* and not the eyes of the TNC managers.

The maquila method preys on people who live in impoverished areas around the globe. The TNC assumes that by locating the factory strategically in these areas it will have an endless supply of labor. One of the ways I witnessed the maquila grooming the women's young children to imagine their future on the assembly line was on August 30, 2017, that year's Día de los Niños (Children's Day). The maquila invited the women to bring their children to the maquila for a tour of the factory. Teresa tells me about her two sons' reaction to the visit,

> Ellos dice, "Mamá, si bonito como trabajas," me dicen [laughs] A ellos le pareció bonito. [She and I both laugh.] Le digo a mi esposo, "Llévalo para que vean. Para que no trabajen así," le digo . . . el día de los niños en la [maquila], hicieron un recorrido dentro de la planta. Llevaron a los niños y vieron como estoy trabajando. Y me dijeron. Le digo, "Hijos yo no quiero que hagan eso así, el trabajo ese entonces es muy cansado." Porque yo trabajo parada.[i]

Teresa teaches her sons la ciencia de la lucha even as the maquila attempts to entice her offspring into imagining their bodies replacing their mothers' on the assembly line. However, the women bear life by teaching their children to see themselves as subject-actors.

Teaching la Ciencia de la Lucha[27]

How then do women teach their daughters and sons to be subject-actors? Mothers, the women tell me, cannot make choices for children. Children

---

i. "They say, 'Mom this work is beautiful,' they tell me [laughs]. They thought it was beautiful. [She and I both laugh.] I tell my husband, 'Take them so they can see. So that they don't work like this,' I say . . . on Children's Day in the maquila, they gave the children a tour of the plant. They took the children and they saw how I am working. And they told me. I tell them, 'Children, I don't want you to do this like this, this work here is very tiring.' Because I work standing up [all day]."

make their own decisions. A mother supports her child and works under difficult conditions she does not want for her own child so that her child will have more options from which to choose. Veronica has two daughters, and she tells me,

> Yo no puedo decir, "Sabes que hija, estudia esto." No. No, que ellas decidan estudiar. Para mi, yo las voy a apoyar hasta donde yo pueda. Pero este, no, la verdad no me gustaría que ellas trabajaran en donde yo estoy. Me gustaría que ellas tengan un futuro. Una vida mejor de la que yo tengo. No me gustaría que pasen por lo mismo que lo que yo estoy pasando . . . yendo a trabajar, dejándolas solas, cada cuatro días. A veces es un infierno.[i]

Veronica describes her hope for her eldest daughter:

> Sueño con que ella quiera ser maestra. Y le digo, "Pues, si te gusta hija, vamos hacer el sacrificio de que lo puedas alcanzar." Porque también ahorita para estudiar una carrera también cuesta. Lleva.[ii]

Veronica connects her work in the maquila with her daughter's life. The sacrifice she describes is not a submission to pain and suffering for the sake of her daughter, a theological construct that is critiqued by feminist theologians. Veronica's sacrifice is the daily activity of pursuing her opportunity to "alcanzar" (reach) for aspirations that are denied to young girls. Veronica models this resistance in her workplace by speaking up for herself. She says,

> Hubo una ocasión que tuvimos una supervisora que malísima. No le importaba que estabas enferma. O si tu bebé está enfermo. Lo que ella quería . . . presente para trabajar, fue que te presentes. Hubo una ocasión igual cuando yo me embarace de mi hija, si fue muy malosa. No sé por qué. Ella no podía tener bebés. Se desquitaba con las embarazadas, mujeres embarazadas. Una vez me intento golpear con un carrito. Cuando yo me estaba yendo caminando con mi carrito para llevarlo así para mi máquina, ella vino y me empujo y sabiendo que yo estaba . . . yo ya estaba grande con mi embarazo, tenia como seis meses cuando me quiso chocar. No solo fue en ese momento. Yo lo primero que hice, yo hablé con ella. Le dije que si se dio cuenta de lo que ella hizo. Porque viendo que estoy embarazada y me choco. Podría haberme causado . . . o que iba abortar a mi bebé, o que el bebe tuviera problemas con mi embarazo. Ni se disculpó. Ni

---

[i]. "I can't say, 'You know, daughter, study this.' No. No. They will decide if they study. For me, I will support them as far as I can. But this, no, I really would not like them to work where I am. I would like them to have a future. A better life than what I have. I would not like them to go through the same thing that I'm going through . . . going to work, leaving them alone, every four days. Sometimes, it's hell."

[ii]. "I dream that she wants to be a teacher. And I say, 'Well, if you like that, daughter, let's make the sacrifice so that you can reach [that goal].' Because also, now, to study a career also costs. It takes a lot."

me dijo nada. Solo me chocó y se dio la media vuelta y se fue. A varias de mis compañeras le hizo la misma, la hacía llorar. Pero muchos decían de que porque ella no podía tener bebé se desquitaba con las embarazadas. Pero yo de allí solo una ocasión tuve problemas con ella por eso y en que falté cuando se empezó a enfermar mi hija yo me fui hablar con el jefe de producción. Llevé la receta de mi hija, explique porque no pude ir.[i]

Veronica is not a helpless victim. She is well aware of the risks she takes by speaking up but she underscores for me how she survives in her circumstances for the sake of the life she is creating. She tells me of incidents of sexual harassment but gives me few details. What she wants me to know is that when she goes through difficulties and experiences despair, she seeks courage within herself to protect life—that of her child and her family. She is her own savior. She does not call herself a "savior" but she does tell me how she confronts her superiors denouncing unjust treatment and prioritizing the needs of "the least of these," which I recognize as actions recorded of a god-man in the Christian sacred texts of my religious tradition. What is clear is that Veronica does not want my sympathy, nor does she need me to "save" her. Veronica's struggle is hers, and she communicates to me how she is exposing evil and working toward liberation for her and her children.

Here, Veronica catches an eschatological fragrance of a future that is emerging in the backbreaking work she does. She does not romanticize her work, "es un infierno" (it is hell), but she works with the conviction that there is life/goodness worth working for. She explains to me how she does this:

Me pongo en la ventalera de que primero están mis hijas. Si me voy a trabajar es por . . . para que mis hijas no les faltara nada. Para eso. Y para superarme también un poco, en cuestiones económicas y también mejorar mi casa también porque también pues . . . mi propósito es ese. Yo no . . . la primera cosa que pasa en mi mente cuando llego a trabajar—digo, "Ya me presenté. Me persigno.

---

i. "There was an occasion that we had a supervisor that was very bad. She did not care that you were sick. Or if your baby is sick. What she wanted . . . [was for you to be] present at work, was that you came to work. There was also an occasion when I got pregnant with my daughter, [and my supervisor] was very bad. I do not know why. She could not have babies. She took it out on pregnant women, pregnant women. Once she tried to hit me with a cart. When I was walking with my cart to take it to my machine, she came and pushed me and knowing that I was . . . I was already big with my pregnancy, I was about six months when she tried to crash the cart into me. It was not only at that time. The first thing I did, I talked to her. I told her that if she realized what she did. Because seeing that I'm pregnant and she tried to crash into me. It could have caused me . . . or that she was trying to abort my baby or cause the baby to have problems with my pregnancy. She didn't even apologize. She did not say anything to me. She only heard me and she turned around and left. Several of my co-workers she did the same to, made them cry. But many said that it was because she couldn't have a baby, she would retaliate with pregnant women. But from then on, only one occasion I had problems with her, because of that and because I was absent when my daughter started to get sick. I went to speak to the production manager. I took my daughter's prescription and explained why I couldn't [come to work]."

Dios mío ayúdame. Que me vaya bien este día y nada más. Y mis hijas primero," digo.[i]

By doing so, Veronica is confronting the practice of ta multinational corporation based in the United States, whose president at the time of this writing is a "sovereign" who has revived racism, Islamophobia, and xenophobia by making popular the phrase, "America first." I do not mean to suggest that Veronica is versed in US politics, but as an assembly-line worker she knows what "America first" means for her family and in light of that, she reminds herself, "My daughters first." She makes choices that are in the best interests of her daughters, bending the will of the multinational corporation to serve her interests. Her embodied practice of making the sign of the cross may appear to be "Christian," but Sylvia Marcos reminds us that it is difficult to separate indigenous spirituality and Christianity.[28] Veronica makes the sign of the cross but also tells me this is not a religious practice linked to the Catholic Church. The Catholic Church, from her perspective, is disconnected from her life in the maquila. What does this symbol point to? I will expand on this point in chapter 4, but for now let me say this symbol reflects the daily deaths and resurrections that take place in the maquila.

This daily lucha occurs alongside a "depression" that washes over her once in a while. She tells me about a day when she had problems with her husband. On that day she arrived at work and her machine was not functioning. A broken machine means she cannot make the production quota for the day and this affects her pay and her employment. She submitted a report to the mechanic to repair her machine. He ignored her and she tells me she knew her supervisor would still hold her accountable to produce more items. She explained why she couldn't: her machine needed repair. Her supervisor did not believe her and she *laughs* as she tells me that in that moment she thought to herself, "Esta bien, no me quieren ayudar con ese problema, por ejemplo. Cuando me pidan también horas extras yo no me voy a quedar."[ii] Whether she actually does this or not is not the point. She draws on the power within herself and validates her sense of agency. If she stays, it is not out of fear of losing her job, it is because of her mantra, "My daughters first." Her laughter affirms her awareness of the options, which include, as Mujerista theologian Ada María Isasi-Díaz notes, "dangerous memories of the personal and communal experiences where life has been begotten and birthed despite the death-dealing

---

i. "I put on the front window that my daughters are first. If I go to work, it's because . . . so that my daughters will not lack anything. For that. And to improve myself a bit, in economic matters and also improve my house also because also . . . the first thing that happens in my mind when I get to work, I say, 'I already showed up. I make the sign of the cross. My God, help me that today will go well and nothing more. And my daughters first,' I say."

ii. "Okay, they don't want to help me with that problem, for example. When they ask me for overtime, I'm not going to stay."

situations in which we have lived."²⁹ She resists the voice of the internalized oppressor by laughing/mocking his power over her.

Veronica describes the mounting pressure to produce and the gaze of the roaming *superintendente* who comes to question her low production rate for the day. She tells him the problem is with the machine and "creo que no soy la única operaria que tiene ese problema con su máquina, hay muchas operarias con el mismo problema. Yo creo que por eso la gente no está sacando su producción. Porque no los está ayudando. A mi no me está ayudando la máquina y me imagino que a los demás también."ⁱ She was successful because, she says, though the *mecánico* did not repair her machine, "de allí no regresaron otra vez a decirme nada."ⁱⁱ She was not shamed by a competitive system that links an assembly-line worker's worth and value to her ability to produce products. Moreover, she speaks to the *superintendente* himself. She knows why the production level is low today overall and has to tell him that women are not machines.

Veronica says this hell has changed her. She describes herself as being "noble" (docile) when she first started working at the maquila:

> Pero, a partir que entre a trabajar allí, a veces . . . o sea hay tantos problemas que ha tenido uno en el trabajo . . . ha veces te aprendes a defender. A defender tus derechos también. Porque también si te quedas callada y no dices nada, pues tampoco te van . . . no te hacen caso. A veces, aunque te están hacienda algo tu no dices nada, pues no te hacen caso. No saben que problema tienes. Tienes que hablar para decir tus problemas. Y yo de allí aprendí a defenderme y a decir las cosas como son.ⁱⁱⁱ

Veronica interprets her ability to speak up for herself as a trait birthed in the anguish of work in the maquila. She gains the knowledge that, as Doña Nayeli says, "el bebé que no llora, no come"ⁱᵛ by experience. The daily deaths of being ignored by macro systems (neoliberal capitalism) and micro systems (maquila management), result in cries for life. She says "aprendí a defenderme" (I learned to defend myself), but this is not a knowledge arising from the suffering. The suffering she endures is evil and nothing good can come

---

i. "I think I'm not the only operator that has that problem with her machine, there are many operators with the same problem. I think that's why people are not meeting their production quota. Because the machine/the mechanic is not helping us. Because the machine is not helping me and I imagine it's the same for others."

ii. "From then on, he did not return again to say anything to me."

iii. "But when I started working there, sometimes . . . that is, there are so many problems that one has had at work . . . sometimes you learn to defend yourself. To defend your rights too. Because, also, if you stay silent and don't say anything, well, they aren't going to . . . they don't pay attention to you. Sometimes although they're doing something to you, you don't say anything, because they don't pay attention to you. They don't know what problems you're having. And I learned from there to defend myself and to say things as they are."

iv. "The baby that doesn't cry, doesn't eat."

of it. Her knowledge flows from something much deeper: a human response to life-threatening danger is to resist. Several of the women tell me how surprised they were to learn that they had it in them to speak up for themselves.

SURPRISING FINDINGS OF THIS RESEARCH

When I began this research, I expected to hear women discuss la lucha in relationship to their experience in the Base Christian Communities and their reading of scripture because that was what I read in the Latina feminist theology of María Pilar Aquino, Nancy Pineda-Madrid, Ivone Gebara, Marcella Althaus-Reid, and the mujerista theologies of Ada María Isasi-Díaz. However, what I failed to recognize is that the point of departure for approaches of Latina feminist theologies and Mujerista theologies is the Christian tradition, and they are written by women and about literate women who engage with the Christian sacred text (the Bible). By contrast, the context in which I found myself among the women in the pueblo mágico was of women who, if they do read and write, do this at an elementary level, women who do not show any interest in biblical interpretation. In other words, Christian hegemony does not seem to have taken root in this pueblo. The sacred text is experienced through oral tradition. The women reference the Christian image of the Virgin Mary, but this imagery has a different history here than elsewhere. My experience with working-class Maya mexicanas did not reflect a strong presence of the Christian church or traditional theology. The women in the pueblo mágico did not discuss Christian sacred texts. I would describe the women as nominal Catholics. While they did engage in practices I might more readily identify as "religious" (praying and bringing an offering to the patron saint), these practices they did apart from the institutional church. As I noted in Chapter 2, more than once they told me the church had "nothing to do" with their lives and especially not with their work in the maquila. My theological education made it difficult for me to hear their story without correcting what I believed were historical errors or errors in reporting, for example, the contextual history of La Virgen de la Asunción, which I will elaborate on below.

I came into this project assuming that I would meet women who draw on Christian sacred texts, such as the Salvadorian women referenced by Marcella Althaus-Reid who live in the context of war and are sustained by their Bible study groups' reading of the Bible. Such groups include illiterate women who "write the Word of God 'in her heart.'"[30] Althaus-Reid asks the question I began with, "What is the place of the Bible as a theological resource?"[31] She wonders how "illiterate communities struggling to survive" use the Bible as a resource in the hermeneutical cycle of action-reflection-action, or what she terms *realidad*-Bible-*realidad*.[32] Althaus-Reid explains that "women's popular theology is basically hermeneutical; that is, it interprets the word and the world simultaneously."[33] What I found was surprising to me in that the Bible was not a common resource among these women and women did not gather in Bible study groups. This caused some fear of the unknown for me as a Christian caregiver who benefits from Christian hegemony and who had quickly assumed that the text and the church would be sources of strength for the women. Perhaps this is a cautionary note to Christian caregivers about the "misunderstandings"[34] to which pastoral theologians committed to practicing and proposing a postcolonial pastoral theology need to be attentive. I struggled to hear the reality of these women's lives because I was blinded by the Christian history and theology I know from my childhood and seminary education. I came with imperial colonialist notions of "gospel" and learned that here the good news is that the pueblo mágico refused to abandon its heritage and sacred past for the gospel of the invading foreigner. The combination of images and practices I recognized as "Christian" was steeped in decolonial practices. One example is in the veneration of the pueblo mágico's patron saint.

Some of the women practice the veneration of the pueblo's patron saint, La Virgen de la Asunción. The women who pray to her tell me they make "promesas" for the health and well-being of their children and their families. This image is important to the women not so much because she is Christ's mother—a Christian figure—but because she is a peasant mother who suffered and is therefore, they feel, able to hear and understand their cries, hopes, and fears. They told me, "Ella sí es milagrosa" (She does miracles). I participated in la fiesta del pueblo on August 11–15, 2018, and learned then that there is an interweaving[35] of the Maya god/goddess and La Virgen de la Asunción. This in itself is perhaps a good example of how the local Maya culture appropriates pieces of Christian traditions, but not the faith wholesale.

Contextual Images of Motherhood in Religious Narratives

There are two images of divine gods/goddesses that shape the context of what it means to be a human and a mother in the pueblo. The first is the aforementioned indigenous image of the Maya maíz god/goddess found in the sacred Maya text Popol Vuh[36] (Popol Wuj), written in the highlands of Guatemala by the Maya royal lineage of the K'iche'[37] people, which presents this god/goddess of maíz. The god/goddess of maíz connects the people to the land and their ancestors, as I discussed earlier. The second image that influences the pueblo mágico's understanding of motherhood is La Virgen de la Asunción (the Virgin of the Assumption). Rituals in the pueblo honor lher , and she is celebrated in the fiesta del pueblo on August 15. It is interesting that both these mother images influence women's connection to bearing life in the pueblo. The god/goddess of maíz connects her to the land and emphasizes her interdependent life within the ecosystem. Meanwhile La Virgen de la Asunción offers an image of a strong woman who is a mother, a poor woman, and a human who never dies and is then taken directly to heaven. These two stories are threads woven into the fabric of women's experience in the pueblo. They provide a backdrop to the scene that comes to the forefront. The women do not discuss these religious narratives overtly; however, the narratives provide significant ontological and epistemological insights into women's experience and especially women's identity in this pueblo.

Interweaving of the Colonizers' Cosmology

When Spanish colonizers invaded the land of the Maya, they intended to impose their religious ideologies and theologies onto the people for the purpose of "evangelizing," through converting the Maya from their indigenous cosmologies/theologies to Christianity. During this time, the Maya preserved their sacred text through deliberate oral tradition and hid their sacred book, the Popul Vuh, from colonizers who might destroy it. Today, the women in the pueblo preserve the oral tradition of the Popol Vuh at the same time as they adapt aspects of their Spanish colonizers' theology.

La Virgen de la Asunción

Two Christian sacred texts (Matthew and Luke) narrate the birth of an illegitimate son of a peasant woman as the hope for the emancipation of the Jews from the rule of an earthly tyrant, the Roman emperor Augustus (63 BC–14 AD). Christian liberation theologies underscore the political revolt the peasant woman's son foments. In Christian theology, mariologies reflect on the mother of the divine child and her ability to intercede in humans' relationships with God. However, the explanation I received from the women about who La Virgen de la Asunción is to them presents elements that contradict the colonialist Christian history with which I am familiar.

Doña Nayeli tells me that La Virgen de la Asunción is one of three sisters, triplets. Her sisters are venerated in nearby villages. The image (statue) of La Virgen predates the arrival of the Spanish. When the Spanish came, they saw that La Virgen was wearing a hipil and told the people they needed to remove that clothing from her. When they removed her hipil, they discovered she was wearing a blue dress with the print of stars all around it. La Virgen's dress matches the ceiling of the local cathedral, which also predates the arrival of the Spaniards. No one knows who painted the ceiling of the cathedral; as they say, "es un misterio."[i] Today, La Virgen in the pueblo mágico is recognized as the first sister, who is wearing her original dress (a veil decorated with embroidered flowers like those on a hipil) and for this reason "los arqueólogos"[ii] want to tear down the cathedral and take La Virgen from the pueblo mágico. However, the people protect her and Doña Nayeli assures me they will not allow los arqueólogos to destroy their cathedral.

This narrative recounted by Doña Nayeli suggests that La Virgen is Yucateca. She, much like the deities in the Popol Vuh, has sisters. The Spanish colonizers removed her traditional hipil but this undressing revealed a mysterious, even divine, connection with the cathedral. The celestial print on her dress and on the ceiling of the cathedral is a treasure the people in the pueblo mágico shield from outsiders who continue to threaten its survival. La Virgen lives in the pueblo mágico and the pueblo celebrates her life-giving tenacity.

Cultural anthropologist Gina Villagómez Valdés describes the pueblo's communal veneration of La Virgen de la Asunción as both sacred ritual and profane practice.[38] The fiesta del pueblo begins with the men of the pueblo constructing un ruedo (arena) where the toreros (bullfighters) and vaqueros (horsemen) lasso twenty to thirty bulls every night. On the first night of the fiesta del pueblo, the priest offers a blessing for the ruedo and the community walks behind him with a portrait of La Virgen and he sprinkles holy water around the perimeter of the ruedo.

Villagómez Valdés explains that women's space in la fiesta del pueblo is in the bailes populares. Here, women enjoy dressing in their regional attire and dancing to traditional jaranas and more frequently modern music introduced by the younger women.[39] The fiesta del pueblo is a family event that also includes games for the children.

The most important event of the fiesta del pueblo falls on August 15. There is a morning misa (mass) followed by a procesión of La Virgen led by los gremios (the guilds). Los gremios are groups of workers from various trades that parade through the pueblo with the image of La Virgen until they arrive at the cathedral. In the pueblo mágico, these gremios are performed differently than in other parts of the Yucatán. Each day the gremio is dedicated to a family member, beginning with the youngest and concluding with the men: children, youth, women, and then men. The community members wear their best clothes and the older women dress in the traditional hipil to attend mass. After mass, they process

---

i. "It's a mystery."
ii. "The archeologists."

Figure 3.5. La Virgen de la Asuncion in the pueblo mágico. Photo taken by the author.

through the pueblo carrying cornstalks, flowers, and candles along the route as tangible evidence of prayers offered for their families' health and well-being. They select a home to house the prayers of the people for a year until the following year's fiesta del pueblo. At this home, the host family offers horchata or Pepsi and pork tacos. The festivities include dancing el baile de cochinito (the pig's dance), a traditional dance in which the head of a pig is placed in a wicker basket and a person dances while holding the basket over their head. The person dancing then selects another person to dance based on who is being honored on the day and passes the basket with the pig's head on to them.

During the fiesta del pueblo, some women honor la promesa (the promise) they made to La Virgen in exchange for a petition La Virgen heard. For example, Araceli's firstborn daughter almost died of malnutrition as an infant. Araceli prayed to La Virgen to save her life and made a promesa to buy a bouquet of flowers every year "en su día"[i] to take to the church if her daughter's life was saved. Araceli explains la promesa as act of gratitude: "Es como que tú le pidieras un favor a alguien y te lo hace, se lo quisieras agradecer."[ii] Araceli will save money from her already small paycheck and request to have this day off from working at the maquila.

What I want to highlight about these rituals is *who* is venerated, namely a peasant mother who is at once Maya and mother of a god-child. This, I believe, is a source of strength for the women in the pueblo. Though the women do not access the spiritual resources of the local parish and though they critique the institution, they believe in the life-giving force of a mother. For example, Celeste says,

> Yo pues no voy en la iglesia, no, no nada, pero yo tengo mucho fe en ella. Y le digo a mi mamá . . . y se que gracias a ella estoy en la [maquila] ahora. Se que ella me ayudó. Porque siempre le estado pidiendo a ella . . . hasta cuando le comenté. Ese día que estaba yo en el palacio pidiendo trabajo para salir a barrer, de eso llega mi cuñada diciéndome, "No pidas nada, tal día entras a trabajar." Sabiendo que yo ya se lo había pedido a ella. Que ella no me iba dejar así, sola.[iii]

Celeste makes the clear distinction between her affiliation with the church and the belief that mothers who practice solidarity make a way for one an-

---

i. "On her special day."

ii. "It's like if you ask someone for a favor and they do it, you would want to thank them."

iii. "I do not go to church, no, no nothing, but I have a lot of faith in her. And I tell my mom . . . and I know that thanks to her I'm in the maquila now. I know that she helped me. Because I've always been asking her . . . even when I tell her. That day I was in the plaza asking for work to go out to sweep, that's when my sister-in-law comes to say to me, 'Don't ask for anything, on such and such a day you are going to begin work.' Knowing that I had already asked her. That she would not leave me like this, alone."

other. Celeste seeks a way to make a living wage in a town where campesinxs land is drying up and meanwhile other women, her sister-in-law and La Virgen, bring good news. Celeste is not alone and she will join women in la fiesta del pueblo because it is the veneration of a woman who like her is a mother doing all she can to shield her child from pain, suffering, and injustice. On the other hand, Celeste and the women do not turn to the institution (Christian church) because the church is a source of added demands that restrict and constrain their flourishing. Veronica tells me she believes in "Dios" but "No, o sea no, no, me ata como para hacer cosas de que no, no voy a salir, o no me voy arreglar, o no debo de comer esto. Porque hay religiones que, que prohíben todo eso. La manera de vestirse."[i] Veronica clarifies this tension between women in the pueblo mágico and the church. The institution's concern is orthodoxy, prescribing rules of conduct instead of standing in solidarity with them as Celeste described. In reality what I found was that the women's gospel was good news for the church. If there is any hope arising from the pueblo mágico, it is not in the church or the maquila, but in matriarchal spaces where women cook and invite all who are near to come and eat.

RELEVANCE FOR PASTORAL CARE AND COUNSELING

The life-giving gospel of the pueblo mágico suggests a necessary revision and expansion of pastoral theologians' theories of hope and of practices of care and counseling with working-class women.

Understanding illness and health in a Mesoamerican cosmology leads caregivers to recognize and value the human in dynamic relationship with all of creation. Pastoral caregivers can enhance their care of persons by studying the internal logic of illness and healing within the Mesoamerican context. For some women, drawing on the healing arts of curanderas may yield a helpful line of conversation. For example, the pastoral caregiver might ask: What natural elements in the material world reflect the struggle you are experiencing? What needs to happen in order to bring equilibrium to the situation?

More importantly, the practices of mothering, which are 1) primeramente madre, 2) sharing resources, and 3) teaching la ciencia de la lucha provide empirical data for what thus far has been mainly a theoretical discourse on class and economics within the literature of pastoral care and counseling.

---

i. "No, or no, no, it doesn't tie me to do things that I . . . no, I can't go out, or I can't get all fixed up, or I shouldn't eat this. Because there are religions that, that prohibit all that. The way you dress."

CARE OF THE SOUL IN A NEOLIBERAL AGE

Pastoral theologian Bruce Rogers-Vaughn in his most recent publication, *Caring for Souls in the Neoliberal Age*, comments on sexism and racism in neoliberalism within the context of the United States. He argues that neoliberalism "mutes and mutates racism and sexism" in order to practice new types of patriarchy and white supremacy. Neoliberalism, argues Rogers-Vaughn, appears to free women to leave unpaid domestic work and enter into occupations once reserved for men. This new avenue of employment, financial contribution to the family, and public work is a deceptive façade, he says, that neoliberalism uses as evidence to support their practice of equality, diversity, and multiculturalism. However, in actuality what is taking place is a dismantling of marginalized groups' collective voice by "muting and mutating" their voices. Rogers-Vaughn explains, for example, that because women are employed they cannot speak of their oppression by virtue of their gender. In other words, the apparent equality "mutates" or is reduced to equal opportunity, a term Rogers-Vaughn links to the market economy. All have access to participate, except not everyone can participate in the same way. The mutation of sexism under neoliberalism invalidates the collective voice of women and consequently the plight of individual women within a patriarchal system is privatized and deregulated.[40]

Castilla Ramos's research agrees with Rogers-Vaughn's observation that women of color are given employment opportunities in the growing number of TNCs in places such as Yucatán. An important point Rogers-Vaughn makes that challenges Castilla Ramos's view of work as empowering women is that their employment is not liberation from sexism and racism but rather a new form of suffering he categorizes as "third-order suffering."[41]

Rogers-Vaughn explains that first-order suffering is suffering as a result of the human condition, such as "death, grief, separation, illness, disability, natural calamities, conflict, physical pain."[42] Second-order suffering, he writes, is suffering brought on by human evil such as: "murder, violence, theft, fraud, deception . . . war, group violence, enslavement, oppressive working conditions, and injustices focused upon identities."[43] In his experience as a pastoral counselor, he notes that caring for first- and second-order suffering takes place in communities of care where there are rituals and opportunities for meaning-making in the midst of pain and suffering. In second-order suffering, the source of suffering can be identified, seen, and resisted through the efforts of communities of care. However, Rogers-Vaughn posits that a unique form of suffering, not previously recognized by pastoral caregivers, has come to the forefront in the neoliberal age. Since neoliberalism "mutes and mutates" systemic violence, it not only breaks apart collectives, it also obscures and persists alongside first- and second-order suffering.[44] Rogers-Vaughn references his pastoral clinical work to illustrate how this new order of suffering emerges in a pastoral care and counseling context. As a pastoral counselor and psychotherapist practicing for thirty years beginning in the mid-1980s, Rogers-Vaughn explains that he experienced an increase in hearing clients express self-blame and what he describes as a sense that they were "teetering on the edge of a precipice."[45] At the same time, he identified a small group of individuals (whom he refers to as "outliers") who spoke with more confidence, "even entitled or defiant."[46] Individuals, he goes on to say, express their suffering in language accessible to them (first- and second-order suffering), internalizing the problem (e.g., "I am depressed"). While Rogers-Vaughn notes that a person's suffering is often "messy mash-ups of the three orders,"[47] pastoral care and counseling approaches to care focus on first- and second-order suffering, but insufficiently address third-order suffering. Rogers-Vaughn calls on the discipline to begin devising new paradigms to assist persons in "finding their footing—to articulate the deep meanings that ground their lives and to strengthen healthy collectives and social movements that hold some residue of transcendental values."[48]

The practices linked to the grounding of transcendental values identified by the women in this study are:

1. Primeramente Madre: Validating and emphasizing women's identity as "mother" and life-giver, one who brings forth life and protects the survival of her children, is a source of strength for women. Providing opportunities for women to speak about their children and their experience as their mothers' children grounds their sense of self in the world. This also gives them the ability to reject the experience-near identity as "assembly-line workers" and supports their daily acts of practicing la ciencia de la lucha.
2. Sharing Resources: Women thrive in collectives with other women where there is a sharing of daily resources necessary to protect the survival of their children and their pueblo. These collectives are matriarchal support systems in which women set the agenda, listen to one another, educate one another's children, and share financial resources with one another. Other activities include gardening, sewing, and working outside the home.
3. Teaching la Ciencia de la Lucha: There is strength in living en la lucha and teaching her children to navigate complex structural relationships with wisdom. Pastoral care and counseling can include opportunities for women to teach their children how to choose which norms to oppose and when to make these decisive moves. Caregivers can also be attentive to how we live in the struggle and not merely view struggle as something to

be overcome or live through. Much of this care takes place organically in life within a woman's home and community. Caregivers who are active in communities can provide care by describing how they see them doing this for their son/daughter and asking follow-up questions like: Why is it important that s/he see or hear you talk about the options you considered and why you chose to respond in the way you did? Storytelling is another way in which care can underscore norms women wish to teach their children to oppose. For example, speaking to their children about work they do not want them to have to do brings them courage to continue their lucha and also supports their voices that stand in opposition to the hope of multinational corporations that there is an endless supply of workers in low-income pueblos willing to endure the conditions they insist upon. Inviting children to listen to the women's preferred futures for themselves, their children and their pueblo, is also a form of care.

4. Resisting Imports of Genetically Modified Corn Seed: Pastoral care and counseling can advocate for policy reform to restrict genetically modified seeds from being imported to Mexico. They can also educate local communities to increase understandings of and responsiveness to the problem. For example, the US agricultural technology company Monsanto is currently the largest producer of genetically modified seed and pesticides. The problem is that Monsanto modifies seeds so that farmers cannot use the seeds from the plants they grow for the following year's harvest. Consequently, farmers become dependent on Monsanto. Though there is legislation prohibiting imports of GMO corn to Mexico, there is a provision to allow designated areas to plant and grow genetically modified seeds. Participating in grassroots protests by campesinxs and transnational organizations[49] can be part of pastoral care. Caregivers can participate in this work alongside careseekers. Tracing the harm to an identified source such as Monsanto and the multiple ways in which this megacompany has caused harm and suffering de-privatizes and regulates the third-order suffering to which Rogers-Vaughn refers. These transnational concerns that underscore the vulnerability of México losing its incredible biodiversity of corn and local campesinxs being pressed to use genetically modified corn or have their milpas contaminated by the genetically modified corn create a supportive collective that resists the crisis that plucks campesinxs from their trade and introduces illness/contaminants to the people and the land.[50]

CONCLUSION

In this chapter, I presented the life-giving gospel by which the women in the pueblo mágico live, which bears life by embodying hope. I tied the relationship between humans and the earth to the narrative of the Maya creation myth in the Popol Vuh. Humans as lxs hijxs del maíz can be "keepers of the days" (time) who contribute to the flourishing of the earth, which is always taking place in what is a complex ecosystem. This activity is always under threat and as a result "illness" and "healing" must find a balance in order to coexist. The hope-practices of working-class Maya mexicanas embrace this tension and confront this complexity with their identities as "primeramente madre" and with their veneration of La Virgen de la Asunción. Women maintain strength in their collectives and teach their children how to practice la ciencia de la lucha. The following chapter focuses on la ciencia de la lucha. There, I turn to the eschatological questions of *where* and *for what* women *hope*. What is the anatomy of la lucha? What practices do women perform in la lucha?

NOTES

1. Duane R. Bidwell, "Eschatology and Childhood Hope: Reflections from Work in Progress," *Journal of Pastoral Theology* 20, no. 2 (Winter 2010): 109–127.
2. Allen J. Christenson, trans., *Popol Vuh: The Sacred Book of the Maya* (Winchester, UK: O Books, 2003).
3. This is a Mesoamerican sport and ritual. There are variations on the rules of the game and variations on how it is played. In Merida, capital of Yucatán, there is a re-enactment for tourists of the ancient ballgame in the zocalo (main plaza). Men are divided into two teams. There is a pole with a circular hoop through which they attempt to launch a rubber ball with their hips through the opening. The Popol Vuh linked the game to the cosmic struggle between dualities and a portal to the Underworld, linking the themes of fertility and death.
4. Juana Batz Puac, "Creation Story of the Maya," Living Maya Time, Smithsonian National Museum of the American Indian, accessed March 15, 2018, https://maya.nmai.si.edu/the-maya/creation-story-maya.
5. Sylvia Marcos, "Sylvia Marcos," Blog de Sylvia Marcos, accessed July 18, 2018, https://sylviamarcos.wordpress.com/sylvia-marcos/.
6. The term "Mesoamerica" refers to the geographical location of mid-México and south to the Central American countries of Belize, Guatemala, El Salvador, Honduras, Nicaragua, and northern Costa Rica. Mesoamerica is the homeland of the Maya, Toltec, Aztec, Zapotec, and Mixtec. Though each of these cultural groups is distinct, Marcos states that Mesoamerican scholars "assume a common cultural core, manifest in similarities of symbolic meanings, rituals and social practices, medical knowledge, architectural elements, and iconographies, writing systems (pictograms, hieroglyphs, pictoglyphs), and measurement of time (calendars) among the diverse people of Mesoamérica." Sylvia Marcos, *Taken from the Lips: Gender and Eros in Mesoamerican Religions*, Religion in the Americas Series 5 (Leiden: Brill, 2006), xx.
7. Marcos, *Taken from the Lips*. (Leiden: Brill, 2006).

8. Marcos, *Taken from the Lips*, 8.
9. Marcos, *Taken from the Lips*.
10. Marcos, *Taken from the Lips*.
11. Marcos, *Taken from the Lips*.
12. Marcos, *Taken from the Lips*.
13. Marcos, *Taken from the Lips*.
14. Marcos, *Taken from the Lips*.
15. Marcos, *Taken from the Lips*, 10.
16. Marcos, *Taken from the Lips*.
17. Marcos, *Taken from the Lips*, 9.
18. Beatriz Castilla Ramos, *Mujeres Mayas en la Robótica y Líderes de la Comunidad: Tejiendo la Modernidad* (Mérida: Universidad Autónoma de Yucatán, 2004), 144.
19. Like a kind of game or hobby that is transmitted from mothers to daughters. See Marcos, *Taken from the Lips*, 145–146.
20. Castilla Ramos. *Mujeres Mayas*, 145.
21. Castilla Ramos, *Mujeres Mayas*, 27.
22. Castilla Ramos, *Mujeres Mayas*, 450–451.
23. The pre-Christian use of the term "gospel" was in the context of military battle. The entry for *euaggelion* in the *Theological Dictionary of the New Testament* explains the usage as an announcement of good news by a messenger who returned to notify the emperor that there was a victory over the opponent and that now those lands and peoples belonged to the victor. Christians appropriated the term "gospel" to challenge the Roman imperial cult and to announce the reign of a rival king, whose kingdom was eternal and not bound by time or space. The Christian community defined itself in relationship to the Roman Empire by appropriating the term "gospel" and assigning the term added meaning by connecting it to the reign of an "eternal kingdom." Christianity retained the military practices that occasioned such "gospels" and these practices are evident in the colonial history of the New World in the fifteenth century discussed in chapter 2 of this book. Here, I use the term "gospel" to refer to the practices of both the maquila and the women in the pueblo. I intend to reveal the gospel of the women as "good news" and as an act of resistance that pushes back against imperialist practices such as the maquilas. Gerhard Kittel, ed., *Theological Dictionary of the New Testament*, vol. 2, trans. Geoffrey W. Bromiley (Grand Rapids, MI: Eerdmans, 1964), s.v. "euaggelion."
24. Loida I. Martell-Otero, "Neither 'Left Behind' Nor Deciphering Secret Codes: An Evangélica Understanding of Eschatology," in *Latinas Evangélicas: A Theological Survey from the Margins*, edited by Loida I. Martell-Otero, Zaida Maldonado Pérez, and Elizabeth Conde-Frazier (Eugene, OR: Cascade Books, 2013), 108–126.
25. Jürgen Moltmann, *The Coming of God: Christian Eschatology* (Minneapolis: Fortress Press, 1996).
26. Trash piling up in the pueblo was a big concern. Neighbors who burned their trash close to the pueblo were berated for the toxic fumes to which they exposed

others. It was expected that each family take its trash to a secluded area in the monte and burn it there. A second expectation was that the pueblo center, the plaza where the capilla is located, be cleaned up by all the women in the pueblo.

27. The science of the struggle. This was a phrase used by Insurgente Erika, a Zapatista, in her opening statement at the International Gathering of Politics, Art, Sports, and Culture for Women in Struggle, March 8, 2018, Chiapas, México.

28. Sylvia Marcos, "La Espiritualidad de las Mujeres Indígenas Mesoamericanas: Descolonizado las Creencias Religiosas," in *Tejiendo Otro Modo: Feminismo, Epistemología y Apuestas Descoloniales en Abya Yala*, edited by Yuderkys Espinosa Miñoso, Diana Gómez Correal, and Natalia Ochoa Muñoz (Popayán, Colombia: Universidad del Cauca, 2014), 143.

29. Ada María Isasi-Díaz, "*Burlando al Opresor*: Mocking/Tricking the Oppressor: Dreams and Hopes of Hispanas/Latinas and *Mujeristas*," *Theological Studies* 65, no. 2 (2004): 344.

30. Marcella Althaus-Reid, *From Feminist Theology to Indecent Theology: Readings on Poverty, Sexual Identity and God* (London: SCM Press, 2004), 117.

31. Althaus-Reid, *Feminist Theology to Indecent Theology*, 117.

32. Althaus-Reid, *Feminist Theology to Indecent Theology*.

33. Althaus-Reid, *Feminist Theology to Indecent Theology*.

34. See Melinda A. McGarrah Sharp, *Misunderstanding Stories: Toward a Postcolonial Pastoral Theology* (Eugene, OR: Pickwick, 2013).

35. I have carefully chosen the word "interweaving" as opposed to "syncretism" because it was my observation that there are several threads of belief and practice that survive as diverse cultures encounter one another. I do not see a blending here as much as a coexistence and intermingling of various traditions.

36. A sacred Maya text written in the K'iche' language. *Popol Vuh* means the "Book of the Community" and it recounts the birth of humans from white and yellow corn, as recounted earlier in this chapter. This is a pre-Columbian Maya text that was committed to memory and passed down through oral tradition, then hidden from Spanish conquistadores in the sixteenth century.

37. The Maya language of Guatemala.

38. Gina Irene Villagómez Valdés and Wilbert Pinto, *Mujer Maya y Desarrollo Rural en Yucatán* (Mérida: Universidad Autónoma de Yucatán, 1997), 157.

39. Villagómez Valdés and Pinto, *Mujer Maya y Desarrollo Rural en Yucatán*.

40. Bruce Rogers-Vaughn, *Caring for Souls in a Neoliberal Age* (New York: Palgrave Macmillan, 2016), 131–161.

41. Rogers-Vaughn, *Caring for Souls*, 109, 125–128.

42. Rogers-Vaughn, *Caring for Souls*, 126.

43. Rogers-Vaughn, *Caring for Souls*.

44. Rogers-Vaughn, *Caring for Souls*, 127.

45. Rogers-Vaughn, *Caring for Souls*, 1.

46. Rogers-Vaughn, *Caring for Souls*.

47. Rogers-Vaughn, *Caring for Souls*, 127.

48. Rogers-Vaughn, *Caring for Souls*, 128.

49. For a history of grassroots movements, see Alfredo Acedo, "Mexico's GMO Corn Ban and Glyphosate Cancer Findings," Environmental and Food Justice Blog, July 20, 2015, https://ejfood.blogspot.com/2015/07/monsanto-in-mexico-report-on-grassroots.html.

50. "Mexico vs. Monsanto: Help Mexico Beat Monsanto," GMO Free USA, accessed August 1, 2018, https://gmofreeusa.org/take-action/mexico-vs-monsanto/.

Chapter Four

La Ciencia de la Lucha: ¡Sí se puede! (The Science of the Struggle: Yes We Can!)

An assembly-line worker leans toward Sofia and says, "Sueñas, me dices?"[i] It is only her second day of work. A few days prior, she had been devastated to learn that her application to work in the maquila had been accepted. She applied for the same reason most of the children of campesinxs do—because any work is better than no work—but this news came to her when she was pursuing a sueño and she was crushed. She never wanted to work on the assembly line of the maquila pegando bolsas de frente (sewing pockets onto fabric), but nevertheless here she was.

In this chapter as in the previous chapter, I use the theological loci of theological anthropology and eschatology to interpret the women's words and describe the practices women exercise to resist the harm that the maquila inflicts. Yet let me be clear: the women did not interpret their experiences in the way I am about to demonstrate in this chapter. I am constructing or imagining a conversation between the women's experience, the political-economic authority of NAFTA, and the Christian doctrine of salvation. The women I came to meet and those I interviewed in the pueblo mágico told stories in the same way I heard Zapatista women tell stories of la lucha. Women narrated long herstories of experiencing abuse (emotional, physical, and sexual), of poverty, illness, loss of land, and cultural appropriation of cosiendo (sewing). These experiences are tied to the broader context of neoliberal capitalism and its effects on their lives. Through their stories, I learned how global capitalism continues the work of colonial imperialism. I also came to *see* what hope is as they explained to me how they practice not just survival, but living/being alive. Continuing to build on Latina feminist Loida Martell's suggestion that for Latinxs eschatology is topological, not chronological, this chapter focuses

---

i. "You say you dream?"

on the eschatological questions of *where* and *for what* women *hope*. I identify Latina eschatological practices and conclude that hope has an anatomy, that it literally lives in women's bodies. I am not claiming that what I delineate in this chapter is the totality of what "hope" is; what I am saying is that when I dissected stories searching for answers to the question of *where* and *what* hope looks like in the experiences of the eleven working-class Maya mexicanas I interviewed, I found an anatomy—a structure of their hope that can be studied. Living in the pueblo mágico also gave me opportunity to see and evaluate the conclusions I reached.

First, I will describe and define women's sueños as tenacious desires for life. I use Sofia's story to introduce the reader to the concept of sueños as a relational telos. Then I turn to the Popol Vuh and Ecuadorian anthropologist Patricio Guerrero Arias to link sueños to sabidurías insurgentes of lxs hijxs de maíz. Next, I discuss epistemicide and the ability of lxs hijxs de maíz to corazonar la vida and thus resist the violence of modernity by engaging in risk-taking actions. These actions are eschatological practices that are hope-filled. I define and describe four practices: hablando (speaking), ignorando (ignoring), insistiendo (insisting), and renunciando (giving up responsibility/quitting). I conclude by reflecting theologically on these practices as everyday deaths and resurrections and the relevance of this for pastoral care and counseling.

SOFIA'S *SUEÑO*

Sofia's dream had seemed possible after finishing her bachiller (high school). At that point it seemed she would avoid the working conditions of the maquila. She had moved in with a physician's family in a neighboring town to care for their infant son and, while living at their home, the physician had tutored Sofia in biology to help her fulfill her dream of working in the medical field. This family had offered to support Sofia in her pursuit of such a career, and Sofia had told me she had wanted to accept this support because she so desperately feels a desire to work in a helping profession. The news about her "successful" application to the maquila had thwarted those dreams. Her father had called her to come home, insisting she could not turn down a job. Intersectionality theory assists pastoral theologians in understanding the complexity of this suffering. Sofia is economically poor, a woman of color, living in a rural area of a country that is increasingly sinking deeper into debt and subject to bilateral and multilateral agreements in a globalized economy. These macro systems account for her particular experience as the daughter of a campesino suffering from the loss of a once-rural economy. Without her father's support to accept the help of the physician's family, she came home and reported to work on the assembly line of the maquila. Understandably, Sofia was crushed that she could not say no to her father and had to come home to work in the maquila.

Sofia is tearful as she tells me this story. Yet she says she has a dream to pursue a vocation in the medical field, a dream she has told other women in the pueblo mágico who also work in the maquila. When I write the word "dream," I am translating the women's "sueños," descriptions of their waking desires communicated to me by their retelling of stories. Sofia is not reflecting on some obscure night vision she experienced in her subconscious that requires the assistance of a trained psychoanalyst to decipher its symbolic meaning, as Sigmund Freud (1856–1939) suggested.[1] Nor is she hinting at some struggle to integrate the longings of her unconscious mind with those of her conscious mind, a task psychoanalyst Carl Jung (1875–1961) identified as the process of individuation in his theory of dreams.[2] Instead, she is speaking of a struggle she engages in during the waking hours of her day, a sueño (dream) that informs her lucha. This sueño is the intended goal (telos) of her work in the maquila. This telos is relational; it is conceived in a community that practices solidarity and sends her adelante (to forge ahead) to engage in the struggle for the sake of her familia and her pueblo.

Many women in the maquila recall coming in to work on those first few days with their sueños (dreams) still alive. For many of the women in the maquila, they quickly learn that once you begin to work on the assembly line your sueños die along with your humanity. A fellow worker tells Sofia, "'Ya estas acá. Y ya después, ni te va, ni te va esto, ni esto. Ya lo vas a olvidar. Ni lo vas a lograr,' me dijo. ¿Y yo? [pause, as she takes a deep breath]. Ah, no puedes. Y yo sigo con la mentalidad que ¡Sí se puede!"[i] As Sofia speaks, I hear what I interpret as a tough resolve to seguir adelante (keep forging ahead) despite the voice of her colonial oppressors that have convinced some assembly-line workers that to soñar (dream) is useless. Such discouragements are the palos (beatings) to which the Mexican-Cuban-Lebanese poet Fayad Jamís (1930–1988) refers when he writes, "Con tantos palos que te dio la vida."[3] The palos of colonialism's subjugation are retained through neoliberal capitalism's expansion around the globe. As campesinxs are plucked from their milpas and distracted from cosiendo (sewing) hipiles while they tend to their children, their way of life and their sueños appear to be unattainable and are in fact difficult to claim because the maquila usurps the pueblo mágico's land and customs. It is difficult to soñar (dream) when your native sacred soil is being desecrated. The golpes (blows) caused by a relentless system

---

i. "'You're already here. And later, this won't go well, that won't go well, not even the other will go well. You're going to forget your dream. You're not even going to achieve it,' he said. And me? [pause] Ugh, you can't. But I hold on to my notions that yes, it can be done."

driven by greed are abusive, but as the poet writes, "Aún sigues dándole a la vida sueños."[i] Jamís articulates a truth I observed in the women of the pueblo mágico who enter the maquila seeking to find Life and instead find it is they who must give to Life the pueblo's sueños.

WOMEN'S *SUEÑOS*

Sofia is not the only woman who shares her sueños with me. Celeste's sueño is to be a beautician and manicurist; her four-year-old daughter's sueño is to be a doctor. Veronica and Maria's sueño is to see their daughters able to pursue the vocation of their choice. Araceli's sueño is to build a house that will be a "gift" for her three children to inherit. Every woman told me soñaban (they dreamed) of building their casa and having milk (meaning, by extension, sufficient food) for their children. The youngest women working in the maquila, Ximena and Sofia, sueñan of building houses for their mothers. In short, women enter the maquila with sueños that are more like *tenacious desires for life*. I would summarize this by repeating a phrase I heard Zapatista women use: "¡Nos queremos vivas!"[ii] As I press Maria to help me understand this struggle for life she says, "Yo no quiero quedarme pobre toda la vida. Y por eso yo quiero seguir adelante. Por eso yo estoy luchando, porque yo tenga un futuro."[iii] As I searched for clarity on what Maria meant by "quedarme pobre" (stay/remain poor), I learned that though Maria does not mention the effects of globalization and neoliberal capitalist policies, she is well aware that in order to survive in the global market economy she will perhaps unwillingly need to replace her agrarian way of life with participation in the modernization project of the global industrial community.[4] She does not want to be economically "poor" and exploited all her life, so she works. However, she also does not view herself as a member of the community of "the poor." She, along with many in the pueblo, talks about "the poor." I was puzzled by such designations and sought clarification on what to me, a privileged outsider, seemed to be conflicting definitions. By all accounts what I saw led me to believe they are "poor." However, the women rejected this classification and explained that those who are cut off from community/family are "poor." In other words, to work in the maquila is to live a relationally and economically "poor" life. Working in the maquila means women's primary need for

---

i. Translation: "yet, even still, you keep giving dreams to life."

ii. This is a difficult phrase to translate but I would propose two approximate English translations: (1) "What we want for ourselves is life!" and (2) "We want us alive!"

iii. "I don't want to be poor all my life. And that's why I want to forge ahead. That's why I'm fighting, so I can have a future."

connection to peers, the earth, and their community is reduced to the competition of market capitalism explored in chapter 2. Though Maria works in the maquila, Maria is not "poor"; she just works in an impoverished system (the maquila and by extension capitalism) that lacks a moral compass. The women enter this morally bankrupt system with the richness of their sueños, and it is their sueños that radically reorder capitalism's patriarchal white supremacy and economic priorities in their own lives.

THE ANATOMY OF HOPE

Hope is made present in and does not exist apart from embodied action. The activity of women in the pueblo mágico who work in the maquila emits an eschatological fragrance of a world they are creating in which they can flourish. This world is one in which their sueños can take root and their children can reap the harvest their lives produce. That world is constructed by what Guerrero Arias calls "sabidurías insurgentes" (insurrectionist wisdoms) grounded in la ciencia de la lucha (the science of the struggle), a phrase I am adopting from Zapatista women who use this expression to summarize the stories of their suffering, stories that narrate their strategies of survival, living/being alive. La ciencia de la lucha is knowledge of the material world gained by experience, observation, narration, and experimentation. La lucha of working-class Maya mexicanas and la ciencia is a study of the struggle, both the structure and the behavior of the struggle.

Women learn how to struggle and, in the struggle, hope grows like the crops planted in the milpa by campesinxs constantly threatened yet persevering. Campesinxs plant hope, like small seeds in the milpa, in their everyday labor on the maquila assembly line. Much like their milpas, neoliberal capitalism invades their land and introduces values and forms of production that are like genetically modified seeds that need to be uprooted. As I discussed in chapter 2, the maquila attempts to devastate the collectivism of tribal life and threatens the livelihood of indigenous life by: 1) assigning individuals the traits of machines, 2) incarcerating women, 3) designing a culture of surveillance, 4) paying women lethal wages, and 5) advancing the religion of the colonizer.

Neoliberal capitalism, as an economic system, needs to be uprooted because, as anthropologist and Marxist geographer David Harvey argues in *A Brief History of Neoliberalism*, neoliberalism is a reconstruction of power for the upper-class elite that increases income inequality between the world's top one percent of earners and the world's poorest.[5] Harvey supports his claim by citing data collected by economists Gérard Duménil and Dominique Lévy in *Capital Resurgent: Roots of the Neoliberal Revolution.* He writes that neoliberal capitalism is "a *political* project to re-establish the conditions for capital accumulation and to restore the power of economic elites."[6] The seed of capitalism is based on policies of liberalization, privatization, and deregulation that are planted in the pueblo mágico through NAFTA and subsequently by the operation of the foreign-owned maquila. The women who work on the maquila's assembly line resist the endangering of their cultural values of collectivism, connection with the earth, and mothering by resisting the pernicious seeds of capitalism. They uproot neoliberal capitalism's seed through their sabidurías insurgentes.

Sabidurías Insurgentes

Guerrero Arias defines "sabidurías insurgentes" (insurrectionist wisdoms) as intuitions that perceive possible paths through life, paths that are carved out of dolor (pain). He expounds on this idea by quoting the teaching of el Viejo Antonio,[7] who says that sabiduría (wisdom) "no consiste en conocer el mundo, sino en intuir los caminos que habrá de andar para ser mejor . . . la sabiduría consiste en el arte de descubrir por detrás del dolor, la esperanza."[8] Said another way, sabidurías insurgentes locate hope by intuiting approaches through life's pain. The hope that is realized has a structure, an anatomy that can be studied. An analysis of the anatomy of hope reveals an epistemology (knowing) in the service of ontological anthro/gynopologies.[9] The subservience of epistemology to ontological anthro/gynopologies can be traced to political uprisings and social agendas in Latin American struggles that propose new forms of government that prioritize the Buen Vivir (well-being) of peasants, Afrodescendants, the earth, women, and children.[10] The concept of Buen Vivir is "a holistic, de-economized view of social life . . . Buen Vivir subordinates economic objectives to the criteria of human dignity, social justice, and ecology."[11] In other words, the quality of life and plants', animals', and humans' access to a good life ought to guide the economic practices and goals of governments in the age of globalization. How do we come to know what a dignified and just life is? Sabidurías insurgentes. In the Popol Vuh, we learn that lxs hijxs de maíz are created with sabidurías insurgentes and this equips them to practice "corazonando la vida" (knowledge gained by feeling-thinking through life). I begin by summarizing the Popol Vuh story before explaining "corazonando."

Lxs Hijxs de Maíz and the Magic of Sabidurías Insurgentes

La sabiduría insurgente is magic. The Popol Vuh[12] gods/goddesses intended to create humans who possessed magic. Guerrero Arias explains that the first humans who were created from mud had words to speak, but no understanding of their own speech. This displeased the gods/goddesses, and they destroyed the humans with water. The gods'/goddesses' second attempt to create humans was to use wood. The wooden humans were sturdier than the mud humans but the gods/goddesses noticed they had no "aliento, corazón, ni sangre en las venas"[13] (breath, heart, or blood in their veins). These humans had words to speak but lacked knowledge because they had no memory or humility with which to "descubrir la sabiduría" (discover wisdom).[14] The gods/goddesses realized they had failed once again, for "los hombres de madera eran demasiado fríos y sin sentimientos, por lo tanto no podrían dar luz a su creación."[15] The gods/goddesses met and consulted about what to do. The task was pressing: they noted that day was about to break and they needed to make humans to populate the land. They then decided to create "un nuevo tipo de hombres" (a new type of humans). This time they breathed and from their breath created humans. They nourished these humans with maíz and the maíz created in humans "el fluido vital que hizo que su corazón cante, encendieron el fuego de la magia de los sueños y se maravillaron con el sagrado milagro de la existencia."[16] The breath of the gods/goddesses and the psychospiritual-relational practice of feeding and eating maíz from the earth resulted in the animation of humans.

The gods/goddesses marveled at this sacred miracle of lxs hijxs de maíz. Their hearts sing. Their dreams are illuminated with the fire of magic. These humans feel, remember, and engage with the world body and soul. As the gods/goddesses step back and evaluate these hijxs de maíz, their admiration turns to fear. These humans are too powerful; one day, the gods/goddesses believe, they might gain more wisdom than the gods/goddesses themselves. To avoid this uprising and potential coup, the gods/goddesses decided to

> opacar, oscurecer, la mirada de los hombres para que no puedan ver sino solo lo intrascendente, aquello que esté frente a sus ojos y no tengan visión sobre el presente y el futuro, que sean incapaces de descubrir la fuerza constructora que tiene la palabra, el amor y la sabiduría.[17]

Guerrero Arias explains that this is why humans cannot hear the wisdom of the heart above the noise of their reason. Moreover, he notes that the difficult work of anthropologists is to "recuperar" (recover) and "revitalizar" (revitalize): dreams, love, hope, dignity, tenderness, and happiness, in order to construct "hombres y mujeres de maíz" (men and women of corn). This is a necessary task because in the recovery of these sabidurías insurgentes, lxs hijxs de maíz regain life. Rationalism, he argues, can ver (look) at reality but cannot mirar (see) reality for all that it is. The challenge for the recovery and revitalization of lxs hijxs de maíz is addressing the effects of a long history of epistemicide so that alternative realities can be given equal validity.

Corazonar and Epistemicide

The term "corazonar" is a combination of the Spanish word corazón (heart) and pensar (think). Tseltal scholar Juan López Intzín[18] and others elaborate on this concept, for example, by speaking about "el poder sentirsaber-sentirpensar" (the power or ability to feel-know and to feel-think).[19] In Spanish the word "poder" can be translated into English in one of two ways, for poder is both "power" and "the ability to do or to be."[20] Corazonar, or sentirsaber-sentirpensar, is not about empowerment. Why use the tool of the oppressor to construct or recover anything if in fact we seek to create *new* life? Corazonar is not interested in power, except to identify how oppressive systems have rendered some of us invisible. Corazonar is about the *capacity* of lxs hijxs de maíz to *be* alive, to affirm the multiple knowledges and ways of being that arise from the hope that nourishes the terrain in which we are planted. Corazonar is not about expanding our territory at the peril of another's survival, nor is it limited to practicing survival. Corazonar is about living, being alive, and creating conditions for life. In order to do this, corazonar decenters, replaces, and fractures the hegemony of modernity's rationalism and privileged empiricism. Reality is not merely what can be seen and logically deduced; reality is also mysterious and magical, and in addition it appears from what is *perceived* and *intuited*. The Popol Vuh preserves a myth to help us remember that lxs hijxs de maíze are created to corazonar, to see beyond what is apparent.[21] Lxs hijxs de maíz see "magical dreams" that are revealed *in* creation through sabidurías del corazón (wisdoms of the heart).[22] Guerrero Arias explains this knowledge (epistemology) that originates outside of the academy:

> No ha sido el resultado de un proceso de reflexión al interior de la academia o de los intelectuales críticos; sino una consecuencia de la lucha por la existencia de los pueblos sometidos a la colonialidad, construidos como "objetos de estudio" de las ciencias sociales, y que hoy transformados en sujetos políticos e históricos; le han impuesto a la academia y a la sociedad el reconocimiento de sus sabidurías y de su existencia.[23]

Guerrero Arias alludes to this deliberative act not just of exclusion but of calculated extinction of knowledges outside of the academe. Epistemicide is a type of violence that undergirds issues of social justice, beginning with assaults on cognition.

Boaventura de Sousa Santos posits that colonialism and by extension global capitalism must first redress "cognitive injustice" in order to address social justice issues. In *Epistemologies of the South: Justice against Epistemicide*, he especially focuses on the injustice of the western Eurocentric academe that fails to see the knowledges of the global south[24] where people live their everyday lives on their terms and make meaning of their lives in different ways than those codified in the theoretical canon of the global north (specifically western Europe).[25] What de Sousa Santos underscores is the neglect and silencing of knowledges other than those produced and theorized in intellectual academic spaces, spaces that are quite disconnected from la lucha of the pueblo. This divide between theory and practice is a concern that practical theology seeks to mitigate in part by beginning the investigation of knowledge from the ground up. However, in order to hear these knowledges into existence we have to work to *see* who people are and see them on their terms and not ours. The challenge is that we who are trained in the knowledge traditions of western Europe, as I am, struggle to remove the veil of universals, abstractions, and positivism, to name a few dominant concepts. These concepts come at the expense not only of the millions of people whose lives and existence are rendered invisible because of our imposition on them of our interpretations, but also at the expense of ourselves, for the practice also diminishes our own humanity. I become less human when I deny or diminish the humanity of the Other. The world is not as I see it, as much as I might be deceived into believing this. The world might actually be more like what the Zapatistas teach, "un mundo donde quepan muchos mundos" (a world where many worlds fit), and therefore our task is to understand the universe as a pluriverse.[26]

The Pluriverse

Eurocentric ontologies present what Colombian American anthropologist Arturo Escobar names "the Mundo Mundial" (one-world world or universe).[27] These ontologies of the Mundo Mundial are "proyectos extractivistas [que] pueden entenderse como estrategias para la ocupación ontológica de los territorios, y por lo tanto las luchas en su contra constituyen, en realidad, luchas ontológicas."[28] In other words, colonial occupation occurs not only through the invasion of an outside group into a defined geographical space. Certainly, the struggle for territory is a political struggle rooted in place, but it is also an ontological lucha where there is a convergence between and among place, people, and worldviews. The women living in the pueblo mágico are rooted in a particular place. Their difuntos antepasados (deceased ancestors) lived on the same land and off the same crops of the milpas. Doña Nayeli explains, "No, no platico mi historia porque no es mía. Yo platicó la de mi abuelo y el platico la de su abuelo porque nosotros todavía estamos creciendo. Es una cadena que se hace."[i] The pueblo mágico's economic practices were linked to relational ontologies connecting land, people, and resources. Practices of extraction, such as those introduced to their pueblo through the invasion of the maquila, were the result of a globalized economy that in practice brings together disparate economies to serve in a one-world world economy. This economic system brings with it additional consequences of the Mundo Mundial/universe, namely ecological harm, poverty, patriarchy, and white supremacy.[29]

The Mundo Mundial/universe is characterized by the confinement of what is to the single reigning reality. This world confines and limits knowledges and only recognizes one experience over and above all others. Any deviation from the Mundo Mundial's/universe's truth is discounted and made invisible. The Mundo Mundial/universe is continuously creating invisibility.[30] The struggle for Buen Vivir (living well) is being led by peasants around the globe and marginalized communities imagining a world where the economy is at the service of the environment, nature, and the well-being of life.[31] A move toward bringing about the reality of a pluriverse requires a turn toward relational ontologies that replace the anthropocentrism of the Mundo Mundial with the biodiversity of the pluriverse.

The pluriverse, as conceptualized by Zapatistas, prioritizes the needs of the earth, then the life of the people (which is connected to the earth), and finally the submission of the government to the flourishing of life. The well-known slogan is "La tierra manda, el pueblo ordena, y el gobierno obedece. Construyendo autonomía."[32] The construction of autonomy in a pluriverse may appear to be an oxymoron. However, as Escobar helpfully clarifies, "autonomies are not institutions but forms of relations."[33] The goal (telos) of the pluriverse is to make a world, a community, out of many communities that share relationship with one another, and to recognize that our well-being is interconnected. The eleven working-class Maya mexicanas in this study embody relational autonomy, that is to say, they live in a pluriverse and assert their presence and way of life in contexts where the Mundo Mundial/universe is imposed. In order to do this, they must first distance themselves from the identity-near experience of assembly-line worker and claim identities as lxs hijxs de maíze.[34]

---

i. "No, no, I do not tell my story because it's not mine. I talked about my grandfather, and he talked about his grandfather, because we are still growing. It is a chain that is made."

THE ANATOMY OF HOPE IN THE PUEBLO MÁGICO

Women struggle to recognize their identity as lxs hijxs de maíz while working on the assembly line in the maquila. Sometimes the life of lxs hijxs de maíz withers and dies because assembly-line workers account for the world's increasingly "poor working class." Women struggle to keep hope alive (by hablando/speaking, insistiendo/insisting, ignorando/ignoring, and renunciando/quitting). At times failed attempts, like dried-up branches, are pruned and watered, meaning women notice when one practice fails and they try another approach that might work. But sometimes hope dies. And when hope dies, because hope dies more frequently than it is revived, women also know that decay and decomposition make up the soil that gives birth to *new* life.

The women of the pueblo mágico possess sabidurías insurgentes and this keeps them alive and struggling for a future they desire. How these sabidurías function is elaborated by Gloria Anzaldúa's concept of la facultad, which is the ability of the marginalized/oppressed to quickly sense the underlying structure of phenomena.[35] She goes on to say, "Those who do not feel psychologically or physically safe in the world are more apt to develop this sense."[36] This sense guides action. La facultad anticipates the danger and intuits how to move in the world. The experience of danger and fear grows la facultad, and the body develops a capacity to intuit and perceive, which then informs the decisive actions an individual might take.

Sabidurías insurgentes and the sensing of la facultad are revealed in stories the women tell me about how they practice survival, living, and being alive in the maquila. There is a difference between these three aspects of practice in the maquila. Survival is when women resist death and struggle to obtain just enough resources to live, but this is not living. Living is the ability to exercise one's will or desire for life, to soñar and imagine a preferred future that is possible. Finally, being alive implies retaining one's worldview and claiming the right to name her/him/them-self. These three aspects of practice coalesce in women's everyday lucha in the maquila, and as I listened to their stories, I learned about the anatomy of hope.

By "hope" I am not suggesting some optimism of a world that will be constructed, because women did not discuss their aspirations for life as a lifegiving practice. Instead, what I heard was that "hope" is a reality revealed *in* the struggle, on the assembly line. Hope is struggle because there is a future that is unfolding and that future is worth a struggle. Hope is both a noun and an action verb—like a gerund, hoping. Hope is creative. Hope brings forth new life when women practice and witness other women practicing hablando (speaking), insistiendo (insisting), ignorando (ignoring), and renunciando (quitting).[37]

Hablando

Celeste establishes the significance of why it is important to hablar (speak). She says, "Si no hablas y así, y no insistes en nada, allá te aplastan cuando quieran."[i] Celeste expresses her vulnerability in the system. She is at risk of being crushed at any point if those in managerial positions decide to make her working conditions more difficult. They could raise her daily quota of items they expect her to produce. They can unexpectedly ask her to work in a different section of the maquila, which means she needs to learn a new task at the same time as maintaining a high rate of production. They could ask her to work all night and tell her this is a voluntary night shift—by which she understands that if she decides not to "volunteer" she may lose her job. There are so very many things they can do to "crush her," including shaming her for not accomplishing tasks they ask her to do that are nearly impossible to complete. In various ways, Celeste is stating that if she does not speak up, the abuse is unrelenting.

Hablando is a strategy for survival in the maquila, and it is a risky endeavor. Hablando is frightening and yet necessary. Itzel tells me of an incident that at once terrified and liberated her:

> Es más, en el trabajo . . . hablando de mi trabajo . . . pues a veces nos regañan, nos gritan. A veces . . . hay cosas que a mi a veces no me parece y no me siento con fuerzas de defender las cosas. Ellos me dicen, me dice hasta el, "Defiéndete. Di las cosas . . ." Pero a mi no, tengo el temor a que yo diga algo, a la burla de mis compañeras o a la burla de . . . O sea, la forma que son mis supervisoras que se burle de mi. De lo que yo diga. O sea, en ese sentido es de que yo mejor prefiero de no, no, no digo nada. En que hace poco veo que esa semana pues semana que pasó, me sentí como que me enojo el bastante. Yo lloré. Lloré lo que me pasó. Porque mi maquina no, esta falle y falle y falle y falle . . . yo no lo aguantaba. Entonces la presión que tenía que me estaban regañando. Vino mi supervisora y me comenzaron a regañar, que porque no saco mi meta. "¡Te cambio de máquina y siempre lo mismo, es lo mismo, es lo mismo contigo!" Y yo en ese sentido, creo que me enojo. Me enojé bastante lo que me estaba diciendo y yo le contesté, "¿Quieres que te saqué mi meta? ¡Repárame mi máquina!" Hablé así. Y si me sorprendí porque cuando yo llegué me dice mi marido (deep breath) yo se lo dije, "le conteste así," le digo. Y dice él, "Está bien, hacía tiempo que quiera que reacciones y le diga "repare la máquina." Ya basta, le dije. Que yo sea su pendeja del mecánico que se esté burlando de mi. ¡Ya basta! Yo ya cambié, yo se los estoy diciendo.[ii]

---

i. "If you don't speak up and like that, and you don't insist on anything, here they will crush you whenever they want."

ii. "What's more, at work . . . talking about my work . . . because sometimes they scold us, they shout at us. Sometimes . . . there are things that sometimes I don't like and I don't feel like I have the strength to defend myself against those things. They tell me, he [her husband] says to me, 'Defend

Itzel's enojo (anger) emerges and becomes visible to her as her supervisor scolds her. She describes wrestling with feelings of shame, worrying about co-workers and managerial staff laughing at her if she speaks. She describes how her "anger" grows as weeks go by and her sewing machine keeps breaking down. This growing rage erupts when her supervisor shames her by inferring that the problem is her, not the machine. Itzel then demands her machine be fixed and maintains that the problem is not her ability, but the faulty machines and that the mechanic is responsible for repairing the machine. What is interesting is that much like Veronica (chapter 3) mentioned that she sensed a change in herself, so does Itzel. Itzel is surprised by her assertiveness and rejection of shame. She is experiencing her ability to defend herself, and this is an unexpected response.

What Itzel describes, I understand through my study of Mesoamerican spirituality (namely, symbolic representation) as being similar to what physicists call "electrostatic discharge." Physicists explain that when two differently charged electrical objects come into unexpected contact with each other, frequently a visible spark is created. These colliding electric forces can range in their visibility.[38] For example, lightning followed by the sound of deep thunder is an electrostatic discharge that can be seen and heard in a very dramatic display of a spark connecting the earth to the clouds. In the pueblo mágico, we often saw this type of electrostatic discharge as the afternoon rains pounded down on the straw roof of our home. However, there are other small instances of such electrostatic discharge occurring inside the maquila. You may not be able to feel or see them as dramatically as the afternoon thunderstorms, but nonetheless we know they are there. Itzel's description of the surprise spark between her supervisor and herself is a point of contact between unequally charged objects, a working-class Maya mexicana and the demands of neoliberal capitalism in a maquila. The force of that moment creates a spark that sounds like low rumbling shaking the foundations of the earth as a bright streak of light zigzags up from the dust, through the clouds, and out into the universe. By speaking, Itzel imposes her mundo into the

---

yourself. Say things . . .' But not me, I have the fear that I will say something, to the mockery of my colleagues or to the mockery of . . . That is, the way my supervisor is mocking me. What I say. That is, in that sense I feel it's better, I prefer to no, no, no, I don't say anything. In that short amount of time, that week, I saw what happened and I felt like I got angry enough. I cried. I cried over what happened to me. Because my machine didn't [work], it fails and fails and fails and fails . . . I couldn't stand it. Then the pressure of the scolding me! My supervisor came and they started scolding me because I hadn't met my goal. 'I changed you to a new machine but it's always the same, it's the same, it's the same with you!' And I in that sense, I think I get angry. I was really angry at what he was saying and I answered him, 'Do you want me to meet my goal? Then repair my machine!' I talked like that! And yes, I surprised myself because when I arrived [home] my husband says to me (deep breath) I told him, 'I answered him like that,' I say. And he says, 'Okay, I've been telling you for some time now to react and speak up and say repair the machine.' Enough, I said, of my being the mechanic's dumb-ass while he makes fun of me. Enough! I have already changed, and I am speaking up and telling them."

Mundo Mundial, and a pluriverse begins to form. Hope is like that, and you can see it and feel it in the maquila.

There are risks to hablando. Mariana explains,

> A veces se lo platicamos a la supervisora. Pero si nos dice a veces si se trata de algo muy así, como, por ejemplo, muy fuerte, pues no. Porque si no nos sacan también. Porque si es algo muy delicado pues no porque si no nos van a sacar. Y si nos sacan no tenemos que hacer después. Tenemos que quedar callados. Sí. Sí.[i]

A woman risks losing her job. There are stories in the pueblo mágico of those who can confirm this cautious approach to speaking up. Just as workers are fired for work injuries, so too they are dismissed for airing their grievances, which can range from sexual assault to the punishment for not volunteering for a night shift. Women listen to their sabidurías insurgentes to guide their

Figure 4.1. After an afternoon thunderstorm in the pueblo mágico. Photo taken by the author.

---

i. "Sometimes we talk to the supervisor. But if you tell us sometimes if it's something like that, for example, very strong, then no. Because they can fire us too. Because if it's something very delicate, then no, because they will fire us. And if they fire us, we don't have another job. We have to stay quiet. Yes. Yes."

survival strategies. Oftentimes, before *hablando*, women attempt *ignorando* (ignoring).

Ignorando

The fear of losing a job in the maquila is constant among the women. There are policies guiding the operations of the maquila that delineate how a worker might request time off from work. However, the women do not express much confidence in their requests being granted, and they tell me there are some values for which it is worth losing the only source of income your family has. Women ignore the maquila's employment policies in order to care for their children. For example, Veronica misses work because her daughter is ill. When she returns to work, her supervisor confronts her, wanting to know why she did not come to work the previous day.

> Yo hable con ella así claro ese día que estaba comentando que se enfermó mi hija. Yo le dije que primero esta mi hija. Primero está la salud de mi hija y después mi trabajo. Si por eso voy a perder mi trabajo no me va a importar. Porque primero está mi hija. Ahí ustedes deciden que hacer, le dije. Yo ya les informé por qué no me presenté a mi trabajo. Ustedes tienen la última palabra. Si por eso voy a perder mi trabajo, no me importa. Pero primero mi hija.[i]

Veronica ignores the policy and does not ask for a day off work because to her there is no choice between caring for her daughter and work. She is *primeramente madre*, as discussed in chapter 3. However, what I want to underscore in this encounter is Veronica's repeated assertion that work, wages, and daily production quotas do not take precedence over her daughter and Veronica's plan for her life. For some values, Veronica is willing to be fired from the only job she has and will not be threatened by the maquila's power over her. She speaks and reveals her goal, leaving the matter of employment to her superiors. She disempowers her supervisor's potential threat by *ignorando*. She reminds the supervisor that losing her job is of little importance to her. She will find some other way, even if that path is not altogether clear at the moment; what is clear to her is that she is a mother and from what little she has, she gives everything to her daughter.

In addition to *ignorando* maquila policies regarding time off, Celeste illustrates how women disregard directives from superiors on the assembly line as a way of building solidarity. Celeste explains that when she completes a

---

i. "I talked to her so clearly that day that I was commenting that my daughter got sick. I told him my daughter comes first. First, my daughter's health and then my work. If I'm going to lose my job, it's not going to matter. Because first my daughter. Here: you all decide what to do, I said. I'd already told them why I didn't come to work. You have the last word. If I'm going to lose my job, I don't care. But first, my daughter."

bulto (70 pieces), they go to "la de calidad" (the woman who works inspecting, quality control). La de calidad checks for stitching mistakes in the fabric. Celeste nurtures a relationship of "respeto" (respect) and it is to this that she attributes the fact that la de calidad does not reject her bultos when there is in fact a defect in the way she's stitched the fabric together. The women get paid per bulto, which means a rejection from la de calidad is a deduction from her pay and women on the assembly line worry about this inspection. Celeste counsels a fellow seamstress not to worry about making a mistake because la de calidad will let it pass inspection if you have a good relationship with her.

> Entonces le digo a mi compañera, "Pues no lo reparo. Dejo así, y lo tiene que pasar así porque es lo que nos tienen dicho a nosotras." Igual, si nosotras le damos respeto y respeto a ella, ella no nos va ha estar fregando.[i]

Celeste knows from experience that respect and building relationships in the maquila is built on a bond of ignorando between her and the supervisors who will do the same. As I hear this story, I am immediately reminded of how I benefit from Celeste and la de calidad ignorando the quality of their work. The maquila intends to sell merchandise to make as high a profit as possible. One reason they employ la de calidad to inspect it is that if there is a defect in the stitching, customers at the local store in the US will expect a discount. As the American-born child of a Cuban refugee single mother, I benefited from the women's ignorando. Upon entering a clothing store in the US, my mother always walked first to the rear to comb through the steep discount bins in search of new clothing to buy for my sister and me. Hope materialized for us when we found an article of clothing with imperfect stitches. As I hear Celeste explaining this practice of ignorando, I express my gratitude for their practice.

Inoperative potentiality is an aspect of the neoliberal apparatus described by Giorgio Agamben and made concrete by women's practice of ignorando. Agamben, influenced by Foucault's understanding of power, draws on Aristotle's concept of potentiality. For Aristotle, potentiality is not only about having the capacity to be but also to *not* be. Agamben develops his political philosophy of inoperativity in conversation with Aristotle's potentiality to discuss freedom and how subjects can enhance their freedom by rendering the apparatus, in this case neoliberal capitalism, inoperative.[39] Admittedly, this practice will not dismantle capitalism, but consider the emancipatory practice of faith that renders the apparatus inoperable (even if only for a moment) and provides wages and life for women on both sides of the border. I

---

i. "Then I said to my coworker, 'Well, I don't repair it. I leave it like this, and it has to happen like that because it is what they have told us.' Likewise, if we give respect and respect her, she will not be messing with us."

see this practice among workers as perhaps a ritual and/or ethical practice, but certainly there is a deep spirituality that is life-giving. Additional qualitative research regarding working-class communities' experiences and resiliencies in the face of hegemonic neoliberal capitalism and its ethos might have the potential to foment an insurrection of nonviolent inoperativity among workers and lead us toward a more just future.

Insistiendo

Insistiendo is when a woman approaches a problem with persistence. Women make multiple attempts to obtain employment in the maquila. Some report submitting their application three years prior to the call inviting them to come take the exam that tests their efficiency and accuracy in completing a tedious task. Maria, the woman with the least formal education, says she took the exam three times before she passed. Though at first she failed the exam, she requested to be allowed to try again to meet the maquila's standards.

Once a woman is hired, insistiendo intensifies. All the women agreed they practice insistiendo (insisting) their machines be repaired. Insistiendo, as a practice, is submitting verbal requests or grievances that are short and direct appeals to a mechanic or supervisor to respond. For example, a common experience on the assembly line is working with sewing machines that constantly need repair. There is one mechanic who is responsible for repairing all the industrial-size sewing machines. The women have experience sewing in their homes but not with industrial machines. This means that they are at the mercy of the mechanic hired by the maquila to repair their machine. Daily they implore the mechanic to repair their machine. Celeste says, "Se lo voy a decir a cada rato. Le estoy insistiendo, 'Tiene esto mi máquina, ¿lo vas a checar?'"[i] The purpose of insistiendo is to learn not to tire of requesting that the mechanic attend to your crisis, even though there is only one mechanic on whom all the women rely.

Insistiendo is also about forcing the maquila to recognize that chronological time is not a commodity. The maquila imposes a view of chronological time and its scarcity in such a way that women express growing presión (pressure) to produce. The women in the pueblo mágico do not relate to time in terms of chronology in their everyday lives. They instead view time as qualitative (kairos) and in relationship to all that surrounds them. Natalia practices insistiendo when she demands that her superiors recognize her particular challenge in relation to the time and space. Natalia is in danger of being fired and she is well aware of this fact.

---

i. "I'm going to tell him every time. I'm insisting, 'My machine has this going on, are you going to check it?'"

> Yo pensé que me iban a sacar. Ya no sacaba mis horas. Me mandaron a hablar, porque no lo saco. Y yo, "Claro," le dije. "No porque yo no quiero, sino porque no puedo sacarlo. Porque tengo que jalar los bultos. Me va llevar tiempo una distancia que tengo que recorrer y llevarlo hasta donde estoy costurando mi bulto que tengo que coser," le digo. "Me va llevar tiempo."[i]

Natalia draws her superiors' attention to the unrealistic expectations they have of her. She cannot complete the task given the layout of the assembly line. She accounts for the longer time she takes by pointing to the source of the problem being their irrational notion of time. She does not turn inward to blame or shame herself; rather, she turns the tables, insistiendo it is their misguided understanding of people, place, and time.

The unrealistic expectations to complete these tasks wear on women's bodies. Veronica tells me about her injured shoulder and how she is trying to decide how much longer she ought to continue working at the maquila. She is trying to avoid a situation that is all too common in maquila work. Women practice insistiendo by reporting work injuries and requesting medical attention. Many of them do this as a last resort because a doctor will get involved who works for the maquila. He evaluates their health and decides if they are able to continue working. The women want to keep their jobs and at times conceal or minimize their pain in order to gain approval for another year of work in the maquila. Veronica tells me about a woman whose arm "no lo podía mover, se le quedó paralizado el brazo."[ii] Although this paralysis may have come while she was home, the woman herself was convinced it was a result of her work in the maquila, so she asked for medical attention from the maquila. Veronica had not seen her for quite some time and she wondered if indeed the maquila had cared for her injury. What she wants me to know is that this woman insisted on care for an injury tied to her work even though the maquila might not want to offer her that kind of sustained care.

Renunciando

Renunciando occurs when women contemplate quitting their job and discuss this with their families and/or other women in the maquila. Most often the results of renunciando are to remain working in the maquila. I learned that women practice renunciando as a way to affirm their agency and subsequent choice to remain in the maquila, despite the less-than-ideal conditions. I ini-

---

i. "I thought they were going to fire me. I no longer reached my daily quota. They called me in to speak with me about my job performance . . . 'Of course,' I said, 'it's not because I don't want to, but because I can't meet the expectation. Because I have to pull the bundles. It's going to take me time. It's a distance that I have to travel and take it to where I am sewing my bundles,' I say. 'It's going to take me time.'"

ii. "She couldn't move her arm, her arm was paralyzed."

tially misjudged this action, understanding it as resignation, as accepting the conditions of the maquila, and as submitting to the abuse. The reason why I jumped to this conclusion was that I did not hear them address the oppressive system of neoliberal capitalism that results in their being hired to work on the assembly line. However, they did know they were sewing clothing they would never be able to purchase because it was not sold in México. They also noted that the fabric that comes to the maquila is from the US and must return to the US. These observations made by the women were often followed by a detailed description of how heavy and thick the fabric is and, depending on the section of the assembly line one is working, that it is difficult to manage this material. After much questioning and checking for understanding, I learned that women believe they *choose* to work in the maquila despite the less-than-ideal working conditions.

From my point of view, I do not see their employment as a free choice they are making for themselves. At the micro level, because of the macrosystems, assembly-line workers are pulled from their agrarian life in the milpa, where collectivism supersedes competition and production is not manufactured goods but reciprocity tied to the creative natural rhythms of nature's seasons. Globalization and neoliberal capitalism impoverish women of the pueblo mágico. Larger systems, such as the international bodies that lend money to countries needing assistance with infrastructure and/or assistance after natural disasters, for example, cause the two-thirds world to live further and further in debt. Moreover, these economically impoverished countries made poor by the International Monetary Fund, the World Trade Organization, and the World Bank are governed through a system of voting that is based on a country's wealth. The decision makers are wealthy men from the richest countries in the world. In descending order, the countries are the US, Japan, China, Germany, the UK, and France.[40] The US alone holds 16 percent of the total voting power—and that is 10 percent more than Japan, the second-highest country with voting power.[41] With a disproportionate amount of power to influence policy in the global market economy, the US then makes regional agreements with neighboring countries on either side of its national borders. NAFTA, reached in 1994, is critiqued for its extractive practices, but on the other hand the location of factories provides jobs for the working class struggling to survive around the world.

Here in the pueblo mágico, the women with whom I speak tell me they choose to work in the maquila and are grateful for the job. I believe they value life and though the global market economy does not value the collectivism they value, they understand that the world economy is moving in a direction they would typically not choose to go but they have to join it in some fashion in order to survive. At the same time, surviving is not living. Surviving is resisting death, destruction, and depravity. Women do not adopt the values of capitalism in their lives; they participate in the neoliberal capitalist system as a means to avoid their complete demise. The struggle is precisely this: participating while not being deceived into believing the way to live is to compete, gain capital, and embrace individualism at the expense of the tribe.

Renunciando is how the women practice socialism. Consider how Veronica discusses renunciando:

> Pues, hasta ahorita estoy allí. Pero, si en dado caso yo decido dejar de trabajar allí o me sacan, porque allí pues . . . si te despiden . . . eh, pues, yo buscaría otro trabajo para ser. Buscaría otro modo de ayudar con el gasto familiar.[i]

Veronica views her work on the assembly line as a choice she makes. She works knowing she can unexpectedly be fired but she also states that she knows she can quit, should she choose to do so. If this job were no longer available as a source of income for her, she is resolute about her capacity to find "another way" to contribute to the economic needs of the family. She tells me that she tells her husband:

> "Yo lo voy a dejar. Voy a buscar también que hacer en mi casa o pongo un negocio. O hago esto. Pero, tampoco me voy a quedar cruzada de brazos esperando a que tú me traigas dinero," le dije. "No, tampoco. Te voy a ayudar también con eso," le dije.[ii]

Veronica communicates a joint struggle in which she intends to participate. She will not leave the economic struggle to her husband alone. Interestingly, she uses the imagery in the idiomatic phrase "quedar cruzada de brazos," which is somewhat equivalent to the English phrase "hands tied." Veronica is not a helpless victim who works on the assembly line, nor would she be one should she *choose* to quit. Veronica is doing what she needs to do in order to care for her family. Sometimes that means adapting to capitalism's imposed modes of production because she is inevitably competing with her co-workers to produce at a higher rate than they are. However, Veronica is not convinced by the promise of capital; she will quit her job when her value for family necessitates this decisive action; and she is confident that she will find "another way" (buscaría otro modo) of supporting her family.

---

i. "Well, for now I'm there. But if I decide to stop working there or they fire me— because there they do fire you—well, I'll look for another job to do. I'd look for another way to help with the family expenses."

ii. "'I'm going to quit. I'm also going to look for what to do in my home or I'll start my own business. Or I'll do this. But I'm not going to stand by and wait for you to bring me money,' I said, 'No, I'm not. I'm going to help you with that too,' I say to him."

Women do quit their jobs at the maquila. But there are also stories of women whom the maquila fires and asks that they "renunciar." Araceli explains:

> Podemos renunciar también. Si puedo. Si vemos que en algún momento no, nos afecta algo allá. Por ejemplo, la semana pasada renunciaron dos. Una que por la pelusa que no le conviene le dio bronquitis, no se que cosa le dio, y renunció. La otra que este, porque ya le duele lo de aquí, el brazo. Ya no lo puede sostener y le dijeron que y no, no puede trabajar con ello así y tuvo que renunciar.[i]

Some women decide to quit their job due to their exposure to harmful substances, such as the case to which Araceli refers. One woman becomes ill, Araceli suspects perhaps with bronchitis, due to the lint in the maquila, and she quits her job. This does not appear to be a calculated strategy but rather a case of the woman's body no longer being able to tolerate the working conditions in the maquila. Her lungs are harmed and she quits because she cannot continue. Araceli gives me this example and then turns to another scenario that is quite different from the one she just presented. The second woman's arm is hurting her, and she likely is not meeting her daily production quota. Moreover, she may not be able to conceal the limited mobility in her arm and might subsequently have been sent to see the doctor, whose office is *inside* the maquila. The doctor judges she is injured and the maquila *tells her* to quit. In this case, there is no choice. There is only the concealment of an employee's work injury and the employer's unlawful firing of her on the basis of this injury.[42] She must go home and find another way. Women see this scenario more often than not, and they practice renunciando because when a woman chooses to quit, she can protect her dignity and exercise her agency. Renunciando is how women resist the maquila's practice of disposing of them as if they are industrial waste. They may not be able to improve their conditions in the maquila, but they find what little control they have and make the choice before it is too late.

LA CIENCIA DE LA LUCHA

Hope is hablando, ignorando, insistiendo, and renunciando. Women draw on their sabidurías insurgentes to guide them through hope. What I mean by this is that they sense and intuit in their body and their environment what aspect of

---

i. "We can quit too. Yes, I can. If we see that in a given moment no, something there will affect us. For example, last week two [women] quit. One because of the lint that isn't good for her [health] it gave her bronchitis, I don't know what [illness] it caused her, and she quit. The other [woman], because she has lots of pain here, her arm. She can't handle [the work] anymore and they told her and no, no she can't work with [her arm] like that and had to quit/resign."

hope they need to draw on (hablando, ignorando, insistiendo, renunciando). Hope brings women courage, and hope is closely tied to risk-taking. From my point of view, it seemed that hope liberated women from the fear of acting. The symbol they rely on to strengthen and inform their hope is "ser madre" (to be mother) and, as you will recall from the previous chapter, to be mother is to bear life. Women's everyday luchas go largely unseen because discussions of globalization and free trade agreements focus on debates about, for example, taxation, the flow of goods, employment costs, capital, revenue, debt, and increased/decreased jobs. These kinds of discussions, argue activists along the US-México border, are focused "on masculine power,"[43] and they omit the direct connection they share with creating the context for their largest workforce, women.

I will leave this masculine discussion on globalization to those who choose to engage in such discourse. I do not want to talk in the language of quantitative data because what I want to foreground is the realities of the complex suffering that develops as a result of globalization and trade agreements, and these realities are revealed in a feminist method that is interested in a different kind of "science." Zapatistas helpfully distinguish between science that answers the question "por qué" (why) and science that answers the question "para qué" (for what purpose).[44] Modernity (the science of "por qué"), with its celebrated technological advances, has a great influence on virtually all our lives. The creation of tools like the internet, genetically modified seeds, and industrial-size sewing machines takes campesinxs far from their cultural roots. Why do campesinxs leave their milpas and work in the maquila? Because the NAFTA decimated their major crop by importing corn that can be sold at a much lower price than the locally grown maíz (corn). Campesinxs then go to the maquila, and though this is not an environment they know well, they are lxs hijxs de maíz and, much as they read the coming thunderstorms and can identify good soil from poor, in the maquila they read the world of their oppressors. They know hope and draw on their many wisdoms to move through la lucha (the science of "para qué").

EVERYDAY DEATHS AND RESURRECTIONS

La lucha is not easy. Some of the women speak of "sacrifice" when they talk with me about what they hope to gain from working in the maquila. One evening while I was lying in my hammock waiting for my host family's relatives to arrive home from the maquila, Sofia's sister came to see me. She told me Sofia needed to talk with me. She wanted to participate in the entrevistas (interviews) I was gathering. I communicated to her that I would be delighted to share a conversation with her. Sofia's sister left and within just a few minutes Sofia appeared at the entrance of our home.

Sofia came with her younger sister and asked me if it was okay for her sister to stay. It was important to her that her sister hear what she had to say to me. Sofia had just showered. Her hair was still wet. There were dark circles under her eyes. I could tell she was very tired by her slumped shoulders and the way she deliberately dragged each foot as if there were bricks tied to her ankles. She moved ever so slowly toward the one chair in the room where she could sit. Sofia was coming to talk with me the evening after working a turno nocturno (night shift). Recall from chapter 2 that these are the unofficially mandatory night shifts that require workers to work for an entire twenty-four-hour period. Though a supervisor might come and *ask* you to work, they also remind you that you signed a document when you were employed that *required* you to apoyar (support) the maquila whenever necessary. It becomes necessary to work a turno nocturno when production is down and the US company demands more goods to sell.

After carefully sitting down in the chair, she looks at me and her eyes well up with tears that flow ever so gently down her cheeks. She is exhausted. She tells me there was a time en la madrugada (at dawn) when she struggled to stay awake. I begin to think about how much danger this eighteen-year-old was in because she was operating machinery while she was drowsy and physically tired from so many hours spent standing up. Sofia says all she wants to do right now is sleep, but first she has to talk with me and her little sister has to listen. She wants her younger sister to know her suffering and hear her sueño. Her insistence that her sister witness this I understand in theological terms. Every resurrection is preceded by a sacrifice and involves witnesses who can preserve what Argentinian Latina feminist theologian Marcella Althaus-Reid calls "theology of memory."

Althaus-Reid reports that Salvadorian women who lived through years of war in El Salvador constructed a "theology of memory" by "counting crosses and resurrections" in communities of women who live in poverty and under constant threat of extinction.[45] Counting crosses in these female communities means to listen to the stories of women and the everyday deaths that occur in their context where poverty, political unrest, and war kill their loved ones and their dreams. Althaus-Reid writes, "Every death changes the lives of the survivors, because some humanity is removed from them."[46] Death is a communal experience. In the pueblo mágico, women count crosses, and Sofia came to erect her cross before her little sister and me.

Sofia tells me about her sueño. That's how I learned about her desire to be educated and work in a helping profession. Sofia explains that she is suffering "porque no todo es fácil" (because not everything is easy). Suffering, she says, is a fact of life. She says her suffering is in her soul and her body, but when her body cannot take it anymore, her soul gives her strength to keep going. Sofia reasons, "Si es cierto, la vida consta de sacrificios. Pero también tiene recompensa."[i] I wonder how or whether this "sacrifice" of which she speaks and the "recompensa" (reward) is related to the discussion of capitalist economy as religion by the Roman Catholic lay theologian Jung Mo Sung, born in South Korea and raised in Brazil. Sung argues there is an alternative to the idolatrous notion that capitalism is the only economic system possible.[47] Moreover, he states that within this system controlled by the assumed greed of the consumer, there is a difference between a "sacrifice" and the "gift of oneself."

To make a distinction between "sacrifice" and the "gift of oneself" may seem like a hair-splitting issue of semantics. Yet Sung carefully defines this nuance. He writes,

> Sacrifices are external impositions in the name of a deified law that goes against the freedom of the victimized person. They are claimed in the name of a deity (or sacralized institution) in exchange for the promise of paradise or for a reward. The gift of oneself is the fruit of love and freedom. It is a movement which is born inside the person and goes in the direction of either the beloved one or the one who nurtures solidarity.[48]

If we follow Sung's train of thought, capitalism as a religion results in Sofia sacrificing herself (her body, soul, desire) and foregoing her freedom. She has no desire to vow any kind of loyalty to the maquila, nor does she have any vision of a reward materializing because of her work in the maquila. She tells me she has a plan to earn one year of wages and then use this small amount of money to support her plan to go to school. She says,

> Ya estoy aquí. Y pues voy hacer todo lo posible para permanecer. Y mi propósito es trabajar todo un año y luego contar mi dinero para luego mi papá no me venga a decir, "Sabes que no te puedo apoyar." Pero ya se que yo tengo un poquito, y con ese poquito puedo dar mucho de mí.[ii]

When Sofia says "dar mucho de mi" (give a lot of me), she is giving the "gift of oneself" to her family, namely her sisters and mother. There is a growing solidarity among the women in Sofia's family, and they practice hope

---

i. "Yes, it is true. Life consists of sacrifices. But it also has a reward."
ii. "I'm already here. And I'm going to do everything possible to stay. And my purpose is to work a whole year and then count my money so my father doesn't come to me to say, 'You know I can't support you.' But I know I have a little bit, and with that little bit I can give a lot of me."

(hablando, ignorando, insistiendo, renunciando), which often means giving of oneself, as a gift, "para que todos estemos bien,"[i] says Sofia.

Death

Brazilian Latina ecofeminist theologian Ivone Gebara underscores the overlooked suffering of women. She suggests that this is due in part to the difference between male and female suffering. Male suffering tends to be public, done in the name of a group, and there is one hero.[49] On the other hand, women's suffering is silenced by the exaltation of male suffering in Christian theology, specifically the crucifixion of Jesus of Nazareth. Some Christian theology—and by extension culture—transforms the tool of torture into a symbol that romanticizes pain. Most often women and marginalized groups are subjected to enduring pain, violence, and abuse on account of Jesus's obedience to his Father even unto death.

I do not hear the women in the maquila speaking about "sacrifice" in terms of their heroic acts. Their hope requires risk-taking that often results in daily deaths. The daily deterioration of women's bodies is a physical dying; however, death is not just a physical dying or decomposition of one's body. Death is being cut off from relationships that are the very sources of life. Women die when they are shamed by their superiors and the voice of their oppressor becomes an unwelcome internal voice limiting their confidence in themselves, not just as assembly-line workers but as mothers, daughters, neighbors, campesinas, and esposas (wives). They know dying is happening when their sueños are uprooted so that they become aspirations for a future so far out of their reach it seems impossible.

Dying does not serve some grand purpose that might legitimize torture. Women "count their crosses," the sites of their daily pain, unhappiness, unjust treatment, and illness, and they gather around each other as witnesses to the evil. This gathering around crosses occurs in the maquila as women encourage one another by saying "¡Sí se puede! ¡Tú lo puedes hacer!"[ii] and it continues when they come home. Sofia's mother, who is too old to work in the maquila, tells her, "Cuando tú estés en alguno que otro sacrificio, yo voy a estar contigo. No voy a dejar que caigas."[iii] Gebara refers to these matriarchal sites of suffering as gathering places to which women come as acts of solidarity that declare "that unjust death does not have the last word."[50] Sofia brings her sister and speaks to me about the unjust conditions in the maquila and in that moment we witness death, name evil, and listen and count the

---

i. "So that we can all be well/live well."
ii. "Yes we can! You can do this!"
iii. "When you are in the midst of various sacrifices, I'm going to be with you. I'm not going to let you fall."

crosses of the daily dying in the maquila. In that same moment we also witness resurrection because, as Althaus-Reid points out, if death is communal, so too is resurrection. She writes: "starting with Jesus' resurrection, a whole community of people who suffered his loss when he was crucified came back to life again."[51]

Resurrection

Althaus-Reid argues that just as death is a communal event, so is resurrection. She points to the images of resurrection in Nicaraguan art that depict recognizable faces of members of the community who participated in la lucha del pueblo. Some are martyrs in the struggle and they rise from their graves "wearing jeans and shirts, smiling at each other, and giving us the impression of a community resurrecting from death."[52] However, not every sacrifice is accompanied with the hope of escape. Gebara correctly points out that sometimes the cross is "a cry without salvation, a call for salvation with no answer."[53] This seems to be the case more often than not in the maquila. Nonetheless, these are all sites of resurrection that contribute to the hope women have.

When hablando results in her discovery of being heard, and the maquila responds with even small requests such as agreeing to host their children for a tour of the maquila on Día de los Niños, women inhale a breath of *new* life. In the same way, when women practice ignorando, insistiendo, and renunciando, they sometimes see the promise of life in death, not because of death but because of women's *tenacious desires for life*. Women are attentive to the everyday resurrections they witness. These are often simple and quiet acts that are powerful.

I witnessed many such resurrections in my time there. At first, I did not see them. I came into the pueblo as a Seventh-day Adventist Christian informed by multiple theories of atonement, all of which focused on the heroic death of a god-man. All I saw was sacrifice with the hope of liberation in a world to come, so I missed the hope of the world in the here-and-now. I did not see how the women's refusal to die was already constructing a more hope-filled world. I subscribed to a soteriology fixated on the unjust death of a man and optimism of a world to come; meanwhile the women I met in pueblo mágico focused on the community of people who reject the authority of the present unjust systems responsible for creating pain and suffering. I needed help to see, but once I saw I could hardly believe my eyes. I experienced a conversion as I witnessed the women's eschatological hope. It was their patient descriptions and conversations about life-in-death that helped me see the world made new. This is not a theory; it is an everyday tangible practice.

The women bear life at the sites of death, and their production of life begins to re-vision the world. Two resurrection sites illustrate what I mean to communicate. First, remember Araceli, whose wrist was broken? Eventually her wrist healed from the fracture, and she returned to work. However, when she returned to work she struggled to meet her daily production quota, but she was able to keep her job. She kept her job by clocking into work, feeling the pressure to produce, sensing the pain, acknowledging the limited mobility her injury caused, and yet stitching together pieces of material; she kept her job by practicing hope. A year later when I returned to the pueblo mágico she was not only still employed, she was also holding a six-month-old baby boy in her arms. Typically, stories like that of Araceli conclude with the worker being fired or asked to quit. Araceli is building her casa. I saw it! Her daughter took me to see the frame of a brick house that will one day perhaps have a roof and maybe even cement floors.

The second resurrection was Sofia's. For an entire year Sofia saved money from her already very low pay. The money she saved turned out to be the poquito (small amount) she had anticipated, but a few days before I arrived at the pueblo mágico she spoke to her father about renunciando. Recall that he was not supportive of investing money in the education of a daughter. He believed Sofia would get pregnant, and the expense of education would be a waste. He also insisted Sofia take the maquila job because this was her chance to earn a steady income. Sofia showed her father the money she'd saved for a year and once again asked him to support her pursuit of an education. Sofia tells me that when he saw she had saved money and he witnessed a year of her "sacrificio" in the maquila, he decided to give her his support. Sofia reports her father responded, "Si tanto quieres ese sueño, ve y lucha por esa meta, no dejes que nadie te diga que no puedes."[i]

Sofia documented this moment by posting on Facebook her father's reply, a note she wrote to him, and stamping the date and time this occurred. I want to highlight some aspects of this resurrection. There is a reorganizing and re-visioning of Sofia's father's beliefs about women and education. The significance of his shift in beliefs and values is influenced by his witnessing Sofia's daily unjust dying in the maquila. As a campesino, he knows unjust treatment and the death of his milpa that has now relegated him to working as a clerk in a minimart owned by a larger grocery company in town but operated by him in the pueblo mágico. He gathers around the site of Sofia's cross and tends to life when he speaks to her. This is one resurrection site. There is a second site of resurrection when Sofia goes to renunciar (quit her job). Facebook is filled with photos of co-workers and maquila supervisors embracing Sofia and

---

i. "If you want that dream so much, go and fight for that goal; don't let anyone tell you that you can't."

wishing her well. Taking pictures in the maquila is not permitted, and yet how could one miss capturing a vision of resurrection? Sofia's story will circulate in the maquila, and I suspect that if a qualitative researcher like me came a year or two or three hence, they would still hear about Sofia's renunciando.

Women in the pueblo mágico teach us that hoping yields everyday deaths and resurrections. Moreover, they claim our sabidurías insurgentes (insurrectionist wisdoms) will guide our path to the creation of a pluriverse, a world where our knowledge and our way of life is valued. ¡Nos queremos vivas! This is la ciencia de la lucha and this book is an invitation to academics and caregivers interested in pastoral care and counseling to come learn to corazonar la vida with us. We need you to build this world where many worlds fit with us. The discoveries explored above make some suggestions that could enhance practices of care and counseling.

RELEVANCE FOR PASTORAL CARE AND COUNSELING

Pastoral care and counseling attends to both the well-being of the polis (at the macro level) and the more intimate responsibility of caring for individuals-in-community (at the micro level). This section of the chapter offers some possible considerations for future trajectories in pastoral care and a framework for pastoral counselors as they care for the working class in the context of neoliberal capitalism.

Pastoral Care

Ryan LaMothe's most recent publication, *Care of Souls, Care of Polis: Toward a Political Pastoral Theology*, written in the context of the United States, may be enriched by considering post-development proposals. Unai Villalba, Professor of Development Studies at the Instituto de Estudios sobre el Desarrollo y Cooperación Internacional (HEGOA), in País Vasco (an autonomous region in northern Spain), explains that discussions on "development" presume the kind of economic growth valued in the West. However, there are approaches to "development" informed by indigenous peoples' concept of Buen Vivir that offer alternatives to "development" in the neoliberal age—"not only 'alternative development strategies' but also 'alternatives to development.'"[54] Similar to "post colonialism," post-development proposals recognize the neoliberal capitalist context and the challenges such proposals assume when transitioning to government policies that adopt values counter to those of neoliberal capitalism. However, I believe political pastoral theology, such as LaMothe describes, can be further developed and enriched by studying the case of Ecuador.

In 2007, Ecuador elected president Rafael Correa based on his campaign promise to begin a transition to implement government policies that explicitly adopted the principles of Buen Vivir. Correa referred to this transition as the Citizens' Revolution and did in fact redraft the country's constitution and proposed a National Development Plan (NPGL) based on the value of the "reproduction of life" as opposed to the "accumulation" models of development. In practice, Villalba notes, the language of the NPGL presents a "de-neoliberalisation' of the country" with no "alternative form of society."[55] However, this may suggest that perhaps transition occurs in stages, and a post-neoliberal society is a first step toward change.

I find that LaMothe's suggestions for a political pastoral care in the US (survival, flourishing, and liberation) align with those of Buen Vivir. However, they can also be enriched by the relational ontology of Buen Vivir. Quechua and Aymara (Andean indigenous peoples), according to Villalba, "view life in fullness mean[ing] a life of material and spiritual excellence expressed harmoniously and in relation to all beings, as well as a community's internal and external equilibrium."[56] LaMothe's discussion privileges care and justice, but could be further enhanced by exploring Mesoamerican concepts of equilibrium, which are radically different from justice as it is discussed in the West. What political pastoral care might look like in the global south is based on principles of complementarity and reciprocity, values rooted in understandings of community/familia, nature (not separate from humans), consensus (not majority votes in a democratic system), living well (not living better), work as joy (not accumulation of capital), and the spiritual world of material and immaterial wealth.[57]

The challenge moving forward is in analyzing how practice complicates the transition from neoliberal capitalism to more communal ways of life. LaMothe presents a useful hermeneutical framework for analyzing political pastoral care. However, this framework is intended to assist faith communities in resisting "systems, structures and groups that destroy/wear away care and justice."[58] The framework needs more emphasis on the dimension of resistance that consists of experimentation and action. Practical theologians, especially those trained in method, can assist in analyzing the case of Ecuador for the purpose of contributing to new proposals we might present to faith communities for response and advocacy in moving beyond neoliberalism. Experimenting means creating communities open to devising multiple actions that are possible, deciding on attempting an action, and anticipating reflection on the action. Experimenting means we forfeit the illusion that we can predict the actions necessary. Pastoral care can move toward a vision of communal care that anticipates failure and seizes these moments as opportunities to come to an ever-expanding understanding of the complexity in which we live.

Pastoral Counseling

In addition to care that is invested in dealing with the macro systems, as LaMothe advocates, there is a need for pastoral counselors to practice care informed by the experience of working-class Maya mexicanas. First and foremost, the above suggests that women do not need counselors to be "agents of hope." In fact, that kind of counseling is not hope-filled; rather, it is a reproduction of power dynamics between women and their maquila superiors. Pastoral counselors may know how hope emerges in their experience; however, hope may look and grow very differently in the lives of those to whom they are extending care. The hope that working-class Maya mexicanas named is something they bring to the counseling relationship. Women are already "agents of hope" for themselves and others. Counselors are or perhaps can be "witness" to this hope when they suspend their role as "agent" in the caregiving relationship. When the counselor is "witness," she observes and listens to women who are "counting crosses." The community gathered in this ritual of counting crosses ought to be chosen by the woman. This research suggests women gather in matriarchal circles and often include women in their family. These matriarchal circles are how the "theology of memory" is preserved. The caring pastoral counselor will trust the process and be attentive to the thin space between life and death, always privileging women's intuition and experimentation over reason (i.e., cognitive-behavioral approaches). This approach will nurture women's sabiduría insurgente (insurrectionist wisdom) and their abilities to corazonar la vida.

When Sofia came to speak with me and brought her sister, she never overtly told me the value of my observing and listening. I suspect the value might be connected to her desire to pursue her own vocation. Her eldest sister, who was married to one of Doña Lucía's sons, often came to help prepare meals and asked me many questions about family in the United States. I shared with her how my mother struggled to earn a college degree and raise both my sister and me as a single parent. I told her how difficult school was and how terrified I was of higher education. She'd asked me about life in the US and specifically wondered, "Están en guerra?"[i] I told her I felt like the country was at war and though I recalled difficult moments in California, such as living through Proposition 187,[59] I was less scared of speaking truth to power. I showed her pictures of my family and also protest marches in which I had participated (the Women's March on January 21, 2017, and the travel ban protest at LAX on January 29, 2017). She asked me, "¿No te da miedo que te van a matar?" (Aren't you afraid they are going to kill you?) I replied by telling her a dicho

---

i. "Are you at war?"

(a wise saying) that my grandmother and my mother told me: "Cuando me muera, prefiero morir con la boca abierta."[i]

Dichos are how our ancestors live on and never die. The elders in our communities pass down their wisdom through philosophical proverbs. Dichos are attached to our actions. I learned this dicho when I witnessed my mother advocating for my medical care and my fair treatment in elementary school. After she spoke truth to power and we walked away from the situation, she repeated this dicho to me, connecting its wisdom to her action for me. My grandmother did much of the same. This proverb accepts death as part of life; what it rejects is dying in silence without speaking your truth. I think Sofia came to talk with me because maybe she suspected she could trust me with her truth because in me lives the wisdom of my ancestors that refuses to die without naming what is unjust.

Sofia spoke to me, a woman with an enormous amount of privilege: born in the United States, a maestra (teacher), and a psicóloga (counselor). She knew the access to power I represent, and she built her bridge on my back. She knew I was collecting stories to write a book that would be read by people who have even more power than I do. I was her link to exposing the reality of life in pueblo mágico. Sofia knew what Gloria Anzaldúa refers to when she writes, "Caminante, no hay puentes, se hace puentes al andar."[60] There is no bridge between the knowledge in pueblo mágico and the academy. Sofia must construct this bridge by her actions, and so she did.

Additionally, the pastoral counselor who understands the anatomy of hope (as described above) can facilitate storytelling that might explore these four practices: hablando, ignorando, insistiendo, and renunciando. These practices are in some ways in conversation with pastoral theologians such as James N. Poling and Kathleen J. Greider. Poling provides a framework for resistance that Greider uses to discuss constructive aggression. In *Deliver Us from Evil*, Poling's framework for resistance has three categories: speaking, silence, and action.[61] All three of these classifications, in my view and as the women demonstrate, are actions. If I were to take what I termed "the anatomy of hope" and use this as a framework, it substitutes silence for ignorar (ignore), and in the examples provided above this ignoring is more like what Greider describes as aggression than it is passive.[62] In addition, the category of action is nuanced by two types of actions in the maquila: insistir and renunciar. What I find helpful in Greider's discussion of aggression is understanding Itzel's "anger" as a constructive force that counters a socially constructed narrative of women as passive and docile.[63] Itzel described a struggle to act, as did many of the women. However, I did not observe women cultivating a spirit of docility in the girls. On the contrary, I observed girls being praised

---

i. "When I die, I prefer to die with my mouth wide open."

for speaking up and having sassy attitudes. Perhaps this is part of their teaching la ciencia de la lucha. Perhaps women were nurturing aggression in their daughters precisely because of the fear they may one day replace them on the assembly line, even though they do not want that future for them.

These practices refer particularly to how hope springs up in situations in the maquila, but I imagine these might also resonate with workers in sweatshop conditions in the US also have to deal with the added vulnerability of not holding US citizenship. However, this added vulnerability needs to be explored, because I suspect it might cause hope to look vastly different than what the women in this study noted. While women here in the Yucatán were risking economic hardship, a sweatshop worker in the US may be risking deportation, separation from family, and separation from their primary identity as parent. Nevertheless, what this research exposes is that women's risk-taking action is liberating, and her contemplation of taking risk that ends in her continuing to endure the oppressive conditions might be a way in which she gains a sense of choice.

Finally, an important way in which women find hope is in teaching children la ciencia de la lucha, and this occurs as children hear and see their mothers "counting crosses" and witnessing resurrections. The eleven working-class Maya mexicanas in this study included their children in every conversation we shared. Children were constantly present, listening and observing the stories of struggle and witnessing their mothers' tears. This witnessing is how children begin to learn about hope in their early formative years.

CONCLUSION

This chapter presented 1) sabidurías insurgentes (insurrectionist wisdoms); 2) the anatomy of hope; and finally, 3) the everyday deaths and resurrections of working-class Maya mexicanas living in the pueblo mágico. Women strategically practice hope through their sabidurías insurgentes, which give them the capacity to corazonar la vida, reject the epistemicide of modernity, and guide their risk-taking actions. These actions are practices of hope that have a structure and behavior—an anatomy. The anatomy of hope realized in these practices is hablando, ignorando, insistiendo, and renunciando. Hope is the site of multiple deaths and resurrections. Women use these sites to construct a "theology of memory" for the preservation of hope in their familias and pueblo.

A more adequate form of care and counseling acknowledges women's sabiduría insurgente and is attentive to learning how to see deaths/resurrections. LaMothe identifies the challenges of class, classism, and class conflict in the context of neoliberal capitalism by demonstrating how pastoral care is political. He proposes that the actions of faith communities (altercapitalist ecclesia) can resist the unjust and uncaring violence of empire and capitalism. To continue the development of such a hermeneutical framework, pastoral care and counseling would benefit from consideration of the case of Ecuador's incorporation of Buen Vivir and the challenges arising from this justice-making. Turning to the micro level, pastoral counseling benefits from being in solidarity with working-class people by witnessing the practice of "counting crosses" and by being available and open to act if and when called upon.

NOTES

1. A. A. Brill, trans., *The Basic Writings of Sigmund Freud* (New York: Modern Library, 1938).
2. Carl G. Jung, *The Essential Jung*, edited by Anthony Storr (Princeton , NJ: Princeton University Press, 1983).
3. "With so many blows/beatings that life gave you." See Fayad Jamís, *Con Tantos Palos Que Te Dio la Vida y Otras Canciones* (Matanzas, Cuba: Ediciones Vigía, 1987), 2.
4. Siroj Sorajjakool and Apipa Prachyapruit, "Qualitative Methodology and Critical Pedagogy: A Study of the Lived Experiences of Thai Peasants within the Context of Western Development Ideology," in *Qualitative Research in Theological Education* (London: SCM Press, 2018), 23–25.
5. David Harvey, *A Brief History of Neoliberalism* (Oxford: University Press, 2005), 17–18.
6. Harvey, *A Brief History of Neoliberalism*, 19.
7. Zapatista spokesman Subcomandante Marcos created this pseudonym to narrate teachings emerging from the Ejército Zapatista de Liberación Nacional (EZLN). The EZLN is the left-wing libertarian-socialist political group from Chiapas, México, that organized the 1994 uprising protesting NAFTA. Many of the sayings and stories of el Viejo Antonio insisted on a utopian cosmovision in which there could be un mundo donde quepan muchos mundos (a world into which many worlds fit).
8. Translation: "Doesn't consist in knowing the world, but in intuiting the paths that we will have to walk so it can be better . . . wisdom consists in the art of discovering behind the pain, hope." Patricio Guerrero Arias, "Corazonar Desde el Calor de las Sabidurías Insurgentes, la Frialdad de la Teoría y la Metodología / Corazonar from Insurgents' Wisdoms Warm, the Coldness of the Theory and the Methodology," *Sophía* 1, no. 13 (December 30, 2012): 200, https://doi.org/10.17163/soph.n13.2012.08.
9. The term "ontological anthro/gynopology" may seem redundant. After all, anthro/gynopology is ontological. But, unfortunately, not all anthropologies acknowledge multiple realities, forms of being, and ways of experiencing the world. For this reason, I emphasize the ontological nature of anthro/gynopologies.
10. Arturo Escobar, *Designs for the Pluriverse: Radical Interdependence, Autonomy, and the Making of Worlds* (Durham, NC: Duke University Press, 2018), 148.

11. Escobar, *Designs for the Pluriverse*, 148.

12. Allen J. Christenson, trans., *Popol Vuh: The Sacred Book of the Maya* (Winchester, UK: O Books, 2003).

13. Patricio Guerrero Arias, *Corazonar una Antropología Comprometida con la Vida: Miradas Otras Desde Abya-Yala la Decolonizacíon del Poder; del Saber y del Ser* (Quito: Universidad Politécnic Salesiana, 2010), 105.

14. Guerrero Arias, *Corazonar una Antropología Comprometida con la Vida*, 105.

15. Translation: "The wooden men were too cold and without feelings, therefore they could not give birth to their creation." Guerrero Arias, *Corazonar una Antropología Comprometida con la Vida*, 105.

16. Translation: "The vital fluid that made their heart sing ignited the fire of the magic of dreams and marvel at the sacred miracle of existence." Guerrero Arias, *Corazonar una Antropología Comprometida con la Vida*, 105.

17. Translation: "Obscure, cloud, the gaze of humans so that they cannot see but only the unimportant, that which is in front of their eyes and have no vision of the present and the future, that are incapable of discovering the constructive force that the words love and wisdom have." Guerrero Arias, *Corazonar una Antropología Comprometida con la Vida*, 107.

18. Within Mesoamerica there are a number of different Maya societies and ethnic groups. Each group has its own particular history, culture, rituals, and language, yet they also share some similarities in linguistic heritage and cosmovision. In the southern state of Chiapas, Maya language groups distinguish themselves by proper names for each dialect: Tzotzil, Tzeltal, Tojolabalis, and Ch'ol. Juan López Intzín is a social anthropologist and scholar of Maya Tzotzil and Tzeltal.

19. Juan López Inztín, "'Ich'el ta muk': La Trama en la Construcción del Lekil kuxlejal (vida plena-digna-justa)," in *Senti-pensar el Género: Perspectivas desde los Pueblos Originarios*, edited by Georgina Méndez Torres et al. (Guadalajara, México: La Casa del Mago, 2013), 78.

20. Mariana Mora, *Kuxlejal Politics: Indigenous Autonomy, Race, and Decolonizing Research in Zapatista Communities* (Austin: University of Texas Press, 2017), 19.

21. Christenson, *Popol Vuh*.

22. Guerrero Arias, *Corazonar Desde el Calor de las Sabidurías*, 201–202.

23. Translation: "It has not been the result of a process of reflection within the academy or among critical intellectuals; but a consequence of the struggle for the existence of the peoples/pueblos subjected to coloniality, constructed as 'objects of study' of the social sciences, and that today are transformed into political and historical subjects; they have imposed on the academy and society the recognition of their wisdom and their existence." Guerrero Arias, *Corazonar Desde el Calor de las Sabidurías*, 202.

24. De Sousa Santos uses the terms "global south" and "global north" as metaphors for populations where there is a concentration of poverty and subjugation, and wealth and privilege.

25. Boaventura de Sousa Santos, *Epistemologies of the South: Justice against Epistemicide* (Boulder, CO: Paradigm, 2014).

26. Marlene M. Ferreras, "Women's Agency in the Context of Neoliberal Capitalism," In *What's with Free Will? Religion and Ethics after Neuroscience*, edited by

Philip Clayton and James W. Walters, 115–117. Used by permission of Wipf and Stock Publishers, www.wipfandstock.com.

27. Arturo Escobar, "Thinking-Feeling with the Earth: Territorial Struggles and the Ontological Dimension of the Epistemologies of the South / Sentipensar con la Tierra: Las Luchas Territoriales y la Dimensión Ontológica de las Epistemologías del Sur," *Revista de Antropología Iberoamericana* 11, no. 1 (January 1, 2016): 11–13, https://doi.org/10.11156.

28. Translation: "Extractive projects can be understood as strategies for the ontological occupation of the territories, and therefore the struggles against them constitute, in reality, ontological struggles." Arturo Escobar, "Thinking-Feeling with the Earth," 14.

29. Arturo Escobar, "Thinking-Feeling with the Earth," 15.

30. For a more detailed discussion of the Mundo Mundial/universe, see John Law, "What's Wrong with a One-World World?" *Distinktion: Journal of Social Theory* 16, no. 1 (January 2, 2015): 126–139, https://doi.org/10.1080/1600910X.2015.1020066.

31. Arturo Escobar, "Sustainability: Design for the Pluriverse," *Development* 54, no. 2 (June 2011): 138.

32. The earth commands, the people order/organize, and the government obeys. Building autonomy.

33. Escobar, *Designs for the Pluriverse*, 166.

34. Ferreras, "Women's Agency in the Context of Neoliberal Capitalism," 118–119.

35. Gloria Anzaldúa, *Borderlands/La Frontera: The New Mestiza*, 4th ed. (San Francisco: Aunt Lute Books, 2012), 60–61.

36. Anzaldúa, *Borderlands*, 60.

37. I have chosen to use the present participle of these words because gerunds are action verbs that function as nouns—meaning the four aspects of hope (hablando, insistiendo, ignorando, and renunciando) are hope (noun) and they are ongoing actions (verbs) that result in the creation of hope in the maquila.

38. Ken Michaels, "Electrostatic Discharge: Causes, Effects, and Solutions—It Only Takes 25 Electrostatic Volts to Irreparably Damage an Integrated Circuit," *EC&M Electrical Construction and Maintenance* 98, no. 10 (September 1999): 16–19.

39. Sergei Prozorov, *Agamben and Politics: A Critical Introduction* (Edinburgh: Edinburgh University Press, 2014), 35–38.

40. "IMF Members' Quotas and Voting Power, and IMF Board of Governors," International Monetary Fund, last updated October 14, 2018, https://www.imf.org/external/np/sec/memdir/members.aspx#3.

41. "IMF Members' Quotas and Voting Power."

42. Hugo Hernández-Ojeda Alvarez and Luis Ricardo Ruiz Gutiérrez, "Mexico: Employment and Labour Law 2018," International Comparative Legal Guide, April 17, 2018, https://iclg.com/practice-areas/employment-and-labour-laws-and-regulations/mexico#chaptercontent6.

43. Wpadmin, "Gender, Globalization and the Women of the Maquiladoras: Before and After NAFTA," Women on the Border, June 15, 2011, http://womenontheborder

.org/2011/06/gender-globalization-and-the-women-of-the-maquiladoras-before-and-after-nafta/

44. Eugenia Gutiérrez, "El Zapatismo, la Ciencia Consciente y la Función del Arco Iris," Radio Zapatista, January 4, 2017, https://radiozapatista.org/?p=20150&lang=en.

45. Marcella Althaus-Reid, *Feminist Theology to Indecent Theology: Readings on Poverty, Sexual Identity and God* (London: SCM Press, 2004), 114.

46. Althaus-Reid, *Feminist Theology to Indecent Theology*, 114.

47. Jung Mo Sung, *Desire, Market and Religion* (London: SCM Press, 2007), Kindle, chap. 1.

48. Sung, *Desire, Market and Religion*.

49. Ivone Gebara, *Out of the Depths: Women's Experience of Evil and Salvation*, trans. Ann Patrick Ware (Minneapolis: Fortress Press, 2002), 111.

50. Gebara, *Out of the Depths*, 115.

51. Althaus-Reid, *Feminist Theology to Indecent Theology*, 113.

52. Althaus-Reid, *Feminist Theology to Indecent Theology*.

53. Gebara, *Out of the Depths*, 115.

54. Unai Villalba, "*Buen Vivir* vs Development: A Paradigm Shift in the Andes?" *Third World Quarterly* 34, no. 8 (2013): 1427.

55. Villalba, "*Buen Vivir* vs Development," 1436.

56. Villalba, "*Buen Vivir* vs Development," 1430.

57. Villalba, "*Buen Vivir* vs Development," 1430–1431.

58. Ryan LaMothe, *Care of Souls, Care of Polis: Toward a Political Pastoral Theology* (Eugene, OR: Cascade Books, 2017), 133, Kindle.

59. A 1994 California ballot initiative that proposed the state screen for US citizenship and prohibit undocumented residents from using health care emergency services, public education, and social services. During this time there was a great deal of racial profiling and I especially recall the fear of speaking Spanish outside the home even though I was born in the US and my mother is a naturalized US citizen.

60. Translation: "Voyager, there are no bridges, one builds them as one walks." Gloria Anzaldúa, "Foreword," in Cherríe Moraga and Gloria Anzaldúa, eds., *This Bridge Called My Back: Writings by Radical Women of Color*, 2nd ed. (New York: Kitchen Table, Women of Color Press, 1983).

61. James N. Poling, *Deliver Us from Evil* (Minneapolis: Fortress Press, 1996), 106.

62. Kathleen J. Greider, *Reckoning with Aggression: Theology, Violence, and Vitality* (Louisville, KY: Westminster John Knox Press, 1997), 69.

63. Greider, *Reckoning with Aggression*, 5.

Chapter Five

Ma'alob (Goodbye and Hello)

The first word I learned in Mayan was "Ma'alob"—goodbye. I heard it every time we had a visitor or went to see family members who lived down the road or bade farewell to maquila workers headed for work. It both marked the conclusion to meaningful moments and signaled the promise of something to come. This final chapter is such a ma'alob from a most hospitable pueblo. Here, I return to the first question Doña Lucía asked me: "¿Y que crece en tu pueblo?"[i]

Back then, I had no idea how or why that question was so important to her, or conversely why it might be important for me to know what grows in pueblo mágico. Here, I summarize what I learned and the implication of this learning for the discipline of pastoral theology. Then, I identify areas for future development in the research and writing of a Latinx feminist pastoral theology. I conclude by reflecting on the progression of this book project and how the experiences I related in it are shaping my ongoing formation as a pastor-scholar-clinician-activist.

LXS HIJXS DE MAÍZ AND RELEVANCE FOR PASTORAL THEOLOGY

What grows in pueblo mágico? Lxs hijxos de maíz grow. They have become for me an image for pastoral care, and more specifically for understanding working-class Maya mexicanas in the age of globalization and neoliberal capitalism. The following image arose from my reflection on the eschatological practices of working-class Maya mexicanas. The interpretation of this

---

i. "What grows in your town?"

136 Chapter Five

image is influenced by a doctrine of creation that believes life is interdependent and thus proposes a relational eschatology based on my learnings from women in pueblo mágico. The inextricable bonds between humans, the earth, and the sacred life force inform my interpretation of this image. Life is about embracing the biodiversity of the planet and recognizing the ongoing cycle of life that gives birth, dies, and provides the necessary compost for the creation of new life. The campesinx exemplifies solidarity with creation and in this way adds experiential aspects to the practice of solidarity as it is theorized by pastoral theologians such as Sharon G. Thornton's *Broken Yet Beloved*. This is the "flesh-and-blood" in relationship with planetary life.[1]

In chapter 2, I demonstrated how neoliberal capitalism is an extension of colonialism. I traced colonial history and the dehumanization of el pueblo indígena from the encomienda system to the hacienda and finally to the

Figure 5.1. Lxs hijxs de maíz as an image of pastoral care. Artwork by William Bredvik.

multinational corporation. The *land* in which women are rooted is desecrated by the invasion of foreigners who subject them to cruel genocidal practices that benefit their global economic systems. These assaults on the women's cultural heritage and wisdom threaten to distort their relationships with the land, themselves, and their communities. But there is a difference between the land and the soil.

Land is the hard surface of the earth that builds over time and becomes solid. Historical violence, such as the story of the Maya in Yucatán, México, is like the land. Violence, oppression, genocide, and epistemicide have taken place across centuries and this is the solid land upon which lxs hijxs de maíz grow. Maya stories collected in this book attest to their growing awareness of how the maquila is a continuation of colonialism. However, despite this hard terrain, lxs hijxs de maíz grow because they know there is a thin layer of nutritious soil, and this makes growth possible.

The soil that covers the land consists of organic remains, clay, and particles of rocks. Soil is unconstrained and malleable. I think of the stories of nuestros antepasados (our ancestors) and los antiguos (the ancients) that I heard recounted during my time in pueblo mágico as such soil. Lxs hijxs de maíz speak of death and suffering as part of life and not as a final state. For life does not end but regenerates itself. The ancestors live on through the dichos (proverbs or wise sayings) that inform the everyday activities of lxs hijxs de maíz. Every time a conversation begins with "nuestros difuntos antepasados decían . . ." new compost is added to the soil and perpetuates life. In other words, lxs hijxs de maíz know that there is a thin but nutritious layer of soil where life and death are connected and constantly creating something new. Their oppressors may steal their land, but only they are in intimate relationship with the soil and the life of the soil continues surviving, thriving, and indeed blooming.

Lxs hijxs de maíz are rooted in place. The future is in constant intimate relationship with the present. The realities of time (the present-as-future) are embodied. Instead of determining exactly when a specific time will arrive, eschatological questions focus on who is present, what is happening, and what is taking place. The question is never about when the future will arrive, for the future is continually emerging. This future that springs up in the present does so bolstered by a matriarchal community and despite violence, oppression, and exploitation. Lxs hijxs de maíz continue to grow because the gods/goddesses created them with the magic of sueños/dreams made possible because they also possess sabidurías insurgentes (insurrectionist wisdoms). Like *the husk* that protects the kernels of corn as they fatten, wisdom protects the women's sueños and gives them the ability to intuit and perceive how and when to draw on their wisdoms to preserve themselves, their families, their tribe, and their soil.

Sabidurías insurgentes (insurrectionist wisdoms) guide the eschatological practices of lxs hijxs de maíz that like *roots* nourish the life they are growing for themselves, their families, their tribe, and their soil. These eschatological practices are hablando, ignorando, insistiendo, and renunciando. These practices are what creates cracks in the hard land and makes way for women to reclaim their preferred futures: land that has been stolen and desecrated, identities as the preservers of life, and the community's cultural and ancestral heritage. These roots depict risk-taking actions that sometimes find resources to keep life going, but at other points in time they must search for different pathways, or grow new roots yet to be discovered.

Practicing survival and discovering how to stay alive is how lxs hijxs de maíz find ways to seguir adelante (keep forging ahead). They are primeramente madre, which means they seek to practice justice-making for the sake of protecting life—specifically of their children, but also of their people and of the earth. Though the maquila (multinational corporation) appropriates their cultural heritage and customs, the women continue to keep alive the art of sewing passed down to them by the women in the community. The sound of sewing machines is heard throughout the pueblo mágico, but this is a radically different type of labor than the labor in the maquila. For this labor is for themselves; it ties the people to their cultural heritage and declares that the maquila cannot transform their art into a business. Pueblo mágico continues to bear life and grow like the long, dark braids of this image; lxs hijxs de maíz produce life rooted in their eschatological practices. And just as their antepasados passed down their cultural heritage of weaving, lxs hijxs de maíz teach their children to engage en la lucha (the struggle). Lxs hijxs de maíz bear life even within death-producing contexts and they pass on these life-giving practices to their children. The young in the community witness how lxs hijxs de maíz are both not afraid to die and also refuse to die because they are primeramente madre. They are the caretakers of their own vulnerable lives. As the reader might recall, in the Popol Vuh we learned that lxs hijxs de maíz were fed corn. Lxs hijxs de maíz grow by eating their own produce. The campesinx may learn about the crops but, in the end, what makes them grow are their own resources.

Lxs hijxs de maíz affirm their interconnected relationship with the earth. With her face raised to the heavens, absorbing the light that radiates from the sun, this image illustrates an ecology of care tied to the well-being of the earth. Lxs hijxs de maíz understand that healing/health of the community is directly linked to the viability of ecological systems. This image invites pastoral theology to consider how anthropocentrism, neoliberal capitalism, and chronological eschatology are inviting death by neglecting the care of place, the interdependency of all life, and the greed that motivates such death-producing practices. What I am saying here is that we are inviting death by noticing; we are neglecting our own survival when we conceptualize care as if human life is separate from the life of the earth. We cannot afford to pretend that deforestation, pollution of rivers and oceans, waste production, genetically modified crops, urban sprawl, depletion of the ozone, melting polar ice caps, and climate change are somehow not related to the care of individuals-in-community. My experience and research findings in pueblo mágico confirm that Ivone Gebara is right: Western thought and patriarchal Christianity result in the support of environmental destruction that results from economic globalization that threatens the life of the land and poor women.[2] Providing care means seeing how the lives of people are connected to the life of the planet. In essence what I am saying is that caring for the relationships present in the biodiversity of the planet is a function of pastoral care.

The pastoral caregiver, informed by the working-class Maya mexicanas in this study, knows that she/he is more like a campesinx than an agent of hope.[3] Campesinxs work on the milpa and they do their work under challenging conditions. They struggle with their milpas being compromised by genetically modified seeds and by trade agreements that make growing and selling their crops more difficult, and they recognize that they are dependent on the unpredictability of the climate. Sometimes the harvest is plentiful and the gods/goddess (Chacc, the rain god) water the land with frequency, but sometimes there is drought. In the face of these challenges, the campesinx regularly checks on how his/her crops are growing. She/he spends time in the field and studies the crop and witnesses the daily dying and reviving of life. Crops grow not solely because of what the campesinx does, but because of the relationship the campesinx builds with the milpa. There is a spiritual dimension that flows through planetary life and the campesinx is like a caregiver who, through decolonial approaches to pastoral care, learns how life continues to grow despite challenges present in the ecosystem. In short, the campesinx illustrates the interdependence of all living things and underscores a worldview in which nature (plants, animals, land, sea, mountains, etc.) is not separate from humans.

The image of pastoral care as hijxs de maíz is a mythical creature presented in the Popol Vuh. This mythical creature's nature as half-human, half-plant emphasizes a hybrid ecological system of care, a worldview that recognizes the need for pastoral theology to move toward a pastoral theology of the earth as we conceptualize the care of persons-in-community. I choose to describe care by naming the elements of land, soil, roots, husk, and braids to connect the biodiversity of life and its dependence on each other. The well-being of any one part relies on the health of each element. I am influenced by the general systems theory developed first out of biological science and cybernetics through the work of biologists Ludwig Bertalanffy from Austria and Humberto Maturana from Chile. General systems theory and cybernetics was influential in the social sciences by assisting the field to conceptualize familial relationships as systems. This laid the foundation for the theorizing of American psychiatrist Murray Bowen's family systems theory that was then the basis for multiple theories based on it: for example, Argentinian family therapist Salvador Minuchin's structural family therapy and American psychotherapists Jay Haley and Milton Erickson's strategic family therapy. Bowen's theory claimed the neutrality of the therapist/caregiver, and lxs hijxs de maíz as an image of pastoral care rejects this unaffected stance by entering into the experience of care with careseekers and naming unjust practices in order to tend to what is birthing life in the midst of challenging circumstance. What follows are some examples of how the pastoral counselor can become more campesinx-aware in the caretaking relationship:

1. Land: Listen for the long history of individuals/families. Consider how their ancestors' experiences of violence and historical trauma are narrated in the present struggle (lucha). Questions for caring conversations might include: How is this connected to the stories of your antepasados/antiguos (ancestors/ancients)? Tell me about your pueblo and what your pueblo is known for. (The second part to this question is because in the Yucatán I learned that each pueblo is known for or has an identity connected to what they make or grow, e.g., shoes, bags, hammocks, etc.) What is made/grows is part of the solid land story and is connected to an alternative economy they once had based on trading with each other locally; such practices are now in competition with globalized and neoliberal policies. These kinds of questions are opportunities to practice lament.
2. Soil: Discover who are the living-dead, meaning what stories and whose life continues to live on in the community (exemplars, relatives, mythical figures). Who are the ancestors? And what of their living and dying continues to shape and inform the community's everyday life? Consider what dichos (proverbs and wise sayings) you are hearing. Pause the individual/family and ask questions if you do not understand something. Also inquire: Is there a favorite dicho you frequently say? What is the significance of that saying to them? What does it mean when someone says this dicho when they _____ (name the activity, event, situation you are discussing).
3. Roots: What risk-taking actions are individuals/families doing or thinking about? Do not focus on weighing the pros and cons and "helping" the individual/family to decide. In a nonjudgmental way, listen to and describe

what you hear, including the risky behavior. Be curious about how those actions resist the harm the individual/family is naming and also pursue justice-making. Ask the individual/family about what they are teaching their children to do by these actions. Why is it important that they teach them to do these things? Who will benefit from these actions? What intended purpose do these actions have?
4. Husk: Recognize that each individual/family is filled with wisdom and has the ability to perceive and intuit paths through life. This is not so much what we call agency as a soulful relationship between the individual/family and the universe. It is almost a kind of magic. Individuals/families have sueños, waking dreams, about the life they are creating. Remain present and cultivate the relationship with the people and their sueños; forgo your "expert" status.
5. Braids: Be curious about and listen to how individuals/families preserve cultural heritage. Whenever possible, ask about how these traditions are passed down. Request to see them do this. For example, tortear/making tortillas is a skill girls learn by the age of five. You might ask how the masa is made, where the corn is ground, how to make the circular form of the masa without it sticking to the candela. This means situating the caretaking relationship in the community, not apart from it. You might also visit a milpa and be similarly curious. Listen for how these practices are tied to the people's sense of self.

These five guidelines are assessing three primary domains: nature deficit disorder, social/environmental ecology, and solidarity. First, American journalist Richard Louv coined the term "nature deficit disorder" to describe the consequences of children growing up in the neoliberal age marked by technological progress. Through interviews and observation, Louv traces the historical progression from children who played in nature to the current solitary play children do on technological devices such as iPads and smartphones. He draws on interdisciplinary research to support his premise that children benefit physically, emotionally, and spiritually when they are connected to nature. He posits that childhood obesity, attention deficit disorder, and depression can be ameliorated by environment-based education.[4] Pueblo mágico is rich in an environment-based education for their children.

Second, the pastoral caregiver is assessing the social/environmental ecology. As the caregiver hears responses to the questions above, she/he is assessing the biodiversity of life described by the careseeker. The caregiver makes this assessment by evaluating what is cross-pollinating and how it is affecting planetary life. The caregiver is being attentive to what new life is birthed because of this cross pollination, and conversely, what is being endangered by this network of relationships. As the caregiver gathers this assessment, she/he feeds this information back to the careseeker and asks the careseeker to judge if the life being born and the life dying is "good" for the ecosystem of which she/he is a part.

The third and final category of assessment is solidarity. The caregiver is assessing the degree to which the careseeker is experiencing solidarity with the fragility of planetary life and how the participation in this struggle for life is impacting the person. The assessment here is to see what life is in danger: in the case of pueblo mágico, the maíz crops suffered with the people and there is a historical tie of henequen suffering with the people as well. If you can find what is dying, you come in contact with what is living and get to know more clearly the conditions surrounding that life so that you can respond more effectively.

The benefits of this image for caregivers extend beyond a Latinx setting. The above invites practical and pastoral theologians to join the conversation emerging within the field of psychology and ecopsychology. Pastoral theologians are uniquely trained and capable of exploring and articulating the spiritual dimensions of planetary life and the healing activity of being in relationship with the sacred geography of place. Furthermore, Gloria Anzaldúa's theorizing on the border (la herida abierta) extends to the religious hybridity[5] of many persons who draw on more than one spiritual tradition. Spiritual mestizaje is "the transformative renewal of one's relationship to the sacred through a radical and sustained multimodal and self-reflexive critique of oppression in all its manifestations and a creative and engaged participation in shaping life that honors the sacred."[6] This is a theoretical framework informed by Latinx spiritualities and applicable to a broader demographic interested in seeking to regenerate life by exploring the sacred histories that come together in all our lives. These sacred histories are what the image above seeks to uncover, especially in the discussion on the land's relationship to pastoral care. I can imagine how a new minister assigned to care for a faith community in a rural setting can draw from this image. She/he will be able to care more adequately for her/his community if she/he uses the image to learn more about the land and the people's relationship to place.

This image has some limitations, and adopting this image comes with some cautionary commentary. This image privileges understanding life through the heart (corazonando la vida) and teaching caregivers to do this means assisting caregivers to hear the heart's wisdom. However, how can a caregiver assess whether a person's heart is leading them toward life-giving practices? In order to learn how to corazonar la vida, caregivers have to embrace death and be open to individuals choosing options for themselves and their families that caregivers might believe are detrimental. I believe choosing death is an option that might be a complication for caregivers.

In pueblo mágico I learned of a goddess of suicide, Ixtab. This goddess dies by tying a rope around her neck and hanging herself. She is the goddess who accompanies suicides to heaven. While in pueblo mágico, I heard a variety of suicide attempt stories and also experienced the attempt of our neighbor who lived directly in front of our home. The means of suicide described (of both the goddess and the neighbor) did not deform the body (gunshot, slitting wrists, etc.). This was a way of honoring the sacredness of the corporeal body. Ixtab is in relationship with those who choose to end their lives and lift the economic burden from their terrestrial family by traveling with Ixtab to heaven.

Further research is needed to understand how the goddess of suicide figures into the indigenized pastoral theology this book is beginning to propose. Nevertheless, what I want to underscore is that the indigenization of care and the use of non-Western pastoral care practices by Western pastoral caregivers pose legal and ethical concerns for their implementation in places like the United States. There is a difference between how multinational corporations dispose of the bodies of women of color as human waste in the production of profit and the conversion of life to death that serves as the compost for the regeneration of life. I understand suicide, as described by the Maya, to be compost, not disposability. This conceptualization of life may not translate to clinical contexts where law and ethics do not allow for more than one view of suicide.

GROWING A LATINX FEMINIST PASTORAL THEOLOGY

This book is a first step toward a much larger project in Latinx feminist pastoral theology.[7] There is so much more to be explored and many possible areas for future research and writing. For example, this book did not explore the experiences of men in the maquila or develop the two theoretical themes of desire and education.

Maquilas in México first employed women; it was only later that men were added to the assembly lines. As their milpas dried up (for lack of rain water and irrigation, water that had been diverted for industrial uses) and their mothers, wives, and sisters went to work in the maquila, earning less than the minimum wage, campesinos joined the women on the assembly line in an effort to survive the devastating effects of neoliberal policies. Their suffering in the neoliberal context is connected to the suffering of women and may share some similarities, but there are no doubt unique aspects of their experience.

Learning from their particular male experience would add to understanding the relational eschatology this book addressed. For example, I wonder about the significance to Sofia of her father supporting her pursuit of a future away from the assembly line. What unspoken relational desire(s), fear(s), and/or concern(s) did Sofia's father have for her? For the family? For himself?

Another avenue of investigation is a gender analysis of labor in the maquila. I learned that there is a gendered division of labor—that women do the detail work of embroidery, sewing pockets, and attaching zippers to jeans, while men do the heavy work of lifting the material at the end of the assembly line when the product is nearly complete. When I visited the maquila, this division of labor was visually apparent: I could see workers segregated by biological sex. In my interview with Ximena, I learned about homophobia, transphobia, and sexism among the workers, and the preschool teacher, Maestra Camila, confirmed this prejudice. Maestra Camila introduced me to the one openly transgender maquila worker who lived in pueblo mágico. On two occasions I noticed they were hitchhiking into town (the only way to travel in and out of pueblo mágico), and I asked the cabdriver to stop and pick them up. This worker was overly appreciative of my sharing a taxi ride with them and I began to wonder what their experience in the maquila was like. Do the matriarchal circles that support life include them? How is their experience different, and where does life spring up for them? In short, I wondered about the construction of gender in the maquila, particularly in suffering and care of persons such as the transgender friend I made in the pueblo mágico, but also of others. These seem to me to be los atravesados within los atravesados to which Anzaldúa refers.

Two theoretical themes, desire and education, were not developed and future research might focus on these themes in order to engage these themes. The first was the theme of desire. Neoliberal capitalism assumes that desires can be disciplined through the open market—in other words, that the demand and supply relationship between goods in the market can reach an equilibrium. This book demonstrated how this is not so in the lives of eleven working-class Maya mexicanas. The market offers them no "equilibrium." Instead it is on their backs that the elite class grows its wealth. Nonetheless, I heard women speaking about desire in a unique way. They referred to desire as a yearning for a vitality in life, an internal longing for the continuance of life. These yearnings and longings were not for what they might gain in a market economy. What I heard sounded like the pursuit of concrete objects that move them toward action(s) and contribute to an imagination that informs their daily activities, for example, the desire for their children to attend school and the financial resources to build a house where they can commune with their family and neighbors. They spoke of desire as a sensation in their body.

Women's bodies know what they "quiero" (love) and "gustaría" (like) and direct their consciousness toward devising strategies to attain the object by activating the imagination. There are subcategories to desire: (1) needs and (2) wants. A *need* is a basic resource necessary for survival. For example, women talked about needing milk for their children. This need informs their activity in the workplace, both to produce more goods and to grow their oppositional consciousness in the quest for fair wages. There are desires that are not necessary for survival but nonetheless are reasonable desires for a change in circumstances: these are *wants*. For example, women want to give their children choices not available to them. They "want" their children to have the option to pursue an education. Then there are "needs" that are also "wants," and when combined these functions as a means toward their strategic decolonizing activities. For example, they sew jeans to earn money so they can build houses. They "need" a home but they also "want" to have a house/land that their children can inherit. I see this as a form of participation in the neoliberal capitalist economy for their survival and for their reclaiming of land. When needs and wants are combined, women can engage in emancipatory practices of faith. This is a gift, an internal revelation (the gestation of "hope"), that reorders the world. By "un poquito de justicia," Mujerista theologian Ada María Isasi-Díaz is referring to a similar concept.[8] I did not gather sufficient information to engage this discussion in a substantial way but am interested in pursuing this topic in a later publication.

MY GROWTH

Having come to the end of my project, I can finally answer Doña Lucía's question: It is naranjas (oranges) that grow in my pueblo, and I am beginning to understand the important ramifications of her question.

When I returned home to Redlands, California, in September 2017, I began transcribing the twenty-two hours of interview conversations. Each ten minutes of conversation took an average of one hour to transcribe. For months, I lived in the audio world of pueblo mágico while I was physically living in Redlands. Rehearing the conversations included ambient sounds—of the thunderstorms, of children playing, of my tiny assistant clamoring for my attention, of children interrupting the conversation to add their recollections to the stories their mothers and aunts were retelling, of kitchen fires crackling, of masa being pounded and hands slapping the tortillas after they are rolled out, and of the strong gust of wind followed by chatter and laughing and the pitter-patter of feet running to pull the clothes off the clothesline before the rain comes. I was hearing the sounds of two worlds at once in a way I had not when I first started this project. Through it, I recognized la herida abierta/ the open wound.

I also began to understand the world in which I live. I have never really felt at "home" in my pueblo. I was born in Orange, California, and moved to the Inland Empire in 1987 at the age of six. My pueblo is here in the Inland Empire, but I had very little connection to the land. When I returned from pueblo mágico, I drove into my driveway and realized that across the street from my house are orange groves. I had not really seen them before.

I stepped out of my car and walked over to the orange groves to see the fruit, the soil, and to take a picture to post on Facebook so I could show Doña Lucía what grows in my pueblo. I began to wonder about the story of oranges and learned that just as the maíz has a painful history, so too do these oranges. A quick Google search alerted me to the history of the orange groves and the exploitation of immigrants from China, Japan, and México who have through the years picked the fruit and packed it.[9] I knew about the Farm Workers Movement and Dolores Huerta and Cesar Chavez, but I had honestly never noticed the realities of that painful history in my pueblo. Maybe that history explains the Chinese pagoda next door to the famous Mission Inn hotel in downtown Riverside. Knowing what grows in my pueblo directs my attention to the struggle (la lucha) of my ancestors and the immigrant community with which I identify. How will I ever understand the soil without knowing how immigrants suffered and continue to suffer right here in my pueblo's land?

A curious thing happened in the process of gathering research and writing. Before coming "home" to Redlands after living in Yucatán, México, for five months between April and August 2017, I went to Cuba and visited my

Figure 5.2. Orange groves in Redlands, California. Photo taken by the author.

mother's pueblo for the first time. I had imagined the place so differently in my mind because my mother's and my grandmother's stories of the place were told with such affection. I had idealized the place as a paradise. It was not. Its parallels with the pueblo mágico struck me. The roads were made of dirt and the taxi driver who took me to my mother's pueblo told me I would not find a way out because public transportation is scarce. The dinner table was small and had only four chairs. The exception to the similarity that immediately struck me was that my family's home and its floor were all made of cement.

Though my mother left this place at the age of thirteen and I was born in the US, this soil immediately felt like "home." I encountered the place where my ancestors lived and this encounter was a meeting of their sueños. I am the sueños of my ancestors going adelante (forging ahead) and that is indeed magical. My family in Cuba showed me what grows in their backyard— giant aguacates (avocados). My mother asked me to bring her back some soil from Matanzas, and I did. I realized we needed it, and have needed it for some time. If "home" is ever truly going to be Redlands, my mother and I needed some soil from her home of Matanzas to nourish our growth in this foreign land.

The process of researching and writing this book was like a return home, a return to myself. I reclaimed my own rebeldía (rebelliousness) and that of my ancestors. Rather than becoming an expert on a narrow topic, I became a student of pueblo mágico and the working-class Maya mexicanas I met. I learned to practice trust in a community that is committed to bearing life. Maybe life does not have a birth date but just keeps on laboring, living, dying, resurrecting, and revealing itself. In this process, my courage grew, as did my ability to corazonar la vida. Staying safe meant trusting my relationship with women who knew I was an outsider, and that was frightening. I had no access to the internet or cell phone reception in pueblo mágico, nor to public transportation. I arrived in the pueblo by taxi but the only way out was by hitchhiking. Doña Nayeli and Doña Lucía showed me how to do this. I still do not know how they knew which vehicles were safe to get into and there was no set time when we went out to find a ride. But they knew, and progressively I jumped into the beds of pickup trucks and the back seats of cars with more courage than I had the previous time.

These experiences have formed me into a more capable practical and pastoral theologian. I am more at home in myself. I found my footing and *realized the caring relationship grows not because of what I bring to it, but because of what emerges from my being present to myself and to others.* I trust the relationship to be enough and I trust that the individuals/families seeking care have resources from which to draw. I also learned to be more confident in my intuition and feelings, and they led me to some incredible truths about myself and about the community in which I was living. Perhaps most importantly, I am no longer afraid of death.

I describe in the preface the eschatological view of God as acting outside of time and in control of an eschaton that only God could bring about. I mentioned my childhood desire to exercise the only control I believed I had in that worldview and much of that was in practicing a life-limiting orthodoxy. I still struggle with living within the rules, but now I care about them less. As a result of this project, I think I can describe the significance of my mother's insurrectionist actions: she was teaching me la ciencia de la lucha. I do not want to live in a present that is focused on a world to come. I am participating in the construction of worlds in the here-and-now and that in itself reorients my experience in the world. As we were parting, an Argentinian woman I met at the Zapatistas Primer Encuentro Internacional Político, Artístico, Deportivo y Cultural de Mujeres que Luchan in Chiapas, México, said, "¡Pórtate mal, porque las mujeres que se portan bien solo van al cielo, pero las demás de nosotras vamos a todos lados!"[i] In short, this whole process has been liberating for me. Araceli, Itzel, Ximena, Doña Lucía, Doña Nayeli, Celeste, Maria, Paloma, Natalia, Mariana, Sofia, Teresa, Veronica, and my tiny research assistant: it is your gospel that brings me life and I am forever grateful. ¡Sí se puede!

Ma'alob and welcome to everywhere!

NOTES

1. Sharon G. Thornton, *Broken Yet Beloved: A Pastoral Theology of the Cross* (St. Louis: Chalice Press, 2002), 123.

2. Ivone Gebara, *Longing for Running Water: Ecofeminism and Liberation* (Minneapolis: Fortress Press, 1999), Kindle.

3. Donald Capps, "The Agent of Hope," in *Images of Pastoral Care: Classical Readings*, edited by Robert C. Dykstra (St. Louis: Chalice Press, 2005), chap. 16, Kindle.

4. Richard Louv, *Last Child in the Woods: Saving Our Children from Nature-Deficit Disorder* (Chapel Hill, NC: Algonquin Books of Chapel Hill, 2005).

5. Gloria Anzaldúa, *Light in the Dark / Luz en Lo Oscuro: Rewriting Identity, Spirituality, Reality*, edited by Analouise Keating (Durham, NC: Duke University Press, 2015), Kindle.

6. Theresa Delgadillo, *Spiritual Mestizaje: Religion, Gender, Race, and Nation in Contemporary Chicana Narrative* (Durham, NC: Duke University Press, 2011), chap. 1, Kindle.

---

i. "Go and misbehave, because the women who behave only go to heaven, but the rest of us—we go everywhere!"

7. I privilege the work of Latinx feminists, meanwhile noting the intellectual genealogy and contributions of feminist political theorists who agree with the notion that care is a political concept. See Diemut Elisabet Bubeck, *Care, Gender, and Justice* (Oxford: Clarendon Press, 1995); Carol Gilligan, *In a Different Voice: Psychological Theory and Women's Development,* (Cambridge, MA: Harvard University Press, 1982); Virginia Held, ed., *Justice and Care: Essential Readings in Feminist Ethics* (Boulder, CO: Westview Press, 1995); Virginia Held, *The Ethics of Care: Personal, Political, and Global* (Oxford: Oxford University Press, 2007); Nel Noddings, *Caring: A Feminine Approach to Ethics and Moral Education* (Berkeley: University of California Press, 1984); Pearl M. Oliner and Samuel P. Oliner, *Toward a Caring Society* (Westport, CT: Praeger, 1995); Fiona Robinson, *Globalizing Care: Ethics, Feminist Theory, and International Relations* (Boulder, CO: Westview Press, 1999); Fiona Robinson, *The Ethics of Care: A Feminist Approach to Human Security* (Philadelphia: Temple University Press, 2011); Selma Sevehuijsen, *Citizenship and the Ethics of Care: Feminist Considerations on Justice, Morality and Politics* (London: Routledge Press, 1998); Joan C. Tronto, *Moral Boundaries: A Political Argument for an Ethic of Care* (New York: Routledge Press, 1993); Joan C. Tronto, *Caring Democracy: Markets, Equality, and Justice* (New York: New York University Press, 2013).

8. Ada María Isasi-Díaz, *Mujerista Theology* (Maryknoll, NY: Orbis Books, 1996).

9. Nathan Masters, "When Oranges Ruled the Inland Empire," Lost LA, KCET, Public Media Group of Southern California, March 11, 2016, https://www.kcet.org/shows/lost-la/when-oranges-ruled-the-inland-empire.

Bibliography

Alston, Lee J., Shannan Mattiace, and Tomas Nonnenmacher. "Coercion, Culture, and Contracts: Labor and Debt on Henequen Haciendas in Yucatán, Mexico, 1870–1915." *Journal of Economic History* 69, no. 1 (March 2009): 104–137.

Althaus-Reid, Marcella. *From Feminist Theology to Indecent Theology: Readings on Poverty, Sexual Identity and God*. London: SCM Press, 2004.

Anzaldúa, Gloria. *Borderlands/La Frontera: The New Mestiza*, 4th ed. San Francisco: Aunt Lute Books, 2012.

———. "Foreword." In Cherríe Moraga and Gloria Anzaldúa, eds. *This Bridge Called My Back: Writing by Radical Women of Color*. 2nd ed. New York: Kitchen Table, Women of Color Press, 1983.

———. *Light in the Dark / Luz en Lo Oscuro: Rewriting Identity, Spirituality, Reality*. Edited by Analouise Keating. Durham, NC: Duke University Press, 2015. Kindle.

Aquino, María Pilar. "Latin American Feminist Theology." *Journal of Feminist Studies in Religion* 14 (Spring 1998): 89–107.

Arjona, Rubén. "The Minister as Curator of Desire: A Model of Pastoral Accompaniment with Young Mexican Men." PhD diss., Princeton Theological Seminary, 2018.

Backhouse, Roger E., and Steven G. Medema. "Retrospectives: On the Definition of Economics." *Journal of Economic Perspectives* 23, no. 1 (Winter 2009): 221–235.

Baklanoff, Eric N., and Edward Moseley, eds. *Yucatán in an Era of Globalization*. Tuscaloosa: University of Alabama Press, 2008.

Baltodano, Sara. *Psicología, Pastoral y Pobreza*. 2003. Reimpresión. San José, Costa Rica: Universidad Bíblica Latinoamericana, 2012.

Bidwell, Duane R. "Eschatology and Childhood Hope: Reflections from Work in Progress." *Journal of Pastoral Theology* 20, no. 2 (Winter 2010): 109–127.

———. "Religious Diversity and Public Pastoral Theology: Is It Time for a Comparative Theological Paradigm?" *Journal of Pastoral Theology* 25, no. 3 (2015): 135–150.

Brill, A. A., trans. *The Basic Writings of Sigmund Freud*. New York: Modern Library, 1938.

Browning, Anjali. "Corn, Tomatoes, and a Dead Dog: Mexican Agricultural Restructuring after NAFTA and Rural Responses to Declining Maize Production in Oaxaca, Mexico." *Mexican Studies / Estudios Mexicanos* 29, no. 1 (Winter 2013): 85–119.

Browning, Don S. *A Fundamental Practical Theology: Descriptive and Strategic Proposals*. Minneapolis: Fortress, 1991.

Brueggemann, Walter. *Sabbath as Resistance: Saying No to the Culture of Now*. Louisville, KY: Westminster John Knox Press, 2014.

———. "Will Our Faith Have Children?" *Word & World* 3, no. 3 (1983): 272–283.

Canto Sáenz, Rodolfo. *Del Henequén a las Maquiladoras: La Política Industrial en Yucatán 1984–2001*. México, D.F.: Instituto Nacional de Administración Pública, 2001.

Capps, Donald. "The Agent of Hope." In *Images of Pastoral Care: Classical Readings*, edited by Robert C. Dykstra, chapter 16. St. Louis: Chalice Press, 2005. Kindle.

———. *Agents of Hope: A Pastoral Psychology*. Eugene, OR: Wipf & Stock, 1995.

Castilla Ramos, Beatriz. *Mujeres Mayas en la Robótica y Líderes de la Comunidad: Tejiendo la Modernidad*. Mérida: Universidad Autónoma de Yucatán, 2004.

Christenson, Allen J., trans. *Popol Vuh: The Sacred Book of the Maya*. Winchester, UK: O Books, 2003.

Couture, Pamela D. *Blessed Are the Poor? Women's Poverty, Family Policy, and Practical Theology*. Nashville: Abingdon Press, 1991.

Creswell, John W. *Qualitative Inquiry and Research Design: Choosing among Five Approaches*, 3rd ed. Thousand Oaks, CA: SAGE, 2013.

Davis, Dána-Ain, and Christa Craven. *Feminist Ethnography: Thinking through Methodologies, Challenges, and Possibilities*. Lanham, MD: Rowman & Littlefield, 2016.

Delgadillo, Theresa. *Spiritual Mestizaje: Religion, Gender, Race, and Nation in Contemporary Chicana Narrative*. Durham, NC: Duke University Press, 2011. Kindle.

Eliade, Mircea. *Myth and Reality*. Translated by Williard R. Trask. New York: Harper & Row, 1963.

Escobar, Arturo. *Designs for the Pluriverse: Radical Interdependence, Autonomy, and the Making of Worlds*. Durham, NC: Duke University Press, 2018.

———. "Sustainability: Design for the Pluriverse." *Development* 54, no. 2 (June 2011): 137–140.

———. "Thinking-Feeling with the Earth: Territorial Struggles and the Ontological Dimension of the Epistemologies of the South / Sentipensar con la Tierra: Las Luchas Territoriales y la Dimension Ontologica de las Epistemologias del Sur." *Revista de Antropologia Iberoamericana* 11, no. 1 (January 1, 2016): 11–13. https://doi.org/10.11156.

Figueroa Deck, Allen. *The Second Wave: Hispanic Ministry and the Evangelization of Cultures*. New York: Paulist Press, 1989.

Finn, Daniel. *Just Trading: On the Ethics and Economics of International Trade*. Nashville: Abingdon Press in cooperation with Churches' Center for Theology and Public Policy, Washington, DC, 1996.
Foucault, Michel. *Discipline and Punish: The Birth of the Prison*, 2nd ed. Translated by Alan Sheridan. New York: Vintage Books, 1995.
Fregoso, Rosa Linda. *Mexican Encounters*. Berkeley: University of California Press, 2003.
Freire, Paulo. *Pedagogy of the Oppressed*, 30th anniversary ed. Translated by Donaldo P. Macedo. New York: Continuum, 2000.
Friedman, Thomas. *The Lexus and the Olive Tree*. New York: Anchor Books, 2000.
Gadamer, Hans-Georg. *Truth and Method*, rev. ed. Translated by Joel Weinsheimer and Donald G. Marshall. New York: Continuum, 2004.
Gebara, Ivone. *Longing for Running Water: Ecofeminism and Liberation*. Minneapolis: Fortress Press, 1999. Kindle.
———. *Out of the Depths: Women's Experience of Evil and Salvation*. Translated by Ann Patrick Ware. Minneapolis: Fortress Press, 2002.
Geertz, Clifford. *The Interpretation of Cultures*. New York: Basic Books, 1977.
Graham, Elaine. *Between a Rock and a Hard Place: Public Theology in a Post-Secular Age*. London: SCM Press, 2013.
———. *Transforming Practice: Pastoral Theology in an Age of Uncertainty*. Eugene, OR: Wipf & Stock, 1996.
———. *Words Made Flesh: Writings in Pastoral and Practical Theology*. London: SCM Press, 2009.
Graham, Elaine, Heather Walton, and Frances Ward. *Theological Reflection: Methods*. London: SCM Press, 2005. Kindle.
Graham, Larry Kent. *Care of Persons, Care of Worlds: A Psychosystems Approach to Pastoral Care and Counseling*. Nashville: Abingdon Press, 1992.
Greider, Kathleen J. *Reckoning with Aggression: Theology, Violence, and Vitality*. Louisville, KY: Westminster John Knox Press, 1997.
———. "Religious Pluralism and Christian-Centrism." In *The Wiley-Blackwell Companion to Practical Theology*, edited by Bonnie J. Miller-McLemore, chapter 43. Malden, MA: Blackwell Publishing Limited, 2012. Kindle.
Grosfoguel, Ramon. "The Structure of Knowledge in Westernized Universities: Epistemic Racisim/Sexism and the Four Genocides/Epistemicides of the Long 16th Century." *Human Architecture: Journal of the Sociology of Self-Knowledge* 11, no. 1 (Fall 2013): 73–90.
Guerrero Arias, Patricio. "Corazonar Desde el Calor de las Sabidurías Insurgentes, la Frialdad de la Teoría y la Metodología / Corazonar from Insurgents' Wisdoms Warm, the Coldness of the Theory and the Methodology." *Sophía* 1, no. 13 (December 30, 2012): 200. https://doi.org/10.17163/soph.n13.2012.08.
———. *Corazonar una Antropología Comprometida con la Vida: Miradas Otras Desde Abya-Yala la Decolonización del Poder, del Saber y del Ser*. Quito: Universidad Politécnic Salesiana, 2010.
Gutiérrez, Gustavo. *A Theology of Liberation*, 15th anniversary ed. Maryknoll, NY: Orbis Books, 1988.

Haring, C. H. *The Spanish Empire in America*. New York: Harcourt Brace Jovanovich, 1975.
Harvey, David. *A Brief History of Neoliberalism*. Oxford: Oxford University Press, 2005.
Helsel, Philip Browning. *Pastoral Power beyond Psychology's Marginalization: Resisting the Discourses of the Psy-Complex*. New York: Palgrave Macmillan, 2015.
Isasi-Díaz, Ada María. "*Burlando al Opresor:* Mocking/Tricking the Oppressor: Dreams and Hopes of Hispanas/Latinas and *Mujeristas*." *Theological Studies* 65, no. 2 (2004): 340–363.
———. *Mujerista Theology*. Maryknoll, NY: Orbis Books, 1996.
Jamís, Fayad. *Con Tantos Palos que Te Dío la Vida y Otras Canciones*. Matanzas, Cuba: Ediciones Vigía, 1987.
Joh, Wonhee Anne. *Heart of the Cross: A Postcolonial Christology*. Louisville, KY: Westminster John Knox Press, 2006.
Jung, Carl G. *The Essential Jung*. Edited by Anthony Storr. Princeton, NJ: Princeton University Press, 1983.
Kittel, Gerhard, ed. *Theological Dictionary of the New Testament*, vol. 2. Translated by Geoffrey W. Bromiley. Grand Rapids, MI: Eerdmans, 1964.
Kubo, Sakae. "UPDATED: The Conflict between the General Conference and the Unions." *Spectrum Magazine*, November 3, 2012. https://spectrummagazine.org/article/news/2012/11/03/updated-conflict-between-general-conference-and-unions.
Kwok, Pui-lan, ed. *Hope Abundant: Third World and Indigenous Women's Theology*. Maryknoll, NY: Orbis Books, 2010.
———. *Postcolonial Imagination and Feminist Theology*. Louisville, KY: Westminster John Knox Press, 2005.
LaMothe, Ryan. *Care of Souls, Care of Polis: Toward a Political Pastoral Theology*. Eugene, OR: Cascade Books, 2017.
Lartey, Emmanuel Y. "Globalization, Internationalization, and Indigenization of Pastoral Care and Counseling." In *Pastoral Care and Counseling: Redefining the Paradigms*, edited by Nancy J. Ramsay, 87–108. Nashville: Abingdon Press, 2004.
———. *In Living Color: An Intercultural Approach to Pastoral Care and Counseling*. London: Cassell, 1997.
———. *Postcolonizing God: An African Practical Theology*. London: SCM Press, 2013. Kindle.
Lassiter, Luke E. *The Chicago Guide to Collaborative Ethnography*. Chicago: University of Chicago Press, 2005.
Laurent, Claire, Michael Platzer, and Maria Idomir, eds. *Femicide: A Global Issue That Demands Action*, 2nd ed. Vienna: Academic Council on the United Nations System, Vienna Liaison Office, 2013. https://acuns.org/wp-content/uploads/2013/05/Femicide_A-Gobal-Issue-that-demands-Action_1.pdf.
Law, John. "What's Wrong with a One-World World?" *Distinktion: Journal of Social Theory* 16, no. 1 (January 2, 2015): 126–139. https://doi.org/10.1080/1600910X.2015.1020066.
Lester, Andrew D. *Hope in Pastoral Care and Counseling*. Louisville, KY: Westminster John Knox Press, 1995.

López Inztín, Juan. "Ich'el ta muk': La Trama en la Construcción del Lekil kuxlejal (vida plena-digna-justa)." In *Senti-Pensar el Género: Perspectivas Desde los Pueblos Originarios*, edited by Georgina Méndez Torres, Juan López Intzín, Sylvia Marcos, and Carmen Osorio Hernández, 73–106. Guadalajara: La Casa del Mago, 2013.

Louv, Richard. *Last Child in the Woods: Saving Our Children from Nature-Deficit Disorder*. Chapel Hill, NC: Algonquin Books of Chapel Hill, 2005.

Luévano, Rafael. "A Living Call: The Theological Challenge of the Juárez-Chihuahua Femicides." *Journal of Feminist Studies in Religion* 24, no. 2 (Fall 2005): 67–76.

Marcos, Sylvia. "La Espiritualidad de las Mujeres Indígenas Mesoamericanas: Descolonizado las Creencias Religiosas." In *Tejiendo de Otro Modo: Feminismo, Epistemología y Apuestas Descoloniales en Abya Yala*, edited by Yuderkys Espinosa Miñoso, Diana Gómez Correal, and Karina Ochoa Muñoz, 143–159. Popayán, Colombia: Universidad del Cauca, 2014.

———. *Taken from the Lips: Gender and Eros in Mesoamerican Religions*. Religion in the Americas Series 5. Leiden: Brill, 2006.

Martell-Otero, Loida I. "Neither 'Left Behind' Nor Deciphering Secret Codes: An Evangélica Understanding of Eschatology." In *Latinas Evangélicas: A Theological Survey from the Margins*, edited by Loida I. Martell-Otero, Zaida Maldonado Pérez, and Elizabeth Conde-Frazier, 108–126. Eugene, OR: Cascade Books, 2013.

Marx, Karl, and Friedrich Engels. *Communist Manifesto*. Translated by Harold Joseph Laski. Chicago: Charles H. Kerr, 1946.

McGarrah Sharp, Melinda A. *Misunderstanding Stories: Toward a Postcolonial Pastoral Theology*. Eugene, OR: Pickwick, 2013.

Meisel, Nicolas. *Governance Culture and Development: A Different Perspective on Corporate Governance*. N.p.: Development Centre of the Organisation for Economic Co-operation and Development, 2004. http://books.google.com/books/about/Development_Centre_Studies_Governance_Cu.html?id=N57VAgAAQBAJ.

Mercer, Joyce Ann. "Economics, Class, and Classism." In *The Wiley Blackwell Companion to Practical Theology*, edited by Bonnie J. Miller-McLemore, 432–442. Malden, MA: Wiley-Blackwell, 2012.

Meyers, Allan D., and David L. Carlson. "Peonage, Power Relations, and the Built Environment at Hacienda Tabi, Yucatan, Mexico." *International Journal of Historical Archaeology* 6, no. 4 (December 2002): 225–252.

Michaels, Ken. "Electrostatic Discharge: Causes, Effects, and Solutions—It Only Takes 25 Electrostatic Volts to Irreparably Damage an Integrated Circuit." *EC&M Electrical Construction and Maintenance* 98, no. 10 (September 1999): 16–19.

Miller-McLemore, Bonnie J. *Also a Mother: Work and Family as Theological Dilemma*. Nashville: Abingdon Press, 1994.

———. "Five Misunderstandings about Practical Theology." *International Journal of Practical Theology* 16, no. 1 (2012): 5–26. https://doi.org/10.1515/ijpt-2012-0002.

———. "The Human Web: Reflections on the State of Pastoral Theology" *Christian Century* 110, no. 11 (April 7, 1993): 366–369.

Moltmann, Jürgen. *The Coming of God: Christian Eschatology*. Minneapolis: Fortress Press, 1996.
Mora, Mariana. *Kuxlejal Politics: Indigenous Autonomy, Race, and Decolonizing Research in Zapatista Communities*. Austin: University of Texas Press, 2017.
Moschella, Mary Clark. *Ethnography as a Pastoral Practice: An Introduction*. Cleveland: Pilgrim Press, 2008.
Orr, Judith L. "Hard Work, Hard Lovin', Hard Times, Hardly Worth It: Care of Working-Class Men." In *The Care of Men*, edited by Christie C. Neuger and James N. Poling, 70–91. Nashville: Abingdon Press, 1997.
Ospino, Hosffman. "U.S. Latino/a Practical Theology." In *Opening the Field of Practical Theology: An Introduction*, edited by Kathleen A. Cahalan and Gordon S. Mikoski, 233–49. Lanham, MD: Rowman & Littlefield, 2014.
O'Sullivan, John L. "The Great Nation of Futurity." *The United States Democratic Review* 6 (November 1839): 426–430. Cited in John C. Pinheiro, *Missionaries of Republicanism: A Religious History of the Mexican-American War*. New York: Oxford University Press, 2014.
Pérez, Altagarcia. "Latina/o Practical Theology: Reflections on Faith-Based Organizing as a Religious Practice." In *Latino/a Theology*, edited by Orlando Espín, 439–451. Winchester, UK: Wiley-Blackwell, 2015.
Poling, James N. *Deliver Us from Evil*. Minneapolis: Fortress Press, 1996.
———. "Pastoral Care in a Time of Global Market Capitalism." *Journal of Pastoral Care and Counseling* 58, no. 3 (2004): 179–185.
———. *Render unto God: Economic Vulnerability, Family Violence, and Pastoral Theology*. Eugene, OR: Wipf & Stock, 2002.
Prieto, Susana. "Obreras Maquileras de Ciudad Juárez." Lecture given in Chiapas, México, March 9, 2018.
Prozorov, Sergei. *Agamben and Politics: A Critical Introduction*. Edinburgh: Edinburgh University Press, 2014.
Quijano, Anibal. "Coloniality of Power, Eurocentrism, and Latin America." Translated by Michael Ennis. *Nepantla: Views from South* 1, no. 3 (2000): 533–580.
Ramsay, Nancy J. "Resisting Asymmetries of Power: Intersectionality as a Resource for Practices of Care." *Journal of Pastoral Theology* 27, no. 2 (November 21, 2017): 83–97. https://doi.org/10.1080?10649867.2017.1399784.
Reinharz, Shulamit, and Lynn Davidman. *Feminist Methods in Social Research*. New York: Oxford University Press, 1992.
Richard, Analiese. "Withered Milpas: Governmental Disaster and the Mexican Countryside." *Journal of Latin American and Caribbean Anthropology* 13, no. 2 (November 2008): 387–413.
Robinson, Cedric J. *Black Marxism: The Making of the Black Radical Tradition*. Chapel Hill: University of North Carolina Press, 2000.
Rodríguez, Jeanette. *Our Lady of Guadalupe: Faith and Empowerment among Mexican-American Women*. Austin: University of Texas Press, 1994.
Rogers-Vaughn, Bruce. *Caring for Souls in a Neoliberal Age*. New York: Palgrave Macmillan, 2016.

———. "Class Power and Human Suffering: Resisting the Idolatry of the Market in Pastoral Theology and Care." In *Pastoral Theology and Care: Critical Trajectories in Theory and Practice*, edited by Nancy J. Ramsay, 55–77. Chichester: John Wiley & Sons, 2018.

Rosewall, Ann L. "Pastoral Theology of Hope: Listening in El Salvador." *Journal of Pastoral Theology* 21, no. 2 (2011): 1–13. https://doi.org/10.1179/jpt.2011.21.003.

Ross, Robert J. S. *Slaves to Fashion: Poverty and Abuse in the New Sweatshops*. Ann Arbor: University of Michigan Press, 2004.

Senate Committee on Finance, U.S. Congress. *North American Free Trade Agreement: Hearings before the Committee on Finance, United States Senate; One Hundred Second Congress, Second Session; on Labor Issues, Business and Labor Views, and Agriculture and Energy Issues Concerning NAFTA; September 8, 10, 22, and 30, 1992*. Washington, DC: U.S. Government Printing Office, 1993.

Simpson, Lesley Byrd. *The Encomienda in New Spain: The Beginning of Spanish Mexico*. Berkeley: University of California Press, 2008.

Smith, Linda Tuhiwai. *Decolonizing Methodologies: Research and Indigenous Peoples*, 2nd ed. London: Zed Books, 2012.

Sorajjakool, Siroj, and Apipa Prachyapruit. "Qualitative Methodology and Critical Pedagogy: A Study of the Lived Experiences of Thai Peasants within the Context of Western Development Ideology." In *Qualitative Research in Theological Education*, edited by Mary Clark Moschella and Susan Willhauck, 18–36. London: SCM Press, 2018.

Sousa Santos, Boaventura de. *Epistemologies of the South: Justice against Epistemicide*. Boulder, CO: Paradigm Publishers, 2014.

Spivak, Gayatri Chakravorty. "Can the Subaltern Speak?" In *Marxism and the Interpretation of Culture*, edited by Cary Nelson and Lawrence Grossberg, 271–313. Urbana: University of Illinois Press, 1988.

Sung, Jung Mo. *Desire, Market and Religion*. London: SCM Press, 2007. Kindle.

Thornton, Sharon G. *Broken Yet Beloved: A Pastoral Theology of the Cross*. St. Louis: Chalice Press, 2002.

Tracy, David. *Blessed Rage for Order: The New Pluralism in Theology*. New York: Seabury, 1975.

Turner, John Kenneth. *Barbarous Mexico*. Austin: University of Texas Press, 1969.

Villagómez Valdéz, Gina Irene, and Wilbert Pinto. *Mujer Maya y Desarrollo Rural en Yucatan*. Mérida: Universidad Autónoma de Yucatán, 1997.

Villalba, Unai. "*Buen Vivir* vs Development: A Paradigm Shift in the Andes?" *Third World Quarterly* 34, no. 8 (2013): 1427–1442.

Washington Valdez, Diana. *Harvest of Women: Safari of Women*. Burbank CA: Peace at the Border, 2006.

White, Michael, and David Epston. *Narrative Means to Therapeutic Ends*. New York: W. W. Norton, 1990.

Wright, Jared. "Pacific Union Conference Approves Fourteen Women for Ordination." *Spectrum Magazine*. September 7, 2012. https://spectrummagazine.org/article/jared-wright/2012/09/07/pacific-union-conference-approves-fourteen-women-ordination.

Wright, Melissa W. *Disposable Women and Other Myths of Global Capitalism.* New York: Routledge, 2006.

Zermeño, Sergio. "Desolation: Mexican Campesinos and Agriculture in the 21st Century." *NACLA Report on the Americas* 41, no. 5 (October 2008): 28–41.

Index

abuse, 99, 110
academic knowledge, 106–7, 132n23
adelante (forging ahead), 62, 101, 138, 147
Agamben, Giorgio, 23, 114
agave (henequén/Kí), 32, 34–35, *36*, 37–39, 56n4, 142
agency, xiii–xiv, 34, 70, 83, 116–17, 119, 141
agriculture, 17, 41–42, 44, 50; during hacienda system, 34–35, *36*, 37–39. *See also* milpas (maize fields)
alcohol, 51, 74–75
Althaus-Reid, Marcella, 85–86, 121, 124
anatomy of hope, 7, 100, 103–8, 109–19, 129–30
ancestors (antepasados), 16, 34, 41, 66, 108, 137, 140, 146–47
Anderson, Jo, 35
anger, 111, 129–30
antepasados (ancestors), 16, 34, 41, 66, 108, 137, 140, 146–47
anthro/gynopologies, 1, 63, 75, 104, 131n9
anthropology, theological, 6, 99
Antonio (el Viejo), 104, 131n7
Anzaldúa, Gloria, 15–16, 18, 19–20, 22, 109, 129, 142, 144

appropriation, 6, 20–21, 44, 70, 72, 96n23, 138
Aquino, Maria Pilar, 2, 85
Araceli, 29–30, 47, 52, 55, 90, 102, 119, 125
Aristotle, 3, 23, 114
Arjona, Rubén, 5
assembly lines, working-class Maya mexicanas on, xii–xiii, 1, 6, 19, 44, 53, 109, 143–44; bodies impacted working on, 29–30, 45–46, 70–72, 119; repetitive tasks of, 21–22, 29–30, 45–46
assessments, pastoral counseling, 141–42
Azteca people, 16

bachiller (high school), 100–101
ballgame (Mayan), 65, 95n3
Banqueros de Nueva York, 35, 37
Barbarous Mexico (Turner), 37
Batz Puac, Juana, 66
Belize, 18, 20
Bentham, Jeremy, 47–49
Bertalanffy, Ludwig, 140
Bible, 56, 85–86
BIP. *See* Border Industrialized Program
Black Marxism (Robinson), 40

159

bodies of working-class Maya mexicanas, xiii, 2–3, 7, 20–21, 68, 123, 143, 144–45; maquilas impacting, 29–30, 45–46, 70–72, 119
Border Industrialized Program (BIP), 16
borders, US-México, 15–20, 22, 120
Bowen, Murray, 140
Bracero Program (BP), 16–17
braids, in pastoral counseling, 141
Brandeis (Justice), 25n13
Brevíssima Relación (de las Casas), 33
A Brief History of Neoliberalism (Harvey), 103–4
Brueggemann, Walter, xiv, 56
Buen Vivir (well-being, indigenous concept), 104, 108, 126–27, 131

"la de calidad" (quality control inspection), 44, 114
California, 12, 39, 134n59, 145–47, 146, *146*
campesinx, 11, 17, 35, 62, 101, 103, 120, 136; rituals of, 41–42, 44; working at milpas, *43*, 66–67, 139
candela (furnace), 12, 75, 141
cansar, 50–52
capitalism, 19, 23, 30, 58n40, 122; global, 21, 99, 107; Zapatistas on, 39–40, 40ni, 44. *See also* neoliberal capitalism
Capital Resurgent (Duménil, Lévy), 103–4
care and caring, 25n17, 74–75, 126, 138–39, 140–42; community, 18, 78–80, 127, 141; neoliberalism and, 1–2, 92–94. *See also* pastoral care
Care of Souls, Care of Polis (LaMothe), 126
Caribbean Islands, 32
Caring for Souls in the Neoliberal Age (Rogers-Vaughn), 92
Carlson, David L., 34–35
Caste War, 38, 57n7
Castilla Ramos, Beatriz, 70–71, 92

Catholicism and Catholic Church, 1–2, 33–34, 54–56, 83
CDI. *See* La Comisión Nacional para el Desarrollo de los Pueblos Indígenas, Yucatán
Celeste, 30, 47, 54–55, 71, 75, 102, 110, 113–14; on religion, 90–91
Cervera Pacheco, Víctor Manuel, 18–19, 20
Chacc (Mayan rain god), 41, 139
Chávez, César, 145
Chiapas, México, 69, 75, 131n7, 148
children, 4, 7, *10*, 52–53, 56, *63*, 102, 141; daughters as, xii, 73–75, 81, 90; education for, 61–62, 144–45; la ciencia de la lucha taught to, 6, 80–85, 130, 138; sons as, 29, 75, 78–80, 88; as witnesses, 9–11, 130, 138
Children's Day (Día de los Niños), 80, 124
chiles, *43*, 50
China, 21–22, 146
choice, 53, 116–19
Christianity, 16, 83, 85–86, 88, *89*, 90–91, 139; Seventh-day Adventist Christian in, xiii–xiv, 124, xvin14; theology of, xiv–xv, 7, 87, 123
church (Christian/Catholic), xiv, 54–55, 83, 85–86, 90–91, 90ni
la ciencia de la lucha (the science of the struggle), 93, 94, 97n27, 103, 119–20, 146, 148; children taught, 6, 80–85, 130, 138
citizenship, US, xii, 130, 134n59
Ciudad Juárez, México, 16–17, 20–21, 47
civil wars, 17
Claremont School of Theology, 20
class, 17–18, 40, 130–31; elite, 19, 35, 37–38, 103, 144. *See also* working-class Maya mexicanas
collective and collectivism, 39–40, 66, 92–93, 103
colonialism, 1–2, 19, 87, 99, 101, 107, 132n23; neoliberal capitalism as

extension of, 6, 136–37; religions of, 6, 54–56; Spanish, 6, 32–35, 37–39, 67
La Comisión Nacional para el Desarrollo de los Pueblos Indígenas (CDI), Yucatán, 79–80
The Communist Manifesto (Marx), 17
communities/communal, 1–2, 19, 41–42, 44, 124, 127, 138; caretaking in, 18, 78–80, 127, 141; faith, xiii–xiv, 130–31; matriarchal, 4, 6, 78–80, 93, 128, 144. *See also* pueblo indígena
competition, 45–46, 45ni, 49, 53, 102–3, 117
conquistadores, Spanish, 32–34
consolation, refusal of, 56
cooperatives, work, 79–80
corazonar la vida (understand life through the heart), 2, 7, 100, 128, 130, 131n8, 142–43; in anatomy of hope, 104, 106–7
corn. *See* maíz
corporations. *See* multinational corporations
Correa, Rafael, 127
cosiendo (sewing), xiii, 99, 101
cosmology, Mayan, 63–64, 67–69, 91
costs, 19, 38, 42, 52–53, 62; maíz, 17, 50, 120
counseling. *See* pastoral counseling
Couture, Pamela D., 5
coyotes (immigrant smuggler), 4
creation story (Mayan), 63–67, 94–95, 105, 132n15–17, 135–36
crops, 4, 42, *43*, 120, 138, 139. *See also* specific crops
Cuba, 33, 62, 78, 146–47; refugees from, xii–xiii, xv, 12
cultural heritage, 15, 20–21, 70–71, 137–38
culture, 18–20, 64–67, 70; of surveillance, 6, 47–48, 50–52
curanderas (healers), 67–69, 91

dancing, 88, 90
daughters, xii, 73–75, 81, 90, 100–101
Day of the Dead (Hanal Pixán), 41
death, 4, 20–21, 26n27, 32–34, 66, 120–25, 128–30; resisting, 109, 117–18; suicide as, xii, 143
death-producing contexts, 4, 18, 83–84, 138–39
debt, 4, 34–35, 37, 57n25, 100
Declaration of Independence of 1810 (Méxican), 37
decolonialism, 1–2, 7, 139
dehumanization, 5, 22, 30, 39, 56; of el pueblo indígena, 32–34, 136–37
de las Casas, Bartolomé, 32–33
Deliver Us from Evil (Poling), 129
demand, 17, 34, 35, 38
dependency theory, xv
desire, 3, 5, 143–45, 148; sueños as, 101–2, 121–22
Día de los Niños (Children's Day), 80, 124
Díaz, Porfirio, 37–38
dichos (proverbs), 128–29, 137
diseases, 32–33, 41
divine authority, 32–34, 37
dreams. *See* sueños
drunken men, 51, 74–75
duality in Mayan cosmology, 67–69
Duménil, Gérard, 103–4

ecology and ecological systems, 18, 108, 138–39, 141
economy and economic systems, 19, 42, 101, 103–4, 122; demand, 17, 34, 35, 38; globalized, 44–46, 71, 100, 117. *See also* capitalism
Ecuador, 126–27, 131
education, xii, 5, 32, 115, 128, 143–45; for children, 61–62, 144–45; Sofia pursuing, 50, 100–101, 125
efficiency, xiii, 44, 49, 71, 115
Ejército Zapatista de Liberación Nacional (EZLN), 131n7
electrostatic discharge (analogy), 111

Eliade, Mircea, 21
elite class, 19, 35, 37–38, 103, 144
El Paso, Texas, 16
El Salvador, 121
employment, xii, xiii, 44–46, 92, 112–13; gender and, 21–23, 70–71, 144; in maquilas, 11–12, 17, 71–72, 102–3, 115–19, 143
encomienda system, 6, 32–34, 37, 54, 136–37
entrevistas (interviews), 2–3, 9–15, 21–22, 120–21, 145
epistemicide, 34, 100, 106–7, 130, 137
Epistemologies of the South (Sousa Santos), 107
epistemology, 2, 67–68, 104
equilibrium, Mayan belief in, 41, 68–69, 91, 127, 144
Erickson, Milton, 140
eschatological fragrance, 62, 82, 103
eschatology and eschatological practices, xiv, 2–3, 6–7, 73, 99–100, 138, 144; hope, 63, 124–25; of working-class Maya mexicanas, 135–36. *See also specific practices*
Escobar, Arturo, 107–8
Europe, 34, 35, 40
everyday deaths, 120–25, 130
experiences of working-class Maya mexicanas, 5–6, 19, 99, 111–12, 128, 140–42; of desire, 144–45; of labor, 17–18; of men, 39, 143–44; of researcher, 7, 14–15, 124–25, 145–48. *See also specific women*
exploitation, 1, 16, 40, 70, 146; resource extraction as, 22, 32–33, 133n28
exploitation colony, 32, 56n3
exports, 35, 37
extraction, resource, 22, 32–33, 37–38, 42, 55–56, 56n3, 107–8, 133n28
EZLN. *See* Ejército Zapatista de Liberación Nacional

Facebook, 125–26, 146
factories, xii–xiii, 1. *See also* maquilas (multinational corporations)
faith communities, xiii–xiv, 130–31
family and familial relationships, 4, 11–15, 46, 122–23, 127, 140, 146–48; fathers in, 50, 100–101, 125–26, 144; during hacienda system, 35, 37; resources shared in, 78–80; wisdom, 141; as witnesses, 120–21, 123–24, 128, 130. *See also* mothers and motherhood; primeramente madre (mothers first)
family systems theory, 140
Farm Workers Movement, 146
fathers, 11–12, 78; support of, 50, 100–101, 125–26, 144
faulty sewing machines, 51, 110nii, 111
fear, xii, 48ni, 110nii, 113, 128–29
feminism, 1–2, 7, 85; Latinx feminist pastoral theology as, 5–6, 135, 142–45; transnational, xv, 2, 7, 14
fertilizer, 42, 50
feudal system, 32, 40
firing, xiii, 45, 112–13, 115–16, 118
first order suffering, 92–93
fluidity in Mayan cosmology, 67–69
forced labor, 32–35, 37
forging ahead (adelante), 62, 101, 138, 147
Foucault, Michel, 23, 49, 114
frameworks, xiii–xv, 2, 129, 142; hermeneutical, 127, 131
freedom, 23, 32–33, 37, 63
free trade agreements, 16–17, 19, 23, 30, 40, 50, 58n44
Freud, Sigmund, 101
furnace (candela), 12, 75, 141
future, 23, 62, 73, 75, 80–82, 102, 109

Gadamer, Georg, xi–xii, xvin1
Galveston, Texas, 18
Gebara, Ivone, 85, 123–24, 139
gender, 2, 45, 123–24, 125; labor and, 21–23, 70–71, 144

general systems theory, 139–40
genetically modified seeds/crops (GMO), 50, 67, 139
genocide, 34, 137
global capitalism, 21, 99, 107
globalization, 3, 16, 42, 102, 135, 139; of economies, 44–46, 71, 100, 117
global south, 107, 132n24
GMO. *See* genetically modified seeds
God (Christian), xiii–xiv
gods and goddesses, Mayan, 41, 75, *76–77*, 86–87, 105, 139, 143
gold, 32
goodbye (ma'alob), 135
gospels (concept), 6, 55–56, 72–73, 94–95, 96n23
Greider, Kathleen J., 129
Grijalva, Juan de, 32
Grosfoguel, Ramón, 34
Guatemala, 18, 20
Guerrero Arias, Patricio, 7, 100, 103–7, 131n8
Gutiérrez, Gustavo, xv, 19–20

hablando (speaking, eschatological practice), 7, 100, 110–13, 124, 129, 138
hacienda system, 6, 32–35, 37–40, 54, 136–37
Haley, Jay, 140
Hanal Pixán (Day of the Dead), 41
Haring. C. H., 32, 56
Harvey, David, 103–4
healers (curanderas), 67–69, 91
healing and health, 3, 22–23, 32–33, 67–69, 91, 116, 138
HEGOA. *See* Instituto de Estudios sobre el Desarrollo y Cooperación Internacional
henequén (agave/Kí), 32, 34–35, *36*, 37–39, 56n4, 142
la herida abierta (the open wound), 15–20, 22
hermeneutics, xi, 127, 131
herstories, xii–xvi, 65, 99, xvin6

higher education, 50, 128
high school (bachiller), 100–101
lxs hijxs de maíz, 6, *10*, 65–67, 73, 95, 104–6, 108–9, 138; pastoral care demonstrated by, 135–36, *136*, 139–40. *See also* sabidurias insurgentes (insurrectionist wisdoms)
hipiles (Mayan garment), 19, 88, 101
Historia de las Cosas de la Nueva España (Sahagún), 67–69
historical trauma, 1, 140
historical violence, 137
history. *See* herstories
homework (tarea), 13, 15
homophobia, 144
hopes, 63, 91, 120, 123, 124–25, 128, 133n37; anatomy of, 7, 100, 103–8, 109–19, 129–30; of working-class Maya mexicanas, 62–64, 72–75, 77–85, 94–95
"horizons" of meaning, xi–xvi
Huerta, Dolores, 146
humans and humanity, 5–6, 19, 107; in Mayan creation myth, 63–67, 94–95, 105
Hunahpu (Mayan figure), 65
Hun Hunahpu (Mayan figure), 65
husk, in pastoral counseling, 141

identity, xv, 2, 5, 15–20, 18, 63, 138; lxs hijxs de maíz as, 6, 65, 108–9; primeramente madre as, 3, 6, 73–75; of researcher, xii–xvi, xvin1
ideology, capitalism as, 39
ignorando (ignoring, eschatological practice), 7, 100, 113–15, 129
illiteracy, 85–86
illness, 67–69, 91, 99, 119
immigrants and immigration, xiii, 1, 4, 16–17, 146
imperialism, 2, 15–16, 55, 99
imports, 4, 17, 94
incarceration, maquilas as, 6, 46–49
income, xii–xiii, 16, 52–53, *54*, 79, 113
indigenization, 5, 143

indigenous, 6, 39–40; resources, 32–33, 34–35, *36*, 37–39. *See also* Mayan people; pueblo indígena
industrialization, 35, 37
inequality, 16, 103
ingeniero (engineer/supervisor), 46–47
injuries, maquila, 22, 45, 52, 112–13, 116, 119; of Araceli, 29–30, 125
inoperative potentiality, 23, 114–15
insistiendo (insisting, eschatological practice), 7, 100, 115–16, 129
Instituto de Estudios sobre el Desarrollo y Cooperación Internacional (HEGOA), 125
insurrectionist wisdoms. *See* sabidurias insurgentes
International Monetary Fund, 16, 117
intersectionality theory, 22, 100
interviews (entrevistas), 2–3, 9–15, 21–22, 120–21, 145
interweaving (concept), 86, 97n35
invisibility, xiv–xv, 11, 107
Isasi-Díaz, Ada María, 1–2, 83–85, 145
Itzel, 30, 46, 48, 51, 73–74, 110–12, 129
Ixtab (goddess of suicide), 143

Jamís, Fayad, 101–2
Japan, 117, 146
Jehovah's Witness, 55
jobs. *See* employment
Jung, Carl Jung, 101
Jung Mo Sung, 122

Katz, Friedrich, 34–35
Kí (agave/henequen), 32, 34–35, *36*, 37–39, 56n4, 142
knowledge, xii, xv, 34, 51–52, 103, 106–7, 108, 132n23. *See also* sabidurias insurgentes (insurrectionist wisdoms)

labor and laborers, xii–xiii, xv–xvi, 7, 14–16, 19, 138; exploitation of, 17–18, 32–35; forced, 32–35, 37; gender division in, 21–23, 70–71, 144; skilled, 38–39, 42, 141; slave, 32–35, 37, 40, 57n25
LaMothe, Ryan, 126–28, 130–31
land, xiv, 1, 39–40, 74, 99, 140, 145–46; theft, 34, 37–38, 137–38
language, xii–xiii, 6, 9, 32, 44–45, 120; Mayan, 97n36–37, 132n18, 135
la promesa (the promise, to La Virgen de Asuncion), 90
Lartey, Emmanuel, 5
Latinx feminist pastoral theology, 5–6, 135, 142–45
Latinxs eschatology, 99–100
lethal wages, 6, 52–53, *54*
Lévy, Dominique, 103–4
liberation, xv, 19–20, 63, 71, 87, 92
life and living, 65, 109, 117–18
life-giving practices, 6, 23, 63, 94–95, 125, 138, 142–43
Liggett Co. *vs.* Lee, US, 25n13
literacy, 32, 61ni
López Intzín, Juan, 106
la lucha (the struggle), xv, 40, 71, 73, 99, 101, 103, 120–26; children introduced to, 6, 80–85, 130, 138; ontology of, 107–8. *See also* la ciencia de la lucha (the science of the struggle)
Lucía (Doña), 11–12, 128, 135, 145–46, 147
Luévano, Rafael, 17

ma'alob (goodbye), 135
machinery, women treated as, 6, 44–46, 71–72
macro systems, 100–101, 117, 126–28
maíz, 4, 35, 65–67, *66*, 138; costs of, 17, 50, 120; goddess, 75, *76–77*, 86–87. *See also* milpas (maize fields)
making tortillas (tortear), 12, 65, 75, 141
Manifest Destiny, US, 15–16
maquilas (multinational corporations), US, 16–18, 38, 58n37, 124, 136–37; appropriation by, 6, 20–21, 44, 70,

72, 138; bodies impacted working at, 29–30, 45–46, 70–72, 119; culture of surveillance in, 6, 47–48, 50–52; employment in, 11–12, 71–72, 102–3, 115–19, 143; faulty sewing machines in, 51, 100–111, 110nii; as form of incarceration, 6, 46–49; la prueba for, 44–46, 115; milpas harmed by, 30, 41–42, 44; policies, 36–37, 46–49, 113–14; profits of, 19, 52, 114; quotas in, 40, 51, 83–84, 113, 116nii, 119, 125; subjugation by, 39, 46–49; women treated as machinery in, 6, 44–46, 71–72. *See also* assembly lines, working-class Maya mexicanas on; injuries, maquila; maquilas (multinational corporations); supervision or supervisors, maquila; wages, maquila

Marcos, Sylvia, 64, 67–69, 83, 95n6
marginalization, 108
Maria, 61–62, 102–3, 115
Mariana, 44, 53, 71, 78, 112
markets (economical), 49, 53, 117, 144
marriage, 53, 54–55, 79, 128
Martell-Ortero, Loida, 73, 99–100
Marx, Karl, 17–18
Matanzas, Cuba, 147
matriarchal communities, 4, 6, 78–80, 93, 128, 144
Maturana, Humberto, 140
Mayan (language), 97n36–37, 132n18, 135
Mayan people, 20–21, 42, 44, 75, 85, 87, 132n18; conception of equilibrium for, 41, 68–69, 127, 144; cosmology of, 63–64, 67–69, 91; creation myth of, 63–67, 94–95, 105, 132n15–17, 135–36; equilibrium for, 41, 68–69, 91, 127, 144; gods and goddesses of, 41, *76–77*, 105, 139, 143; Spanish colonialism impacting, 32–35, 37–39, 54. *See also* pueblo indígena
McCormick Harvesting Machine, 35

means of production, 17, 25n14
memory, 66, 111, 121, 130
men, 4–5, 16, 28, 45, 53, 70, 123–24; drinking by, 51, 74–75; experiences of, 39, 143–44
mercantilism, 58n40
Mérida, Yucatán, 18–20, 38, 71, 78–79, 95n3
Mesomaerica, 67, 95n6
mestiza identity, 15, 18, 142
methodology, research, 2–3, 6–7, 14
Méxican immigrants, xiii, 146
México, 15–20, 21–23, 22, 30, 56n1, 65–67; Chiapas, 69, 75, 131n7, 148; hacienda system in, 6, 32–35, 37–40, 54, 136–37. *See also* Yucatán, México
Meyers, Allan D., 34–35
milk, 52–53, 102, 145
mill (molino), 67, 78–79
milpas (maize fields), 12, 66, *66*, 143–44; campesinxs working on, *43*, 66–67, 139; maquila industry harming, 30, 41–42, 44
minimum wages, xii–xiii
Minuchin, Salvador, 140
modernity, xi, 100, 120, 130
molino (the mill), 67, 78–79
Moltmann, Jürgen, 73
Monsanto, 50, 94
mothers and motherhood, xii–xiv, 5, 11–12, 30, 40, 50, 53, 91, 129; as act of resistance, 72–73, 81–82; hopes of, 62–64, 72–75, 78–85; refusal of consolation by, 56; religions on, 86–87. *See also* working-class Maya mexicanas
mothers first. *See* primeramente madre (mothers first)
mud (in Mayan creation myth), 64, 105
las Mujeres del Mayab (textile business), 79–80
Mujeres Mayas en la Robótica y Líderes de la Comunidad (Castilla Ramos), 70

multinational corporations, US, xii–xiii, 1, 3, 11, 21–23, 143. *See also* maquilas (multinational corporations), US
Mundo Mundial/universe (concept), 107–8, 111–12
Muslim people, 32
Myth and Reality (Eliade), 21

NAFTA. *See* North American Free Trade Agreement
Natalia, 45, 115–16
National Development Plan (NPGL), Ecuador, 127
nature deficit disorder, 141
Nayeli (Doña), 41, 49, 79–80, 87–88, 107, 147
needs, 145
neoliberal capitalism, 2, 5–6, 40, 65, 101–4, 111, 135, 136–37; globalization and, 42; NAFTA exemplifying, 19; as oppressive, 117; post-development and, 126
neoliberalism, 1–2, 3, 14, 58n42, 92–94, 143–44
New World (the Americas), 32–34
New York, 38
night shifts, voluntary (turno nocturno), 48–49, 48niv, 110, 112, 121
North American Free Trade Agreement (NAFTA), 16–17, 19, 23, 40, 58n44, 67, 99, 117, 120, 131n7
NPGL. *See* National Development Plan, Ecuador

ontology, 54, 107–8; anthro/gynopologies, 1, 104, 131n9
the open wound (la herida abierta), 15–20, 22
oppression, 22, 117, 137
oral traditions, Mayan, 75, 85, 87
Orange, California, 146
oranges, 145
Ormex de México (US maquila), 70, 72
O'Sullivan, John L., 15–16

la palapa (palm roof dwelling), *13*, 41, 47nii–iii
Paloma, 30, 45, 51–52, 55, 79
panopticon, 47–49
parents, xiv, 11–12, 23, 28, 128; fathers as, 100–101, 125–26, 144. *See also* mothers and motherhood
pastoral care, 5, 6–7, 91, 126–27, 130–31; lxs hijxs de maiz demonstrating, 135–36, *136*, 139–40
pastoral counseling, 6–7, 91, 126, 128–31, 140–42
pastoral theology, xv–xvi, 1–2, 19–20, 22–23, 25n17, 142; indigenization of, 5, 143; Latinx feminist, 5–6, 135, 143–45; lxs hijxos de maíz informing, 135–43; practical theology and, 5, 18, 25n16
patriarchy, xiii, 92, 139, xvin1
Piketty, Thomas, 58n39
Pineda-Madrid, Nancy, 85
pluriverse, 7, 107–9, 111–12, 126
policies, maquila, 36–37, 46–49, 113–14
Poling, James N., 129
Polk, James K., 15
pollution, 3, 42, 75m 96n26, 139
poor people and poverty, 99, 100–101, 102–3, 129
Popol Vuh (Maya sacred text), 7, 86–87, 101, 104–6, 138–39; creation story, 63–67, 94–995, 105, 132n15–17, 135–36
post colonialism, 2, 126
post-development, 126
potentiality and possibility, 3, 23, 114
poverty. *See* poor people and poverty
power, 22–23, 45, 103, 106, 114, 117, 128–29; of Spanish colonizers, 32–34; of surveillance, 47–48
practical theology and theologians, xii, xv–xvi, 1, 14, 107, 127, 142; pastoral theology and, 5, 18, 25n16
primeramente madre (mothers first), 3, 6, 72–75, 80–85, 93, 113, 138
privilege, xv, 2, 18–20, 128–29

profits, 17, 37–38, 40ni, 42, 48, 62; of maquilas, 19, 52, 72, 114
the promise (la promesa, to La Virgen de Asuncion), 90
Proposition 187, California, 128, 134n59
proverbs (dichos), 128–29, 137
proximity (in Mayan cosmology), 67–68, 69, 75
la prueba (test) for employment, 44–46, 115
el pueblo indígena, 37, 103; dehumanization of, 32–34, 136–37
pueblo mágico, Yucatán, *13, 36, 112*. *See also specific topics*

qualitative research, xi–xii, xv, 2–3, 21–22
quality control inspection ("la de calidad"), 44, 114
quitting, 45, 118–19. *See also* renunciando (resignation, eschatological practice)
quotas, production, 40, 51, 83–84, 113, 116nii, 119

race and racism, 5, 40, 70, 92, 134n59
"race to the bottom," 17, 25n13
Radio Zapatista, 39–40, 40ni
Redlands, California, 12, 145–47, *146*
Reform Laws, 1856 (Méxican), 38
refugees, xii–xiii, xv, 12, 17
relationships/relational, 15, 23, 32–34, 49, 75, 100–101, 108, 138; eschatology, 136, 144. *See also* family and familial relationships
religions, 1–3, 6, 54–56, 67, 85–88, 90–91, 122. *See also specific religions*
renunciando (resignation, eschatological practice), 7, 100, 116–19, 125, 129, 138
repair for sewing machines, 51, 115
repetitive tasks, assembly line, 21–22, 29–30, 45–46

research, xv–xvi, 4–5, 85–88, 90–91, 100; interviews for, 2–3, 9–15, 120–21, 145; methodology, 2–3, 6–7, 14; qualitative, xi–xii, xv, 2–3, 21–22
researcher, xi–xvi, xvin1; experiences of, 7, 14–15, 124–25, 145–48
resignation (renunciando, eschatological practice), 100, 116–19, 138
resilience, 22–24
resistance, acts of, 70–71, 99, 129; against death, 109, 117–18; mothering as, 72–73, 81–82
resources, 78–80, 93; extraction, 22, 32–33, 37–38, 42, 55–56, 56n3, 107–8, 133n28; indigenous, 32–33, 34–35, *36*, 37–39
resurrections, 120–26, 130
rights, 24n9, 83, 84, 84niii
risks and risk-taking, 4, 110–11, 130, 138, 140–41; of being fired, 112–13, 115–16; hope and, 120, 123
rituals, 41–42, 44, 67, 70, 75, 87–88, 89, 95n3; appropriation of, 6; marriage, 79
Robinson, Cedric, 40
Rogers Vaughn, Bruce, 92–93

sabidurias insurgentes (insurrectionist wisdoms), 7, 120, 126, 128, 130, 137–38; in anatomy of hope, 104–6, 109; in la ciencia de la lucha, 103; sueños linked to, 100; survival and, 112–13
sacrifice, 81, 120–25
Sahagún (colonizer), 67
Santiago (Don), 11
the science of the struggle. *See* la ciencia de la lucha
second order suffering, 92–93
self-surveillance, 47–50, 54
Seventh-day Adventist Christianity, xiii–xiv, 124, xvin14
sewing (cosiendo), xiii, 99, 101
sewing machines, *31*, 51, 100–111, 110nii, 115, 138

sexism, 5, 40, 70, 92, 144
sexual violence, 3–4, 51, 74–76er 5, 112
shame, 84, 111, 116, 123
Sheppard, Phillis, 5
silence, 54–56, 107, 123
similarity (in Mayan cosmology), 67–68, 69, 75
single parenting, xiv, 23, 28
skills and skilled labor, 38–39, 42, 141
slavery and slave labor, 32–35, 37, 40, 57n25
Smith, Adam, 40
social status, 12, 71–72, 141
Sofia, 9, 50–51, 125–26, 128–29, 144; sueños of, 99–102, 121–22; suffering of, 100–101, 120–24
soil, 35, 42, 44, 137, 140, 146–47
solidarity, 6, 90–91, 136, 141–42
soteriology, 124
Sousa Santos, Boaventura de, 34, 107, 132n24
Spain and Spanish colonialism, 6, 32–35, 37–39, 54, 67
Spanish (language), xii–xiii, 32
speaking (hablando, eschatological practice), 100, 110–13, 138
spirituality, 2–3, 6, 23, 83, 111, 127, 139
status (social), 12, 71–72, 141
stories and storytelling, 9, 94, 99, 101, 129, 137, 140
stratification, social, 32–34
the struggle. *See* la lucha
subjugation, 3, 22, 30, 101, 132n24; via debt peonage system, 34–35; via maquilas, 39, 46–49
sueños (dreams), 103, 137, 141, 147; of Sofia, 99–102, 121–22
suffering, 1, 18–20, 25n17, 52, 63, 103, 142, 143–44; gender and, 123–24; pastoral theology on, 5–6, 19–20; Rogers-Vaughn on, 92–93; sexual violence and, 3–4; of Sofia, 100–101, 120–24; of Veronica, 83–85
sugar cane, 38

supervision or supervisors, maquila, 46–49, 82ni, 110–13, 110nii, 116; quotas and, 51, 83–84
support, 78–79, 121; of fathers, 50, 100–101, 125–26, 144
surveillance, culture of, 6, 47–48, 50–52
survival, 22–24, 109–13, 117–18, 138, 143–45
symbolic representation in Mayan cosmology, 67–69
systemic violence, 92–93

Taken from the Lips (Marcos), 67
tarea (homework), 13, 15
tattoos, 75, *76*
taxes, 16–17, 25n13, 120
taxis, 11, 46ni, 144, 147
Tecform Engineering Limited, xii–xiii
tejiendo (weaving), 20–21, 42, 70–71, 138
telos, relational, 100–101
Teresa, 30, 46, 80
Texas, 16, 18–19, 52
textile company, US, 20–21, 34, 70. *See also* maquilas (multinational corporations), US
theft, land, 34, 37–38, 137–38
theology/theological, xiii, 99, 121, 130; Christian, xiv–xv, 7, 87, 123; Latinx feminist pastoral, 5–6, 135, 142–45. *See also* pastoral theology; practical theology and theologians
third order suffering, 93
"third world," 15, 21–24
Thornton, Sharon G., 5, 136
Tijuana, México, 38
time and temporality, 22, 26n31, 63, 73, 115, 137
TNC. *See* transnational corporations, US
tortear (making tortillas), 12, 65, 75, 141
trade laws and agreements, 16, 35
transgender people, 144
transnational corporations (TNC), US, 39–40, 61, 80, 92

transnational feminism, xv, 2, 7, 14
transportation, 11, 38, 46ni, 144, 147
trauma, 1, 15, 140
the traversed (los atravesados), 18, 144
Treaty of Guadalupe-Hidalgo, 15–16
Truth and Method (Gadamer), xi
Turner, John Kenneth, 37
turno nocturno (voluntary night shifts), 48–49, 48niv, 110, 112, 121

understand life through the heart. *See* corazonar la vida
Underworld (Xibalba), 64–65
unemployment, 17
United States (US), xv, 1–2, 12, 34, 92, 117, 128, 147; citizenship, xii, 130, 134n59; immigrants and immigration in, xiii, 4, 146; imperialism, 15–16; México border with, 15–20, 22; pastoral care in, 5, 127; transnational corporations, 39–40. *See also* maquilas (multinational corporations), US
upper class, 35, 37, 103
US. *See* United States
US-México border, 15–20, 22, 120

Valentina (Doña), 13
Veronica, 30, 45, 54, 102, 111, 113, 118; as primeramente madre, 73–75, 81–85
Villagómez Valdés, Gina, 88
Villalba, Unai, 126–27
violence, 20, 22, 62–63, 82, 82ni, 100, 137, 140; sexual, 3–4, 51, 74–75, 112; of Spanish colonialism, 32–34; systemic, 92–93
la Virgen de la Asunción, 64, 85–88, *89*, 90–91
Virgen of Guadalupe, 55, 55ni
voting, 117
Vucub Hunahpu (Mayan figure), 65

Wáajil kool (Mayan agricultural ritual), 41, 44
wages, xii–xiii, 32–35
wages, maquila, xii–xiii, 6, 16–17, 52–53, *54*, 56n1, 70–71
Walker-Barnes, Chanequa, 5
wants, 145
wealth, 32–33, 35, 37, 40ni, 117, 144
weaving (tejiendo), 20–21, 42, 70–71, 138
well-being, 126, 139–40. *See also* Buen Vivir (well-being)
Western thought, 14, 107, 139
wisdom, xii, 6–7, 18–19, 23–24, 104–5, 131n8, 132n23, 141; ancestral, 34; of la ciencia de la lucha, 93; dichos as, 129; matriarchal, 78. *See also* sabidurias insurgentes (insurrectionist wisdoms)
witnesses, 9–11, 125, 138; family as, 120–21, 123–24, 128, 130
women of color, 14, 20, 21–24, *63*, 70, 92, 100, 143–44; bodies of, 2–3, 123, 143–45; education and, 50, 61–62, 100–101, 115, 125; El Salvadorian, 121; exploitation of, 1, 40; wisdom of, 18–19; Zapatista, 75, 99, 102–3. *See also* working-class Maya mexicanas
wood (in Mayan creation myth), 64, 105, 132n15
workday (hours), 22, 26n31, 29, 47
working-class Maya mexicanas, xv, 1, 17–18, 23–24, 58n40, 128, 139, 144; as los atravesados, 18–19; choices of, 116–17; dead bodies of, 20–21, 26n27; eschatological practices of, 135–36; hopes of, 62–64, 72–75, 77–85, 94–95; lethal wages for, 6, 52–53, 54; maquilas as incarceration for, 6, 46–49; as primeramente madre, 6, 113, 138; subjugation of, 39, 46–49; sueños of, 102–3; treated as machinery, 6, 44–46, 71–72. *See*

also bodies of working-class Maya mexicanas; experiences of working-class Maya mexicanas; lxs hijxs de maíz; maquilas (multinational corporations); *specific women*
World Bank, 16, 117
World Trade Organization, 117
World War II, 16
Wright, Melissa W., 21–22, 44–45

Xbalanqu (Mayan figure), 65
Xibalba (Underworld), 64–65
Ximena, 30, 47–48, 102, 144

Yucatán, México, 1, 11, 70, 80, 92, 145–47; hacienda system in, 6, 32–35, 37–40, 54, 136–37; Mérida, 18–20, 38, 71, 78–79, 95n3

Zapatistas, 7, 97n27, 99, 102–3, 108, 120, 131n7; on capitalism, 39–40, 40ni, 44
Zapatistas Primer Encuentro Internacional, 148

About the Author

Marlene M. Ferreras, PhD, is assistant professor of practical theology at the HMS Richards Divinity School at La Sierra University. Her research focuses on decolonial approaches in care and counseling with working-class Latinx women. Marlene is the first American-born daughter of a single-parent Cuban refugee mother. She is an ordained Seventh-day Adventist minister with fourteen years of experience in pastoral ministry serving in communities around the Loma Linda, California, area. She holds two MA degrees in theology, from Fuller Theological Seminary and Claremont School of Theology, and an MS degree in marital and family therapy from Loma Linda University. She is registered as an associate marriage and family therapist with the California Board of Behavioral Sciences.

www.ingramcontent.com/pod-product-compliance
Lightning Source LLC
Chambersburg PA
CBHW021356300426
44114CB00012B/1252